COLLECTIONS AND THE ENFORCEMENT OF MONEY JUDGMENTS

Library of Congress Catalog Card Number: 84-60393
ISBN Number: 0-942954-30-0

COLLECTIONS AND THE ENFORCEMENT OF MONEY JUDGMENTS

Editors-in-Chief

Jack L. Getman
Robert B. Frank
Richard J. Miller

Contributing Authors

Gabriel J. Ferber, Esq.
Raymond L. Fink, Esq.
Ronald Forster, Esq.
Michael J. Kaplan, Esq.
Marvin Krumholz, Esq.
Richard A. Nicoll, Esq.
Bradley E. Rock, Esq.
Bruce B. Roswig, Esq.
Francis P. Weimer, Esq.
Prof. Barry L. Zaretsky

New York State Bar Association
1986

NYSBA

TABLE OF CONTENTS

TABLE OF FORMS AND PLEADINGS

CHAPTER NINE: Procedures During Litigation

CHAPTER ELEVEN: Evaluating Collection Prospects

CHAPTER TWELVE: Procedures

CHAPTER THIRTEEN: Effect of Bankruptcy Act

DETAILED TABLE OF CONTENTS

CHAPTER FOUR: Demand Upon the Debtor

CHAPTER FIVE: Debt Collection Restrictions

CHAPTER SIX: Alternatives to Litigation

CHAPTER SEVEN: Instituting Suit

CHAPTER ELEVEN: Evaluating Collection Prospects

CHAPTER FOURTEEN: Miscellaneous Provisions

CHAPTER ONE

DETERMINING PROPER PARTY DEFENDANT

Gabriel J. Ferber, Esq.

I. PRELIMINARY CONSIDERATIONS

The obligor of any debt referred in for collection can normally be obtained from a simple review of the referral document. Initial determinations must be made as to whether there is more than one obligor and as to the basis of each obligor's indebtedness. Such determinations are important in order to insure that all appropriate parties are named if suit becomes necessary and to comply with any rules of pleading that may be applicable. If more than one entity is involved, a determination has to be made as to whether each entity's liability for the debt in question is that of a primary obligor, as in the case of a cobuyer, comaker or cosigner, or whether such liability is secondary, as in the case of a guarantor.

In the case of a guarantor, a determination must be made as to whether the guarantor is a "guarantor of payment" or "guarantor of collection." A "guarantor of payment" is liable upon the default of the primary obligor and demand. A "guarantor of collection" is liable only if the creditor is unable to collect from the primary obligor after exhausting all legal remedies, including demand, suit, judgment and the return of unsatisfied execution. Under New York State's Statute of Frauds, General Obligations Law, sec. 5-701 (a)(2), a guarantor's liability must be evidenced by a writing.

II. PARTIES NOT NAMED ON DOCUMENTS OF INDEBTEDNESS

Certain entities may be liable for a given debt even though they are not specifically identified on a creditor's referral documents. These might include the general or limited partners of a partnership, individuals or business entities doing business under an assumed name, the individual members of an unincorporated association, or the individual directors or officers of a corporation where the debt was incurred through *ultra vires* action. The names of partners or those doing business under an assumed name can normally be obtained from a review of certificates covering these entities filed in the County Clerk's Office. Partnership Law sec. 81; General Business Law sec. 130. However, it should be noted that these certificates are not always current. Frequently, a filed certificate of partnership will not have been amended to list partners who became members after the filing of the original certificate.

Pursuant to CPLR sec. 1025, actions against partnerships can be sued in the partnership name and actions against unincorporated associations can be instituted by naming the association's president or treasurer in such capacity. However, this provision appears primarily designed for expediency of suit. A subsequent judgment, while enforceable against jointly held assets of the partnership or association, could not be enforced against the individually owned assets of parties not served with process. CPLR, Article 15. Moreover, a suit instituted against an unincorporated association, in the name of its president or treasurer, bars a subsequent suit against the association's individual members until the judgment on the first suit is returned unsatisfied. General Associations Law secs. 16, 17.

Therefore, if suit is initiated against a partnership, the individual partners who were unknown at the time the suit was instituted should be identified through discovery and joined as defendants so that a subsequent judgment will have a broader base for enforcement. In the case of an unincorporated association, unless the association is known to have jointly held assets sufficient to satisfy a judgment, the better practice would appear to be to bring the action against association members individually, naming those known, and joining those later identified through discovery.

III. WHETHER PARTY LIABLE IS A CORPORATION

Occasionally, a collection matter may identify the debtor only by a business name, without indicating its status as a corporation, partnership or sole proprietorship. In such case, a review of the assumed name, partnership and corporate indices in the County Clerk's Office should be made to determine the defendant's status. It should be noted that under section 130 of the General Business Law, a corporation may do business under an assumed name. If a local search is unavailing, a search of certificates of corporations filed with the Secretary of State in Albany should be instituted (*see* form letter, Appendix A). Certain lawyer service agencies, such as Infosearch or Servico, can perform this service at a nominal charge. If the status of the defendant is still unknown, suit should be instituted against the individual who incurred the indebtedness, placing the burden on such individual to raise the defense that such indebtedness was incurred by a corporation.

IV. EXTRINSIC FACTORS AFFECTING IDENTIFICATION OF PARTY

The ease of identifying a proper party defendant is normally a function of the thoroughness of the creditor's records. However, factors which are extrinsic to what is otherwise a straightforward debtor-creditor relationship may complicate the task of defendant identification. For instance, when an infant is a debtor, the infant can appear only by a proper representative who should be named as a defendant in such capacity. CPLR sec. 1201. Where a creditor has furnished "necessaries" to an infant or a spouse, the parent or other spouse, under certain circumstances, may be held liable for the indebtedness incurred. *See* 47 NY Jur.2d Domestic Relations secs. 664 *et seq*. Where a committee for an incompetent debtor has been appointed, the identity of the committee must be determined and the committee named. CPLR sec. 1201. Where an individual debtor has died, an examination of the Surrogate's Court's records should be made to determine whether an estate representative has been appointed, whether it is necessary to seek the appointment of an estate representative, or whether, under certain circumstances, the distributees or testamentary beneficiaries of the estate should be named defendants. *See generally* SCPA, Article 18. Under Business Corporation Law sec. 1006(a)(4), a dissolved corporation can still be sued in the corporate name. Under section 61 of the Partnership Law, a partnership's liability is not terminated by its dissolution, and thus the liability of partners on predissolution obligations continues. *Reed v. Pelley*, 112 Misc. 2d 382, 447 N.Y.S.2d 98 (1982).

V. CURE FOR NON-JOINDER OR MIS-JOINDER OF PARTY

It should be noted that the failure to join all parties liable for a given debt can sometimes be the basis for dismissal of a creditor's cause of action. CPLR sec. 3211(a)(10). However, liberal amendatory mechanisms are available under Article 10 of the CPLR to cure such defect. Article 10 also contains provisions for the substitution of appropriate parties in the event of the death, incompetency or, in the case of a corporation, dissolution of a party defendant.

Appendix A

GOLDMAN, COSTA, GETMAN AND BIRYLA
ATTORNEYS AT LAW

KARL GOLDMAN
PETER L. COSTA
JACK L. GETMAN
RICHARD J. BIRYLA

705 BRISBANE BUILDING
BUFFALO, N. Y. 14203-2173
716 853-4340

October 12, 1984

Secretary of State
Division of Corporations
Albany, New York 12231

Re: NAME: -
ADDRESS-

Dear Sirs:

Kindly advise whether your office has any record of a corporation by the above name or any closely similar name. If so, please advise date of incorporation and its principal offices.

Yours truly,

GOLDMAN, COSTA, GETMAN
& BIRYLA

JLG:df

(NOTE:- The Secretary of State will only honor one request per letter. If you include more than one name on your request, it will generally be returned without action. The Secretary of State will reply to your inquiry by postcard in approximately two weeks.)

CHAPTER TWO

EVALUATING THE CLAIM

Francis P. Weimer

I. INITIAL EVALUATION

One of the initial actions undertaken by an attorney engaged to collect an overdue account on behalf of a creditor should be carefully and systematically to evaluate the claim. A telephone conversation with the creditor prior to receiving the underlying documentation will not always supply you with all relevant information regarding the claim. Institution of legal action, or even formal demands on the debtor for payment of the claim, should be avoided without a prior review of the creditor's documents unless prior dealings with the creditor leave no doubt that all relevant information has been supplied during the initial referral.

Care should be taken during the initial conversation with the creditor to ascertain any possible statute of limitations problems, or notice requirements under section 2-702 of the Uniform Commercial Code or section 546 of the United States Bankruptcy Code. If the client deals in materials used in the construction industry, further investigation should be directed towards the dates on which materials were shipped. This is in an effort to ascertain whether or not there are any potential deadlines in connection with notice requirements contained on payment bonds, and to further insure against an inadvertent lapse of the time limit within which to file a Notice of Mechanic's Lien. If it appears that your client may have "trust fund" rights under Article 3-A of the New York State Lien Law, section 77 of the article should be reviewed for its additional time limitations.

If no time constraints arise as a result of this conversation, you should request forwarding of copies of all documents in the creditor's file as well as copies of correspondence sent to and received from the debtor. If the client has kept a log of telephone conversations or personal contacts with the debtor, request a copy of this log as well. It is suggested that copies be requested in lieu of originals in order to safeguard these items from inadvertent mishandling prior to the time they may actually be needed in any eventual trial. If in the alternative your conversation results in a finding that time may be of the essence, advise the creditor accordingly, indicating the time frames which you believe may be important and secure whatever additional information is needed in order to satisfy the relevant time constraints.

II. REVIEWING DOCUMENTATION

Assuming, as is the case most often, that time permits a careful review of the documents prior to instituting action, upon their receipt use a systematic review of all documents and correspondence forwarded by the creditor in order to insure that all appropriate steps are taken to protect your client's interest and maximize the chances of recovery. In the great majority of cases claims will result from open account sales of goods, wares and merchandise delivered to a debtor or from the rendering of services. Initially documents should be reviewed with an eye towards identifying all possible defendants. An invoice or statement may list what your client believes is the proper debtor, but oftentimes guarantors appear on earlier credit applications or separate guarantee agreements which had been completed at the creditor's request some time earlier but were subsequently overlooked. Oftentimes this initial review will result in establishing liability on third parties. Documents such as credit applications and guarantee agreements may also provide you with information concerning the debtor's proper legal composition and may further provide information helpful to your process server in his/her efforts to effect service of summons and complaint.

Makers of dishonored notes or drawers of checks returned due to insufficient funds may also be ascertained if copies of these documents have been forwarded with the claim and the individual maker or drawer can be held liable on the particular instrument, notwithstanding their lack of clear connection to the primary debtor. In the case of a creditor who renders services to a debtor, if the debtor appears to be a minor, the documentation will often list the names of responsible parents or other third parties.

Claims involving the sale of construction materials or the rental of construction-related equipment require a careful review in order to ascertain the possibility of lien rights, bond rights or trust fund rights. Care should be taken to review invoices and delivery receipts for indications that the material in question may have been delivered to a particular job site. The creditor's documentation will help to develop information concerning delivery times for purposes of establishing lien rights. These same delivery receipts may also be critical with respect to notice requirements often contained in payment bonds filed in connection with major private improvements and most public improvements, some of which can be as short as ninety days following delivery. Very often a creditor will overlook these other possible avenues for enforcing collection of a claim and a failure to review the documents initially may have the undesired result of precluding your efforts to perfect these rights at a later date.

Referrals of claims in some instances occur on transactions between a creditor and debtor which have occurred within time parameters as short as ten days. A vigilant credit manager, after authorizing delivery of merchandise to a debtor, may learn of a bankruptcy proceeding initiated by the debtor or other act indicating that payment will not be forthcoming. If the initial telephone interview with the client or subsequent review of the documents establishes such a fact pattern, demand pursuant to Uniform Commercial Code section 2-702 and/or United State Bankruptcy Code section 546 may be the initial action that is necessary. Failure to protect your client's rights within the stringent ten-day limit imposed by both of these sections may result in an inability to secure a positive result for your client at a later date.

The documentation supplied by your client will also establish in most instances whether the claim is a commercial claim or consumer claim with its statutory venue rules requiring that venue be laid in either the county where the transaction occurred or the county where the debtor resides. A failure to ascertain that an item is in fact a consumer-related claim can result in a lawsuit which is jurisdictionally defective and a corresponding delay in securing judgment. Even in nonconsumer-related matters, agreements are oftentimes executed by parties consenting to a particular jurisdiction or even agreeing to arbitration. Reviewing a file prior to the institution of suit will preclude later defenses which may be interposed by a debtor's attorney demanding arbitration if such an agreement exists or requesting a change of venue based upon contractual provisions. Failing to note these problems when evaluating a claim can cost your clients money if the debtor's financial situation continues to deteriorate.

From time to time claims may be referred that initially appear to be based upon open account transactions. A subsequent review of the client's documents may nevertheless indicate that a security interest in the debtor's property had been taken by the creditor. In such event, an action to recover the chattels in question may be the appropriate remedy if the amount involved is substantial. The creditor may not even realize its original security agreement and corresponding Uniform Commercial Code filings cover the material delivered to the debtor at the later period; it is, therefore, essential that every effort be made to ascertain client's status as either a secured or unsecured creditor prior to recommending action. In the case of a debtor who subsequently files bankruptcy, a failure to note your client's secured position may result in losing the only effective remedy he/she has with which to enforce recovery.

Returning to the claim which is most often referred for collection, that being the claim based on open account sales to a debtor, invoices and statements also serve an important function in those cases where a concern exists as to the possibility of the debtor interposing an answer following service of summons and complaint. Very often the answer interposed by the debtor may consist of a general denial. If such an answer is anticipated, a complaint may be prepared pursuant to CPLR sec. 3016(f) using the invoices and statements in the complaint pursuant to the section, thereby precluding the use of a general denial by the debtor. This greatly enhances the prospect that a motion for at least partial summary judgment may be successful following service of the answer, assuming that the debtor does not dispute each and every item on the client's statement. The statement itself can also be used to set up a second independent cause of action as an account stated if same has previously been accepted by the debtor without dispute.

There are other reasons why a careful review of the creditor's documentation should be made prior to the institution of suit. One of the major items that is in some instances overlooked is the agreement by the debtor, oftentimes contained in either a credit application or contract, to pay attorneys' fees in the event the claim is referred to attorneys for collection. In some instances the agreement concerning attorneys' fees is overlooked by the creditor who merely forwards a claim requesting suit on the principal balance then due and owing on the claim. Since attorneys' fees are oftentimes granted for amounts in the vicinity of 20 percent of the principal balance of the claim, it is an important item to have a constant awareness of since more and more creditors do attempt to secure such agreements before entering into open account transactions with the debtor. These same credit applications or agreements can also provide for interest in excess of the normal 9 percent interest demanded in lieu of an agreement.

III. SECURING DEBTOR'S NOTES

In some instances when creditors are unable to secure collection on their past due accounts from their debtors, they attempt to secure notes executed by the debtor. It is very often only after the debtor defaults in payment on the note that the claim is referred to an attorney's office for collection. A review of such a file will result in the attorney being able to recommend action based both on the open account and the note. Thereafter if an answer is interposed on behalf of the debtor, a complaint drafted setting up both causes of action will more often allow for a quicker disposition of the matter on a motion for summary judgment on the note. The availability of a note in the creditor's file further allows you as attorney for the creditor to serve with the original summons a notice of motion for summary judgment with supporting papers pursuant to CPLR sec. 3213. The motion papers would thus be served in lieu of the complaint. In such a case where a client has been able to secure a note prior to the forwarding of the claim, if it is felt that there is no genuine defense to the cause of action on the note, it is very possible that you may be able to improve the opportunity to obtain accelerated judgment.

The availability of a note may also serve to save a claim that would otherwise be barred by the statute of limitations provision in connection with goods, wares and merchandise contained in Uniform Commercial Code sec. 2-725.

IV. CONCLUSION

Following the institution of suit, whether it be an action based on goods sold and delivered, services rendered, promissory note, account stated or other cause of action, the debtor may appear through an attorney and interpose an answer. In some instances the answer, in addition to a general denial, sets up affirmative defenses and/or counterclaims. It is at this stage that the other correspondence requested earlier from the creditor, concerning all correspondence sent to and received from the debtor, becomes important. Very often correspondence or telephone contacts between the parties, prior to the time the claim was referred for collection, will evidence a pattern of activity on the part of the debtor which may contradict substantially the answer interposed on his/her behalf. A careful review of this correspondence initially may put you in a position where prior to the institution of suit you would have knowledge as to whether or not an answer containing affirmative defenses of counterclaims was to be anticipated. In fact this documentation may have resulted in the choice to pursue one remedy over another that was available to your client. But in any event, having received the answer on behalf of the debtor from his/her attorney, with this documentation now in hand you are in a position to incorporate same into applicable affidavits for execution by the client. Very often, depending upon the quality of the documentation in the creditor's file, you may now be in a position to successfully move for summary judgment and avoid the additional time and expense of discovery proceedings.

CHECKLIST

I. Identify transaction—causes of action

A. Goods, wares, merchandise sold and delivered
B. Services rendered
C. Account stated
D. Promissory note
E. Replevin (recovery of chattel)
F. Lien rights, bond rights or trust fund rights
G. Reclamation
H. Other, credit card purchases, NSF checks, deficiency actions

II. Identify relevant statutes of limitation

A. CPLR sec. 213 - 6-year statute on contracts, notes, other causes of action with no other limitation
B. UCC sec. 2-725 - 4-year statute in contracts for sale
C. CPLR sec. 214 - 3-year statute for damage to property or action to recover chattel or to recover damages for taking or detention of a chattel
D. UCC sec. 2-702 - 10-day limitation on reclamation demand
E. USBC sec. 546 - 10-day limitation on reclamation demand
F. UCC sec. 6-111 - 6-month statute on Bulk Sales Transfer violations
G. Lien Law sec. 10 - 4-month limitation on filing mechanic's lien on single family dwelling,
8-month limitation on filing mechanic's lien on other real property
H. Lien Law sec. 12 - 30 days after completion acceptance on filing mechanics' liens on public improvements
I. Lien Law sec. 77 - 1-year limitation following completion to enforce fund claim
J. Miscellaneous notice requirements and limitation requirements in payment bonds

K. Agreements on contracts between parties fixing time limitations

III. Identify all possible defendants

A. Original debtor as per invoices, etc.—correct legal composition
B. Guarantors on credit applications, etc.
C. Makers, drawers, endorsers of commercial paper
D. Responsible parents for minor children
E. Bonding companies and/or general contractors
F. Owners of real estate where merchandise was used
G. Banks for improper dishonor of negotiable instruments

IV. Miscellaneous

A. Agreements allowing for addition of attorneys' fees
B. Agreements allowing for addition of late charges and interest
C. Debtors in bankruptcy—prepetition vs. postpetition transactions and their differing rights
D. Arbitration clauses prohibiting suit
E. Agreements on venue and venue rules, CPLR 501-513
F. Consumer vs. nonconsumer claims

CHAPTER THREE

PRELIMINARY INVESTIGATION AND AIDS

Jack L. Getman, Esq.

I. INTRODUCTION

Collecting the claim and earning a fee will depend in a large part on your investigating and evaluating not only the claim but also the debtor. It will be a waste of your client's money (for disbursements) and your time to proceed with a claim against a debtor who is totally uncollectible. This chapter will deal with some of the tools and aids available to investigate the collectibility of a debtor. How many of these aids will be used and to what extent they will be used will depend in a large part on the amount of the claim; obviously some claims may not warrant the time or expense entailed in the use of all of these aids.

II. AIDS IN INVESTIGATING A DEBTOR'S COLLECTIBILITY

A. Client's File

Ask for and review your client's collection file, statements and invoices. Often these documents contain information that the client does not perceive as important to the collection of his/her claim. Look for:

1. Credit reports obtained by the client on the debtor.

2. Letters or purchase orders from the debtor which will reveal the full and correct name, telephone number, names of officers, and branch offices of the debtor.

3. Memoranda of telephone numbers and names of people that the client may have talked to in their attempt to collect the claim.

4. Notations of debtor's bank account or copies of checks from prior payments.

5. Any letters or memoranda from the debtor acknowledging or disputing the claim.

B. Directories

1. Telephone directories should be checked both in the white pages and the yellow pages for telephone numbers and information concerning the debtor.

2. City directories will provide information based both on names and addresses. Often they give some information about the nature of the debtor's business or employment. Code symbols used in the directories will indicate whether the premises are owner occupied and if there are other occupants at the premises. If the debtor is the owner of the property, the existence of other occupants would suggest that the debtor may have rental income.

A review of the samples of "directory" pages in Appendix A will demonstrate the kind of information available from these sources.

C. Court Records

The review of court and other government records can reveal a wealth of information concerning the debtor. Some of the records to check are:

1. Assumed name, partnership and corporation indexes. If the claim is against an entity other than an individual, it is imperative to check the indexes to determine the exact composition of the debtor before you can accurately check any other records. If you start out with the wrong name, the information you develop will be useless. Also, the indexes may provide useful information. The partnership records may give you the full name and address of all partners, and if a limited partnership, the extent of each partner's liability. Also, the Assumed Name and Partnership Certificate index may show a more accurate address or a change of address. The Certificate of Incorporation will include the name of the incorporator and the attorneys who filed the certificate, either of whom may be willing to discuss the claim with you. If the Certificate

of Incorporation is not filed locally, you can request information as to the correct name of the corporation, its current status, and the name of the attorneys filing the certificate, from the Secretary of State in Albany, by mail. They will provide this information at no charge.

2. A Judgment Docket indexed by defendant's name will reveal whether there are judgments against the debtor, and if they are still open or have been satisfied, and the name of the plaintiff and his/her attorney. This type of information is a good indication of the debtor's collectibility; and the attorneys for the judgment creditor will usually give you some indication of their experience with the debtor. If the judgments are satisfied, it is a good indication that the debtor may be solvent. The Judgment Docket also lists State Tax warrants which indicate whether the debtor is paying his/her taxes.

3. Security Agreement. A search for UCC-1 filings will tell you if the debtor has chatteled his/her assets. And on the useful side, the UCC-1 also gives you a description of the debtor's assets and how long they have been chatteled. If the assets have been chatteled for a lengthy period of time, you might assume that the debtor has some equity in those assets. The UCC search will also reveal federal tax liens against the debtor. A UCC search can be done in person or through the mail by using Form UCC-11 and paying the appropriate fee (*see* Appendix B).

4. Motor Vehicle Lien Search. Liens against a debtor's motor vehicle (1973 or newer) are not discoverable by a UCC search. Motor Vehicle Lien records are maintained by the New York State Department of Motor Vehicles in Albany and can be searched by use of M.V.-Form 905 (*see* Appendix C).

5. Tax Assessor's Office. A telephone call or visit to the appropriate tax assessor's office will tell you if the debtor owns the real property for which you have addresses.

D. Telephone Call

A telephone call may be the quickest and cheapest form of information. First, it will tell you if the debtor is still at his/her address, and if he/she is in business, the nature of his/her business. Second, it will give you an opportunity to make a demand on the debtor and to discuss his/her ability to pay the claim. If the telephone call is made in a courteous manner, you may engage the debtor in conversation which will develop information about his/her income, job, property, bank account, motor vehicles, and other assets.

E. Personal Inspection

Sometimes the size of the claim warrants someone from your office making a personal inspection at the debtor's address, particularly if the debtor is a business. A personal inspection will reveal if the debtor is at the address given, the general nature of the business, and the nature and volume of his/her assets.

F. Certified Trace or Letter

If the debtor is not at the address given by the client, you may be able trace his/her new address by use of Certified Mail, Return Receipt Requested Form (*see* Appendix D). With postage costs of approximately $2.00 the post office will return the receipt indicating where your letter was delivered. Make sure that the return receipt is properly filled out and that that you have clearly indicated that you desire the address where the letter was delivered. Use your demand letter in the envelope and if it reaches the debtor, you will have accomplished two purposes —obtaining the address and making your demand for payment.

G. Employment Confirmation

If you have information concerning the debtor's employment, you can try to confirm that employment by a letter to the employer (*see*

Appendix E). Although the employer is not required to reply, most employers will reply if you furnish them with an easy way to respond and a self-addressed, stamped return envelope.

H. Bank Accounts

If you have the name of a bank account and the debtor's bank account number, you can call the bank and determine if the debtor has an open account. However, the bank will not reveal information concerning the amount in the account or other personal information.

I. Law Journals

The local legal newspaper gives information concerning judgments, tax liens, real estate transfers, mortgages, recently filed assumed names, recently filed corporations, pending cases, and bankruptcies. If you read the paper on a daily basis, it will provide you with current information concerning the debtors against whom you have claims.

J. Previous Experience

It should be your office practice to check new claims against your other open or closed files. You may find that you have previous files against the debtor which will assist you in dealing with the debtor in collecting the new claim.

K. Private Detectives

Sometimes the clients have to be reminded that your law office is not and cannot be a private detective agency. If the client desires detective work, an outside agency should be hired. However, this should not be done without the client's consent and approval as to the expense involved; and if your office is contracting the hiring, it is preferred that the client advances the funds for the anticipated expense. The detective should be given specific information or a specific goal; without such specific instructions, the expense may get out of hand. In commercial cases, the detective's job is usually limited to either locating the defendant or locating some specified assets.

L. Other

The nature of the claim may require or suggest other forms of investigation. For example, if the claim involves materials or services supplied to the improvement of real property, information can be obtained from the owner, the general contractor, and from the accessor's records. Such information may indicate that the client has some Mechanic's Lien or payment bond rights. If such rights exist, they should be pursued along with any action on the money claim itself, as they may be the ultimate source of payment.

Appendix A

ALPHABETICAL DIRECTORY
WHITE PAGES

(h) HOUSEHOLDER (r) RESIDENT OR ROOMER

BLUE COLLAR WORKERS

EMPLOYED WOMEN

correct full name — Landon Edw G & Charlotte D; servmn B F Goodrich h1215 Oak Dr ◎

occupation and employer — Landon Fred M & Mary E; supvr Reliance Elec h60 Norman Av ◎

Landon Kenneth A & Carol L; clk First Natl Bk h1400 E Main St Apt 14

complete street address including apartment number — (h1400 E Main St Apt 14)

Landon Kenneth A Jr studt r1400 E Main St Apt 14

student 18 years of age or older — (Landon Kenneth A Jr studt)

Landon Virginia E r1641 W 4th St

Lane See Also Layne

cross reference of surnames — (Lane See Also Layne)

Lane Allen M & Joan M (Allen's Bakery) h1234 Grand Blvd ◎

Lane Avenue Restaurant (Ernest G Long) 216 Lane Av

out-of-town resident employed in area — Lane James M & Betty B; brkmn Penn Central r Rt 1 Jefferson O

armed force member and branch of service — Lane Marvin L USA r1234 Grand Blvd

Lane Robt B & Margt E; retd h1402 N High St ◎

Lane Walter M r1234 Grand Blvd

Layne See Also Lane

Layne Agnes E Mrs v-pres Layne Co h2325 Eureka Rd

wife's name and initial — Layne Albert M & Minnie B; slsmn Hoover Co h19 Bellows Av ◎

corporation showing officers and nature of business — Layne Co Inc Thos E Layne Pres Mrs Agnes E Layne V-Pres Edw T Layne Sec-Treas bldg contrs 100 N High St

homeowner –
suburban designation
retiree
business partnership showing partners in parenthesis
husband and wife employed
"r" resident or roomer
"h" householders
owner of business showing name of business in parenthesis
bold type denotes paid listing
business firm showing name of owner in parenthesis
unmarried and unemployed resident
more than one adult in household
church showing name of pastor

Layne Edw T & Diane E; sec-treas Layne Co h140 Oakwood Dr ◎
Layne Ralph P & Gladys M; formn Layne Co h1687 Maple Dr ◎
Layne Thos E & Agnes E; pres Layne Co h2325 Eureka Rd ◎
Leach See Also Leech
Leach Wm E USMC r1209 Ravenscroft Rd (EF)
Lee Alf M & Celia J; retd h2106 Oakwood Dr
Lee Bros (Louis J And Harry M Lee) plmbs 151 Abbott St
Lee Harry M & Karen L (Lee Bros) h2023 Stone Rd
Lee Louis J & Martha B (Lee Bros) h1616 Fulton
Lee Martha B Mrs ofc sec Lee Bros h1616 Fulton
Lee Minnie M Mrs h87 Eastview Dr ◎
Lee Muriel E r810 LaForge St
Lee Sterling T & Nadine S; mtcemn Eastview Apts h202 Wilson St Apt 1
Lee Thos W & Effie M (Tom's Men's Wear) r Rt 23
LEE'S PHARMACY (Lee A Shaw) Prescriptions Carefully Compounded, Complete Line Of Toiletries And Cosmetics, Fountain Service, Greeting Cards, 1705 N High St (21505) Tel 245-9040
Leech See Also Leach
Leech Doris E tchr North High Sch h1323 W McLean St ◎
Leech Joseph B & Lucy V; slsmn Metropolitan Dept Store h824 Wilson St ◎
Leech Joseph B Jr studt r824 Wilson St
Leech Marcia M clk Community Hosp r1323 W McLean St
Lewis Anne M Mrs clk County Hwy Dept h914 Wilson Av
Lewis Ernest W studt r914 Wilson Av
Lewis Harold G & Anne M; mgr Cooper Paint Store h914 Wilson Av ◎
Lewis Robt B lab County Hwy Dept r1410 Union Hwy Rt 2
Lewistown Methodist Church Rev John R Allen Pastor 515 Maple Valley Rd

ADDRESSAKEY FEATURES

Complete Street Name → CALE AV SW 44720 ← Zip Code

NORTH CANTON

4403	IRWIN HOWARD L	484-4278 +4
4406	KIRBY PAUL	484-4097 3
	TOZZI GRILL	**484-4412** 2
4434	**P K PRODUCE CO**	**484-1820**
4499	**STANDARD OIL CO THE**	**484-3755** 8
4501		00
4510	STOFFEL GEO P	484-1875 +4
	STOFFELS WELL DRLNG	**484-1875** 2
4515		00
4602	MCCLURE LEWIS W	484-2749
4603	MCROBIE KATHY	484-5104 +4
	RODGERS ALLAN	484-5104 7
	RODGERS DON C	484-3171
4607	GIFFEN MARGARET	484-2296
4612	SMYTHE KENNETH A	484-4148
4613	PFOUTS C	484-6560 9
4623		00
4627	YUTZEY RAY A	484-2752
4630	DIERKING ERNEST	484-2740
	DIERKING JOYCE	484-2740
4636		00
4637	VALENTINE PATK	484-6570 6
4702	HUDSPETH R	484-3569 7
4707	BAER DONALD IRVIN	484-2343
4713	ORDUVENSKY STEPHEN	484-2818
4717	ROHRIG PAUL A	484-1402
4726	**GRANGE INS AGCY**	**484-2506**
	MCLAUGHLIN YOHE AGC	**484-2506** +4
4728	**US PST OFC NO IND**	**484-5200**
4730	**SPEE D FOODS 04**	**484-1662**
4735		00
4801	KLEPTACH JOHN G	484-2159 2
4811	MARKLE RUSSELL H	484-2074
4815	MCCLELLAND JOHN M	484-4245
4827		00
4837	**BOWLINGS USED CARS**	**484-2096**
4840	DAUGHENBAUGH F P	484-2767
4841	HOWARD P D	484-2802
4846	REICHMAN E D	484-2849
4847	DEVAULT N	484-2789
4901	**CONE CORNER**	**484-1822** 6
4961	BARR L E	484-2634
5013	HANEY WM	484-2761 +4

Multiple Residential Listing → (4602 / 4603)

+ Symbol is New Listing Identification Current Year ← (484-5104 +4)

More than one person in same family listed with same phone number → (4630)

9 or more years at this address with same phone number ← (484-2740)

Multiple Business Listings with same phone number → (4726)

Business or Non-Residential Identification **Printed in bold type** ← (484-5200)

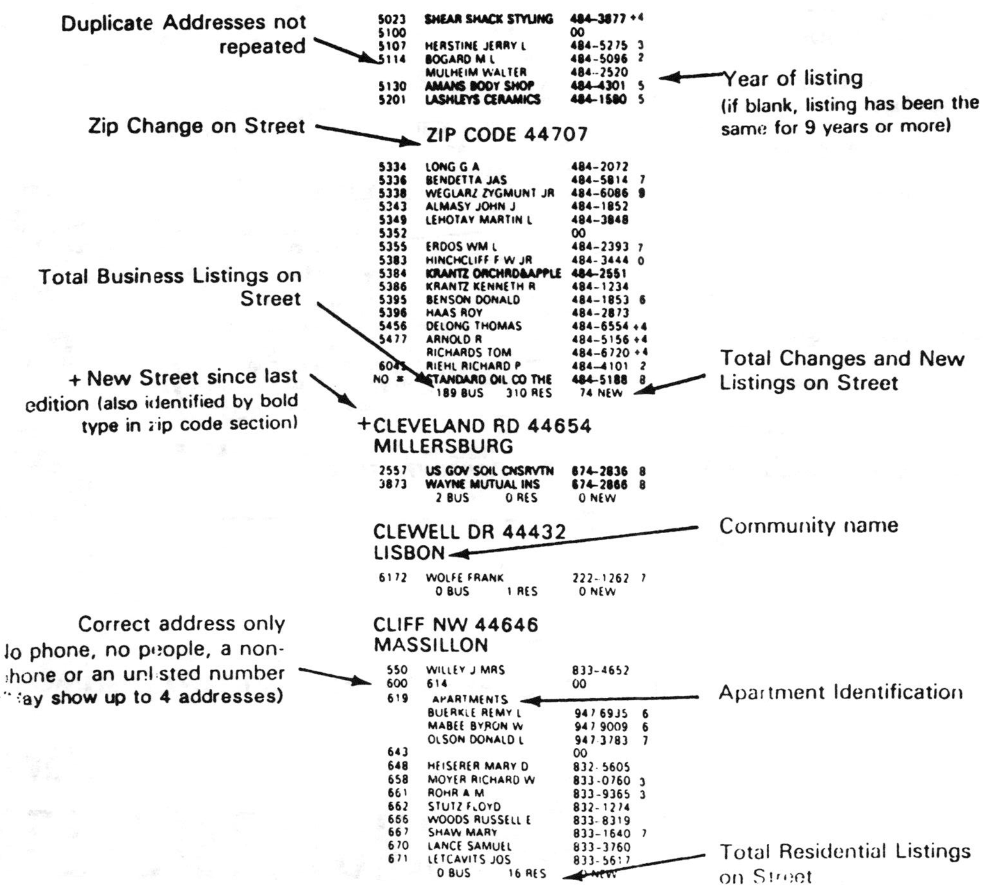
Duplicate Addresses not repeated
Zip Change on Street
Total Business Listings on Street
+ New Street since last edition (also identified by bold type in zip code section)
Correct address only
No phone, no people, a non-phone or an unlisted number
(may show up to 4 addresses)
Year of listing
(if blank, listing has been the same for 9 years or more)
Total Changes and New Listings on Street
Community name
Apartment Identification
Total Residential Listings on Street
5023 SHEAR SHACK STYLING 484-3877 +4
5100 00
5107 HERSTINE JERRY L 484-5275 3
5114 BOGARD M L 484-5096 2
MULHEIM WALTER 484-2520
5130 AMANS BODY SHOP 484-4301 5
5201 LASHLEYS CERAMICS 484-1580 5
ZIP CODE 44707
5334 LONG G A 484-2072
5336 BENDETTA JAS 484-5814 7
5338 WEGLARZ ZYGMUNT JR 484-6086 9
5343 ALMASY JOHN J 484-1852
5349 LEHOTAY MARTIN L 484-3848
5352 00
5355 ERDOS WM L 484-2393 7
5383 HINCHCLIFF F W JR 484-3444 0
5384 KRANTZ ORCHRD&APPLE 484-2551
5386 KRANTZ KENNETH R 484-1234
5395 BENSON DONALD 484-1853 6
5396 HAAS ROY 484-2873
5456 DELONG THOMAS 484-6554 +4
5477 ARNOLD R 484-5156 +4
RICHARDS TOM 484-6720 +4
6045 RIEHL RICHARD P 484-4101 2
NO # STANDARD OIL CO THE 484-5188 8
189 BUS 310 RES 74 NEW
+CLEVELAND RD 44654
MILLERSBURG
2557 US GOV SOIL CNSRVTN 674-2836 8
3873 WAYNE MUTUAL INS 674-2866 8
2 BUS 0 RES 0 NEW
CLEWELL DR 44432
LISBON
6172 WOLFE FRANK 222-1262 7
0 BUS 1 RES 0 NEW
CLIFF NW 44646
MASSILLON
550 WILLEY J MRS 833-4652
600 614 00
619 APARTMENTS
BUERKLE REMY L 947 6935 6
MABEE BYRON W 947 9009 6
OLSON DONALD L 947 3783 7
643 00
648 HEISERER MARY D 832-5605
658 MOYER RICHARD W 833-0760 3
661 ROHR A M 833-9365 3
662 STUTZ FLOYD 832-1274
666 WOODS RUSSELL E 833-8319
667 SHAW MARY 833-1640 7
670 LANCE SAMUEL 833-3760
671 LETCAVITS JOS 833-5617
0 BUS 16 RES 0 NEW

STREET DIRECTORY

GREEN PAGES

◎ HOMEOWNER SYMBOL ★ NEW NEIGHBOR SYMBOL

NEW NEIGHBOR

HOMEOWNERS

1

ANSON AV—FROM 718 MAIN ST SOUTH, 1 WEST OF PARK CIR — complete street description

ZIP CODE 23652 — zip code

28 Hardee Wm A ◎ 256-0740 — homeowner
29 ★Smith James M ◎ 256-1350 — new householder this edition
30 Hope Robt M ◎
41 Ashley Walter B 256-6052 — telephone number
50 ★Ross Kenneth E
53 Vacant
56 Geisler Albert H ◎ — homeowner without telephone
57 Under Constn — under construction
HIGH ST INTERSECTS — intersecting street
101 Royal Court Apartments — apartment building and occupants
A Grady Carol A Mrs
B ★Strickland Geo L 256-2171 — complete street address including apartment number
C Poole Anne M 256-7626
D Fowler Martha A Mrs 256-7680

FAMILIES WHO RENT

TELEPHONE PAY STATION

"VACANTS" AND UNDER CONSTRUCTION

PROSPECTING

- By Neighborhood
- By Area of Section of City
- By Occupation, Job Title

110 Sinclair James L Jr bldg contr ◉ 256-1025 — business operated out of home
rear ★Sinclair Henry B
MEADOW ST INTERSECTS

2

ARLINGTON ST (UNIONTOWN) FROM 900 S 26TH AV WEST — suburban designation

ZIP CODE 23653
702 Galkins Shell Service gas sta 256-3632 — possible pay telephone not normally listed in telephone book
705 Arlington Building — office building showing room number and occupant of each office
Rooms
100 Bristol Barber Shop
101 Modern Beauty Shoppe 256-8515
102 Vacant — vacant
103 Johnson Harlan G lwyr 256-6553 — nature of business shown when not self explanatory
104 Packard Victor O phys 256-4493
105 State Union Insurance Co 256-8515
710 First National Bank (Br) 256-5961 — branch of business firm
STEWART AV INTERSECTS
801 Arlington Street Market groc 256-7854 — multiple purpose address, business firm and residence at same address
Walters Clyde B 256-7854
806 Patterson Thos A — renter without telephone
807 Francis Fred F ◉ 256-6170
810 Danko Mattie M Mrs ◉ — nearest telephone
825 City Hall — government offices showing department and telephone number
Floors
1st Fl City Clerk 256-2620
1st Fl City Manager 256-2622
2d Fl City Engineer 256-2626
2d Fl City Treasurer 256-2624
STREET CONTINUED

827 Safeway Plumbing & Heating 256-1121
878 West End United Methodist Church
831 Toby's TV Sales & Service 256-2802
833 Standard Oil Co gas sta 256-0476

CLASSIFIED BUSINESS DIRECTORY

EXPLANATION OF INFORMATION IN THIS SECTION

business classification — **BOOKKEEPING SERVICE**

complete name and street address — Blackstone Ronald J 310 College St Rm 101

professional style extended information listing includes telephone numbers — Dixon J E & Co Suite 600 Dix Bldg 125 S Maple St
Tel 282-1675 Res Tel 285-6972

Local Bookkeeping Service 642 E Pine Rd

BOX MANUFACTURERS

all firms are listed without cost under their principal classification — Karton Box Co 142 Bishop Mill Rd (RV)
Union Box & Bag Inc 301 Ragsdale St

BUILDING MATERIALS AND SUPPLIES

heavy black type (bold type listing) denotes paid listing — **GOLDSTONE BUILDERS SUPPLY INC, 1645 Battle Av, PO Box 7549, Anytown, USA (27840) Tel 285-1849**

Hedgewood Home & Building Supply Co 401 Janesville Rd

suburban designation — Nelte Lumber & Building Materials 525 Adams Rd (TC)

Names appearing under headings marked thus (*) are inserted only when specially contracted for.

ACCOUNTANTS

Alico Kenneth N S4280 S Buffalo St (OP)
Almquist Leonard J 12 Main St (H) Rm 104
Buccieri And Buccieri 72 Hamburg St (EA)
Caffarelli Anthony C 19 Rainbow Ter (OP)
Computing By US 151 Queensway Rd (E)
Elma Tax Service 260 Girdle Rd (E)
Ferraro And Ferraro S3656 Abbott Rd (H)
Gould And Swanson 1 Main St (H)
Green Danl J 7625 Seneca St (E)
Hamms Geo D 6398 W Quaker St (OP)

KIEFER ELMER J & CO
4219 CLARK STREET
HAMBURG NEW YORK (14075)
TELEPHONE 649-7550

Lillie Marvin M S6786 Woodland Dr (H)
Majewski Income Tax Accounting Firm 5710 Seufert Rd (OP)
Mason-Benz-Atkinson S3605 Eggert Rd (OP)
Mercer R A & Co S3576 California Rd (OP)
Mumbach Donald J 40 Main St (H)
Philipps & Co 765 Main St (EA)
Povinelli Thos P 204 Pierce Av (H)
Rozbicki Alf B 3997 Ockler Pl (H)
Schrobacz Joseph S4280 S Buffalo St (OP)
Schultz Raymond S4728 Kennison Pkwy (H)
Schwabel Wm S4230 N Buffalo Rd (OP)
Selle & Co 85 Main St (H)
Whittall Maurice D 2725 West Blood Rd (E)
Zablonski Leonard 3718 Sowles Rd (H)

ACCOUNTANTS—CERTIFIED PUBLIC

Chamberlain Paul 19 E Union St (H)
Gaines Emhof Metzler & Co 6507 E Quaker Rd (OP)
Paulus & Co 49 Buffalo St (H) Rm 203
Sawers Edw J 7 George St (H)
Sixt Edward L 1075 Davis Rd (AUR)

ADVERTISING AGENCIES

ELLIS SINGER WEBB & ASSOC 1035 Delaware Av (Buffalo; 14209), Tel 884-8885
Flagler & Nelson Inc S6200 South Park Av (H)
Hamburg Penny Saver Inc 50 Buffalo St (H)
Heppner Advertising 25 Colony Rd (OP)
Southtowns Advertising Plaza Pk (H)
Ted's Sales 1901 Woodard Rd (E)

W L K COMPANIES INC
MAINSPRING/W L K
ADVERTISING
120 DELAWARE AVENUE
4TH FLOOR
BUFFALO NEW YORK (14202)
TELEPHONE 853-6755

*ADVERTISING—CITY DIRECTORY

POLK R L & CO
15 RIVERVIEW BUSINESS PARK
300 COMMERCIAL STREET
MALDEN MA 02148
TELEPHONE (617) 322-0500

ADVERTISING—DIRECT MAIL

Alpha Advertising & Printing 112 Lake Av (BL)
Guastella And Associates Inc 4927 Southwestern Blvd (H)
Lad Enterprises 227 Thorn Av (OP)

NUMERICAL TELEPHONE DIRECTORY

BLUE PAGES

This Directory takes the "mystery" out of blind numbers. It lists telephone numbers in numercial sequence, making it easy to "decode" blind phone numbers in classified ads—especially valuable for real estate agencies, used car dealers, etc.

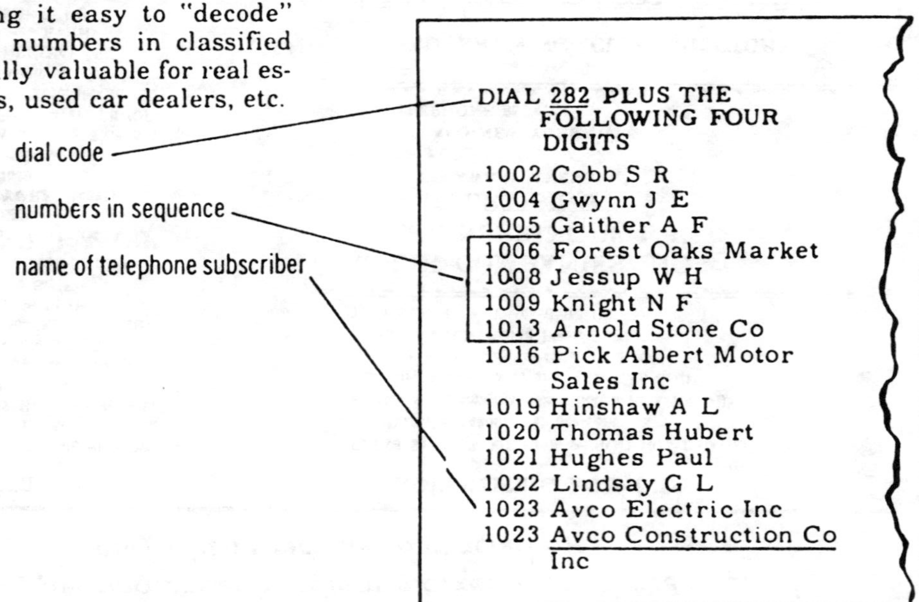

WHAT'S IN A PHONE NUMBER?

ABOUT THE FIRM:
Who called me? When your call back message gives a telephone number only—or includes a common surname such as Jones, Smith, Brown, etc.—this Numerical Telephone Directory will assist in determining correct firm name. Make use of both Alphabetical and Street Guide information to establish names of officers, owners or partners, products and services, and correct address. Properly identify firm and caller and have needed records, file or correspondence on hand before returning call.

ABOUT THE INDIVIDUAL:
Who called me? When only a telephone number is known, this Numerical Telephone Directory will assist in determining the name of the subscriber—with this information combined with other sections of your Polk Directory you may quickly establish such information as wife's name, place of employment, job title, home address, business address and telephone number.

BUFFALO **THE HAINES DIRECTORY** 1984 **6TH AV**

1ST AV		14120 CONT	
75	XXXX	00	
75	SCHUBERT DONALD J	692-6280	0
77	FEZER C	692-1103	9
	HURKO HENRY	692-9247	
	SANDERSON DONALD P	693-6484	3
112	WASIELEWSKI FRANK	693-0854	
114	LORICH HAROLD	693-2061	3
120	LORICH KENNETH	694-2782	3
124	FIRE M A	694-4254	0
	ZARZECZNY A	692-6579	2
125	XXXX	00	
126	SOBOCINSKI STANLEY	693-2261	
*	1 BUS 55 RES	4 NEW	

2ND 14219 BLASDELL

3626	GOVENETTIO M A	822-6588	+4
3629	KARALUS EDWARD J	825-0048	+4
3631	NENDZA LEO	822-4592	1
3633	ZAHM L M	825-1516	1
3640	OBERST RAYMOND	825-3097	1
3641	CLARK K T	823-5271	1
3643	SCHROEDER MARY J	823-5203	1
3644	CLARK RICKY	823-0746	+4
3647	PALMER CLYDE F	822-7207	1
	TAYLOR N H	826-3756	3
3650	PATTON GLENN A	824-7086	1
3654	LOKUTA SUE	825-5920	3
3659	TOMAKA FRANK	823-7854	1
3660	PYZIKIEWICZ JULIUS	825-8130	3
3662	WALTERS S	825-0335	+4
3666	MALLERY PETER	825-6478	1
3669	KEKONI JULIUS	823-4396	1
3671	PELLIEN J	827-8765	1
3676	RUCHALSKI JOSEPHINE	824-0738	1
3677	PINTER MICHAEL JR	823-7953	1
3684	OLENIACZ JOSEPH W	825-0739	1
3688	ZUKOWSKI THOMAS J	822-1539	1
3692	HAYES FRANCIS L	822-3189	1
3696	PEACOCK CLARA M	823-9938	1
	RIVERA W M	822-0465	1
3698	BROWN JERRY	825-8620	+4
	HRYCYSZYN WILLIAM	823-0560	1
3700	SCHWEIKERT MARY L	823-9365	1
*	0 BUS 28 RES	5 NEW	

2ND AV		14120 CONT	
50	NELSON BARBARA	695-3994	1
53	BRZEZINSKI RICHARD	694-4781	5
54	CIESIELSKI PAUL L	694-0501	9
	GERBEC JAMES	694-0586	7
	LYONS K G	694-8808	3
55	XXXX	00	
57	FEATHERSTONE R A SR	693-1142	
60	NUGENT WILLIAM G	694-2864	0
61	CUNNINGHAM ALEX	693-9067	
62	XXXX	00	
66	MCCABE LLOYD S	693-4717	
67	CROWE RENE	694-3158	3
	VONA CLAUDE	693-5933	
67½	GIBSON EDGAR D	695-3561	+4
72	HABUDA STANLEY	695-1932	
73	POCHEPAN JACOB	692-8457	5
75	KUKUCKA JOS	693-3305	
78	NOVOSAT STEPH F JR	694-4812	
114	XXXX	00	
117	LACHUT STEPH	693-1545	
118	COPP ROBERT L	692-9038	2
125	BIRCH KEVIN	692-7241	3
	BRONSCHIDLE SCOTT L	694-3364	0
	KALOTA K	693-9307	+4
	WILSON P	694-3741	1
126	MOGAVERO MICHAEL F	693-6773	+4
NO #	HEAPS J	694-0219	2
*	0 BUS 51 RES	5 NEW	

3RD 14219 BLASDELL

3613	XXXX	00	
3614	PELKEY CLIFFORD J	825-6786	1
3650	SCHROEDER ELMER	826-3084	1
3651	SCHUMACHER KENNETH	823-8282	1
3654	ROGERS ALAN G	826-1024	1
3657	SMITH JOHN Z	823-8315	+4
3660	BOLGA J	822-3432	2
3663	DURUSKI ANDREW	823-2761	1
3666	OLENIACZ I M	822-8334	1
3667	GEARHART T	826-2663	+4
	SCHWEIKERT CHARLES	823-3667	2
3670	BURKE DOUGLAS	823-6314	1
3674	PETTIS ROBERT A	824-7623	1
3675	SCARSELLA E	824-5158	+4
3678	GEARHART JOHN V	825-5915	1
3680	CLARK JAMES J	822-5236	1

3RD AV		14120 CONT	
113	BELVISO PHILIP D	694-7635	
114	XXXX	00	
118	ROGERS THOMAS	692-6729	2
119	AMBRUSKO L	692-8530	
122	JASINSKI WALTER	692-3163	
123	WASIELEWSKI HELEN	693-3313	
125	FRELEWICZ ELIZ	692-5084	
126	WILSON RON	692-3509	3
*	0 BUS 37 RES	2 NEW	

4TH 14219 BLASDELL

3653	PLARR GEO D JR	823-7611	2
3654	WOJTKOWSKI C	825-4297	3
3657	PLARR GEORGE D	825-1187	1
3664	BALICKI RONALD J	827-8899	1
	SCHLITZ EDW	824-6639	2
3669	ENGLER PAUL	826-0586	+4
3670	CASSIDY FOREST L	824-4854	1
3672	BAXTER DONALD D JR	824-1030	3
	KOLB JOHN E	824-6492	1
3675	LENAHAN PAUL F	824-0268	+4
3680	MARDINO ANTHONY R	822-2293	2
3681	LEIBOLD LOUIS	825-1885	1
3684	JONES EMERSON	823-1829	1
3685	PASSINAULT KENNETH	824-4591	3
	SOBASZEK JOSEPH JR	824-4558	1
3690	SMOLAREK MAUREEN	822-5058	2
3697	DUENGFELDER JOHN JR	826-7494	1
*	1 BUS 16 RES	2 NEW	

4TH 14201 BUFFALO

SOUTHWEST FROM
266 WEST GENESEE

X	W GENESEE		
X	WILKESON		
X	COURT		
X	GEORGIA		
X	CAROLINA		
X	VIRGINIA		
X	MARYLAND		
443	HARPER L M	854-6377	+4
X	HUDSON		

4TH		14201 CONT	
553	XXXX	00	
554	MCKAIN LENORE	849-0083	3
558	XXXX	00	
561	APARTMENTS		
	GRICE CURTIS	847-0632	2
	HALE HARRIET C	855-5033	3
	HERNDON GENEVA	856-4142	
	NORAT ANTONIO R	845-6374	+4
	REARDON S	856-1335	2
561			
562	BLANKS BESSIE MAE	854-1188	3
	CARUSO ANGELINE	847-6941	9
	DOMINO FRANK	854-5031	
	PEDANO M	847-6936	9
565	APARTMENTS		
	CLAYTON NAOMI	855-0514	3
	LAXTON ARTHUR	855-2422	5
	MEDINA GERTRUDE	856-5976	2
	MOORE LUCILLE	852-4009	+4
	TROUTMAN I	856-3195	1
	WEAVER MCKINLEY REV	854-1665	
565			
566	PARK I J	855-0179	5
	TUCKER W M	855-2119	3
	WORTHY B	856-5792	2
569	XXXX	00	
572	BUCHOLTZ F	854-5460	1
575	HOLT G	847-2073	3
X	JERSEY		
617	XXXX	00	
619	ADIMEY C	886-1007	8
	ADIMEY ROBT	886-2875	
621	XXXX	00	
629	UNITD TELEVISN SYS	886-2551	0
X	PORTER AVE		
*	1 BUS 127 RES	16 NEW	

4TH 14072 GRAND ISLAND

2227	DLUGOKINSKI ALEXNDR	773-5877	
2248	COLEMAN WALTER	877-4027	
	LYNCH ROBERT J	773-0903	+4
2256	ZAUNER RALPH	773-4735	
2257	CLARKE RICHARD C	773-1250	8
2276	TICKNER RONALD L	773-3179	C
2289	HOLMES GEORGE	773-6288	6

2ND 14227 S CHEEKTOWAGA

2 GAWRON WALTER R 683-0922 2
* 0 BUS 1 RES 0 NEW

2ND 14057 EDEN

2746 DUMOND FRANCIS A 992-9476
2749 XXXX 00
2750 HUGHEY W 992-3119
2753 TWIST PAUL F 992-4203
2757 LOEBER D 992-4529 0
2758 HARMS ROBT L 992-2976
2761 GAVIN JOHN W 992-4863 9
2762 XXXX 00
2781 LAHRS DAVID G 992-4304 0
2782 COCINA JOSEPH JR 992-4612 3
2785 SCOTT RICHARD L 992-2130
2789 HANNEMAN GLENNA 992-9267 +4
SPACKMAN PAUL R 992-9096 9
2795 REMILY NORMA C 992-3885
2796 OCONNOR WALTER D 992-4814 3
2810 KLEIN MARVIN 992-4573
2813 DRESSER CHARLES JR 992-4365 7
2820 XXXX 00
2823 CHAPMAN JAY W 992-3997
* 0 BUS 19 RES 1 NEW

2ND 14072 GRAND ISLAND

2225 CHRZANOWSKI LEO 773-7037 3
2242 WROBLEWSKI JOS V 773-4748
2269 CLARKE GILLMAN H 773-3282
2282 DIMARCO VINCENT J 773-2802 5
2291 RICOTTA JOHN J 773-2183 9
2300 XXXX 00
2305 OCHS HENRY 773-3765 9
2337 ACCARDI H 773-7187
2344 GOUPIL DANIEL A 773-6097 5
2352 MISTRETTA RUSSELL 773-4318
2371 ZYGMUNT JUDITH 773-1645 3
2384 XXXX 00
* 0 BUS 12 RES 0 NEW

2ND W 14043 DEPEW

23 ATLAS LEO J 684-5735
26 LEWANDOWSKI HOWARD 683-0464
32 GANGLOFF R 683-6196 1
38 NOSKY DONALD E [illegible]

3681 RZEPECKI LOUIS F 822-4420 1
3684 RUSSELL CHARLES T 826-0685 1
3689 LIEDY ROSE 823-0997 1
ROWLAND WM J 826-4149 1
3693 RENZI M 822-5841 2
* 0 BUS 21 RES 3 NEW

3RD W 14043 DEPEW

10 SHARP RALPH JR 681-4678 3
21 ELWOOD CLIFFORD SR 683-2274 6
22A BARONE C 681-1849 0
27 DENZEL LARRY 681-0997 3
28 DOMKOWSKI KENNETH L 684-0130 +4
WESLEY JAMES F 683-4145 3
33 MEYER JAMES P 681-0532 1
SCHEELAR DALE A 681-1864 1
39 MINNECI C A 681-8119 8
SCOTT RANDY L 681-8567 +4
45 SAVASH JOHN A 683-8225 8
YOUNG GERALD E JR 681-1624 +4
* 0 BUS 12 RES 3 NEW

3RD AV 14221 WILLIAMSVILLE

385 IVINS GREG 631-9628 2
391 XXXX 00
397 KREHL PAUL W 631-8170 2
399 BLOOM HENRY J 634-9722 +4
401 BRYK JEROME E 634-5712 2
403 UTTS NORMAN L 631-0221 6
405 BUSCH CHARLES H 633-2808
407 PUNSKY A 634-9557 +4
409 XXXX 00
411 BERES EDWIN 633-5174 1
413 CLANCY M 634-9009 8
414 SZYMANSKI A 634-2389 1
415 CLARK L A 633-6531
417 XXXX 00
419 HIGGINS WILLIAM 634-7619 +4
420 ZEHLER JOSEPH D 631-3989 7
421 XXXX 00
423 ESCHNER CHARLES G 632-7028
425 KOREN S M 634-899[illegible] 3
426 SCHUMANN FRANKLIN P 631-9775 1
429 CAULFIELD CHARLES 634-7510 0
431 XXXX 00
433 JACOBSON BRADLEY 631-3720 +4
435 HUGHES CLARENCE 633-8814 2

445 ASKEW J 854-4340 3
447 DEJESUS OBED 855-3518 3
448 WHITE THOMAS A 854-0210 +4
453 APARTMENTS
GOODWIN VICTORIA J 845-6274 9
KIRKLAND ANNIE 852-2910 +4
RAMOS ALEJO 842-1463 1
REED M 855-3822 0
ZIMMERMAN GRACE I 845-6996 9
453
454 CARUSO JOSEPH 854-5096
LYLES K 847-0949 3
MILLER R 854-1165 7
457 DIXON J 852-6749 +4
DORSETT G 856-4945 2
GOODRUM LENORA 855-3899 3
LILLARD I 849-0838 7
458 APARTMENTS
ASHTON R 845-6954 3
BRANT WILLIE 855-2596 +4
DAVIS CHARLES 855-2350 2
EDWARDS MINERVIA 856-2247 2
HEASLIP V D 842-1050 9
NOACK D 856-3756 0
ROBERTS G 856-4559 0
SALTER RUDY MRS 852-4389 5
458
461 XXXX 00
462 XXXX 00
464 XXXX 00
465 XXXX 00
466 SHATTUCK A G 852-8261 3
467 XXXX 00
473 XXXX 00
475 DAVIS D 847-2032 3
476 XXXX 00
477 XXXX 00
478 TRIBBLE B 855-1978 +4
479 XXXX 00
480 XXXX 00
483 DAVI I 856-1272 3
HORRIGAN A 856-3308 8
484 COCHRAN DAVID 856-1146 +4
SMITH M P 856-7636 2
487 KESSEL ROBERT C 84[illegible]-106[illegible] 3
DONALD H 842-0464 9
H E P 856-0244 3
[illegible] M 855-3405 2
488 APARTMENTS
COTTON E R 852-5514 0
COTTON MINNIE L 856-2031 2

* 0 BUS 7 RES 1 NEW

4TH W 14043 DEPEW

8 ZIELINSKI THOMAS 681-0980 9
14 CANFIELD THOS C 683-4014
15 HESS NORMAN G JR 681-8953 +4
TURZYNSKI BROWNIE 685-4292 9
20 PERRY BERNARD A 683-9004
26 ARENA RUSSELL M 683-5218 9
* 0 BUS 6 RES 1 NEW

4TH AV 14086 LANCASTER

9 XXXX 00
12 FAULHABER MARK 681-4180
13 MARTZOLF I M 683-3603
17 RECZKA DANIEL 681-0933 2
20 SWIAT JOHN T JR 684-2752 +4
21 NAJUCH LEON 683-8[illegible]
24 MINGOIA JOS 683-7840
25 XXXX 00
28 MEYER E J 683-7941
32 HAAG L J 683-5993 1
45 STOLDT HERBERT 683-1530
46 ANGIELCZYK MAX F 684-2536 5
49 BAUER R J 683-8377
50 OVERHOLT JAY E 684-8582
52 AYRES ATHERTON 683-1945
55 XXXX 00
56 ALLEN E M 683-1832 3
60 PETERS WAYNE 683-7135 2
61 LAROSE PAUL J 683-5968
64 HUBBARD CHESTER J 681-1167 2
65 CZUWIT ANTHONY H 683-2597
66 WINIASZ STANLEY 683-9066 +4
67 CHAMBRON JOEL 681-5657 +4
70 GUARINO THOMAS F JR 681-1879 6
71 SEKUTERSKI RON 683-1567 +4
75 XXXX 00
77 STUDLEY CARROLL R 683-3433
81 XXXX 00
87 XXXX 00
88 KOSCIELNIAK ALAN 684-4846 +4
92 SAGLIANI M 681-7310 3
95 FINK THECKLA S MRS 683-2986
99 DELZER KENNETH W 683-8614
100 GILBERT PHILIP 683-9354
101 AMBROSE GASTON [illegible]

Appendix B

Uniform Commercial Code — REQUEST FOR INFORMATION OR COPIES — Form UCC-11

JULIUS BLUMBERG, INC. N. Y. C. 10013

IMPORTANT — Read instructions on back before filling out form

REQUEST FOR COPIES OR INFORMATION. Present in DUPLICATE to Filing Officer.

1. Debtor (Last Name First) and Address:	Party requesting information or copies: (Name and Address)	For Filing Officer: Date, Time, No. Filing Office

☐ INFORMATION REQUEST: ☐ COPY REQUEST:

Filing officer please furnish certificate showing whether there is on file as of ______________, 19___ at __________ ___ M., any presently effective financing statement naming the above named debtor(s) and any statement of assignment thereof, and if there is, giving the date and hour of filing of each such statement and the name(s) and address(es) of each secured party(ies) therein. The statutory fee is enclosed. Filing officer please furnish exact copies of each page of financing statements and statements of assignment listed below, which are on file with your office. Enclosed $ ______________ fee for copies requested. In case any of said statements contain more than one page the undersigned agrees to pay the statutory fee for each additional page payable in advance.

Date ______________________ (Signature of Requesting Party) ______________________

File No.	Date and Hour of Filing	Name(s) and Address(es) of Secured Party(ies) and Assignees, if any

CERTIFICATE: The undersigned filing officer hereby certifies that:

☐ the above listing is a record of all presently effective financing statements and statements of assignment which name the above debtor(s) and which are on file in my office as of ______________________, 19 ______ at ____________ ___ M.

☐ the attached ________ pages are true and exact copies of all available financing statements or statements of assignment listed in above request.

COPY 1

______________ Date ______________________ Signature of Filing Officer

(5/82)

STANDARD FORM — FORM UCC-11 — Approved by Secretary of State of New York

APPROVED FOR USE IN MOST STATES

Appendix C

MV-905 (12/78) TITLE BUREAU — NEW YORK STATE DEPARTMENT OF MOTOR VEHICLES

LIEN RECORD/VEHICLE INFORMATION REQUEST FORM

Date Requested ____________________

1. Check appropriate box below. Use separate form for each request. This form should not be used to request insurance, driver license or registration information.
2. Print or type all information available.
3. Mail to: Title Bureau, New York State Department of Motor Vehicles, The Governor Nelson A. Rockefeller Empire State Plaza, Albany, New York 12228.

Request for Owner's Lien Record(s) .... $2.00 ☐ $2 Enclosed ☐ Dept. of Motor Vehicles' Charge Only

(Payable to COMMISSIONER OF MOTOR VEHICLES)

Name of Owner	Date of Birth	Year and Make of Vehicle
Address		Body Type
		Vehicle Identification Number
Name of Requester		Current Plate No. (if available)
Address		THIS BOX FOR MOTOR VEHICLE DEPARTMENT USE ONLY
		Request Code / Requester / Abstract Code

MV-905 (12/78)

RECEIPT FOR ABSTRACT

Please enter in this box, the name and address to which this abstract is to be mailed.

Name of Requester

Name of Owner (if available)

Year and Make of Vehicle (if available)

Vehicle Identification Number (if available)

Your File Number

MV-905 (12/78)

Name of Owner (if available) .... ______

Year & Make (if available) .... ______

Vehicle Identification No. (if available) .... ______

Indicate name and address of account to be charged in this box.

☐ Check or Money Order — $ ______ ☐ Dept. of Motor Vehicles Charge — $ ______

Appendix D

EXPOSE ADHESIVE — REMOVE TO EXPOSE ADHESIVE

UNITED STATES POSTAL SERVICE
OFFICIAL BUSINESS

PENALTY FOR PRIVATE USE TO AVOID PAYMENT OF POSTAGE, $300

SENDER INSTRUCTIONS
Print your name, address, and ZIP Code in the space below.
- Complete items 1, 2, 3, and 4 on the reverse.
- Attach to front of article if space permits, otherwise affix to back of article.
- Endorse article "Return Receipt Requested" adjacent to number.

RETURN TO

GOLDMAN, COSTA & GETMAN
(Name of Sender)

705 Brisbane Building
(Street or P.O. Box)

Buffalo, New York 14203
(City, State, and ZIP Code)

PS Form 3811, Dec. 1980

RETURN RECEIPT, REGISTERED, INSURED AND CERTIFIED MAIL

● SENDER: Complete items 1, 2, 3, and 4.
Add your address in the "RETURN TO" space on reverse.

(CONSULT POSTMASTER FOR FEES)

1. The following service is requested (check one).
   - ☐ Show to whom and date delivered .... ___¢
   - ☐ Show to whom, date, and address of delivery.. ___¢
2. ☐ RESTRICTED DELIVERY ___¢
   (*The restricted delivery fee is charged in addition to the return receipt fee.*)

TOTAL $____

3. ARTICLE ADDRESSED TO:

4. TYPE OF SERVICE: ☐ REGISTERED ☐ INSURED ☐ CERTIFIED ☐ COD ☐ EXPRESS MAIL — ARTICLE NUMBER

(Always obtain signature of addressee or agent)

I have received the article described above.
SIGNATURE ☐ Addressee ☐ Authorized agent

5. DATE OF DELIVERY — POSTMARK

6. ADDRESSEE'S ADDRESS (*Only if requested*)

7. UNABLE TO DELIVER BECAUSE: — 7a. EMPLOYEE'S INITIALS

Appendix E

Attn: Personnel Department

Gentlemen:

Would you please advise if you are presently employing on full or part basis

NAME ______________________________

BADGE NO. __________________________

SOCIAL SECURITY NO. ________________

ADDRESS ___________________________

____

For your convenience you may indicate your reply at the bottom of this letter and return in our enclosed self-addressed envelope.

Any information given will of course be treated as confidential. Thank you for your courtesy and cooperation.

Yours truly,

BY:

CHAPTER FOUR

DEMAND UPON THE DEBTOR

Jack L. Getman, Esq.

I. PURPOSE

A telephone or written demand upon the debtor should be made on the same day a claim is received. The demand for payment upon the debtor is as important to your law firm as it is to the client. It establishes the date when you commenced work on the claim. If the debtor makes payment direct to the client after you receive the claim, but before you make the demand, it is difficult to justify your fee to the client.

II. FORM

It is good practice to always send a written demand to the debtor. The letter should be direct and simple and should contain the name of the creditor and the full amount of the claim (*see* Appendix A). If the letter contains too much information or includes attachments, or is too long, it may give the debtor something to dispute or argue about. A demand letter should be sent even if the client has authorized immediate legal action; it establishes your presence in the case while the summons and complaint is being prepared and served.

The demand letter should not violate any of the debt collection restrictions discussed in Chapter Five. For example, if you know your client will not authorize legal action, you should not threaten legal action. General Business Law, sec. 601(8).

III. TELEPHONE DEMAND

The size or nature of the claim may warrant a personal telephone call. This call not only can serve as a demand for payment, but also can serve as a source of information. Even if the debtor tells you he/she cannot or will not pay, if you give him/her an opportunity to talk or explain his/her position, you may well develop information that will ultimately help you enforce a judgment.

IV. FOLLOW-UP

Whether you use an oral or written demand, it is imperative to develop a follow-up system. Several systems are available in the forms of diaries, tabs, ticklers, etc., which bring the file back to you in a given number of days. Don't rely on the debtor's answering your demand letter to bring the claim out of your filing system; it won't happen.

If your follow-up is a second demand letter to the debtor (*see* Appendix B), the claim should be diaried ahead for a day certain.

When you have determined that legal action is necessary, you should request and obtain suit authority from the client before proceeding with issuing a summons and complaint.

V. PAYMENT AGREEMENT

If your demands have resulted in the debtor agreeing to payment or a payment plan, you should confirm the agreement by letter to the debtor. If the payment date is in the future, or is to be in installments, your letter should request the debtor to confirm his agreement. This can be done easily by providing the debtor with an extra copy of your letter and asking him to confirm his agreement by signing the letter and returning the copy in an envelope you provide to him (*see* Appendix C). If the debtor signs your letter, you have his written acknowledgement of the debt. If the debtor receives and keeps your letter without response, you have a justifiable inference that the debtor does not dispute the debt. In either case, the letter can be helpful in establishing the debtor's liability if he/she fails to pay and tries to contest your legal action.

The anticipated return of your letter and the proposed payment dates should be diaried for follow-up action in the event the debtor does not keep his/her agreement.

Appendix A

GOLDMAN, COSTA AND GETMAN
ATTORNEYS AT LAW

KARL GOLDMAN
PETER L COSTA
JACK L GETMAN

RICHARD J BIRYLA

705 BRISBANE BUILDING
BUFFALO, N. Y. 14203
716 853-4340

Re: Claimant
Amount

The above named claimant has retained our office to collect their claim against you. Please send the amount indicated above directly to our office. If you have any questions concerning this claim, please call the undersigned.

If we do not hear from you immediately, we will recommend to our client that legal action be brought against you to enforce this claim without any further notice to you.

Yours truly,

GOLDMAN, COSTA & GETMAN

Appendix B

GOLDMAN, COSTA AND GETMAN
ATTORNEYS AT LAW

KARL GOLDMAN
PETER L. COSTA
JACK L. GETMAN

RICHARD J. BIRYLA

705 BRISBANE BUILDING
BUFFALO, N. Y. 14203
716 853-4340

Re: Claimant -
Amount -

Inasmuch as we have not received any payment from you with respect to the above claim, we can only assume that you do not intend to pay it voluntarily and that it will be necessary to proceed with legal action.

Unless we receive payment or hear from you immediately, we will recommend to the claimant that legal action be brought against you without further notice.

Yours truly,

GOLDMAN, COSTA & GETMAN

Appendix C

GOLDMAN, COSTA, GETMAN AND BIRYLA
ATTORNEYS AT LAW

KARL GOLDMAN
PETER L. COSTA
JACK L. GETMAN
RICHARD J. BIRYLA

705 BRISBANE BUILDING
BUFFALO, N. Y. 14203-2173
716 853-4340

Re: Claimant:
Amount :

Dear

This will confirm your agreement to pay the above claim. As agreed, your payment(s) will be due:

Please confirm this agreement by signing the extra copy of this letter and then returning it in the enclosed envelope; thus, avoiding the necessity of any other legal action being considered in this case.

Yours truly,

GOLDMAN, COSTA, GETMAN
& BIRYLA

JLG:df
Enc.

The above payments are agreed to:

CHAPTER FIVE

DEBT COLLECTION RESTRICTIONS

Raymond L. Fink, Esq.

I. INTRODUCTION

The exercise of good common sense is, indeed, the most successful way of insuring that a creditor does not run afoul of the various statutes and regulations which pertain to debt-collection procedures. The statutory enactments of the General Business Law of New York and the Federal Commerce and Trade Act primarily focus upon debt collection activities insofar as they pertain to consumer debtors. Notwithstanding these provisions, which do create restrictions on the types, methods and manners of communications which may be transmitted, it is important to be mindful of the possible criminal ramifications for certain types of overreaching conduct.

II. RESTRICTIONS IN NEW YORK

Under certain egregious circumstances it is, indeed, possible for a debtor to seek vindication through the criminal process by specifically alleging a violation of section 240.30 of the New York State Penal Law. Specifically, this provision addresses itself to conduct known as Aggravated Harassment, and the statute provides as follows:

> A person is guilty of aggravated harassment when, with intent to harass, annoy, threaten or alarm another person, he:
>
> 1. Communicates, or causes a communication to be initiated by mechanical or electronic means or otherwise, with a person, anonymously or otherwise, by telephone, or by telegraph, mail or any other form of written communication, in a manner likely to cause annoyance or alarm;
>
> 2. makes a telephone call, whether or not a conversation ensues, with no purpose of legitimate communication.
>
> Aggravated Harassment is a Class A misdemeanor.
> N.Y. Penal Law sec. 240.30 (McKinney 1980)

There have been certain cases where criminal prosecutions have been sustained based upon collection efforts and although these holdings are somewhat dated, they still remain good law to this date. *See People v. Globe Jewelers*, 291 N.Y.S. 362 (1936), and *People v. Loveless*, 84 N.Y.S. 1114 (1903). In the former case of *People v. Globe Jewelers, supra*, a creditor's conviction was based upon a communication it issued to a debtor which was a facsimile of legal process and appeared to be a judicial command that the debtor pay a debt. In the latter case of *People v. Loveless, supra*, the creditor threatened to disclose to other third-party creditors that the complainant debtor was not paying his bill. This threat was the basis upon which a conviction was sustained.

III. COMPARISON OF STATE AND FEDERAL LAW

The trend towards consumer protectionism coupled with the apparent overreaching conduct of certain creditors or their agents have resulted in the enactment of certain statutes by the New York Legislature, as well as the United States Congress. Each of these statutes attempts to curtail certain types of collection practices. Specifically, the General Business Law of the State of New York (hereinafter referred to as the "GBL") was amended in 1973, whereby Article 29-H entitled "Debt Collection Procedures," *see* N.Y. General Business Law, sec. 600 *et seq.* (McKinney, 1984), was added. This statute predated the Federal Fair Debt Collection Practices Act of 1977, 15 U.S.C.A. sec. 1692 *et seq.* (hereinafter referred to as the "Fair Debt Collection Act"). Needless to say, both the New York and Federal statutes should be read in conjunction with each other. For the purposes of this analysis, a comparison of certain salient critical points will be rendered.

The most glaring distinction between New York State's Debt Collection Procedures statute and the Fair Debt Collection Act is that the former contains no statutory right for the institution of a private cause of action upon an alleged violation of the statute, whereas the latter authorizes both private party and class actions. *See* section 602 of the GBL and 15 U.S.C. sec. 1692k. However, it was held in *Kohler v. Ford Motor Credit Co., Inc.*, 447 N.Y.S.2d 215 (1982), *modified on other grounds*, 462 N.Y.S.2d 297 (1983), by the Supreme Court in Albany County that a private cause of action under section 602 of the GBL does exist for an aggrieved debtor. The definitional provisions with regard to the protected class of parties of each of the statutes is approximately the same. Section 600(1) of the GBL defines the term "consumer claim" as any obligation of a natural person for the payment of money or its equivalent which is or alleged to be in default and which arises out of transaction where credit has been extended or offered to a natural person and the money, property or service which is the subject of the transaction was primarily for personal, family or household purposes. Included specifically therein are any obligations of a natural person who would also be deemed a comaker, endorser, guarantor or surety. Section 600(2) of the GBL proceeds to define a "debtor" as "any natural person who owes or is asserted to owe a consumer claim." In comparison, 15 U.S.C. sec. 1692a(3) of the Fair Debt Collection Act defines a "consumer" as "any natural person obligated or alleged to be obligated for the payment of any debt." Then 15 U.S.C. sec. 1692a(5) proceeds to define a "debt" as "any obligation or alleged obligation of a consumer to pay money arising out of a transaction in which money, property, insurance or services, which are the subject of the transaction, are primarily for personal, family or household purposes, whether or not the obligation has been reduced to a judgment." While the Fair Debt Collection Act does not specifically address, within the definitional section, whether or not an individual comaker, guarantor or endorser would also be afforded protection under the statute, it would appear as though the spirit and intent of the statute would extend its protection to such a contingent or indirect third-party debtor.

The definition of the creditor under the New York State statute would appear to be narrower than the Fair Debt Collection Act. Specifically, it defines "principal creditor" as "any person, firm, corporation or organization to whom a consumer claim is owed, due or asserted to be due and owed, or any assignee for value of said person, firm, corporation or organization." *See* GBL sec. 600(3). Thus, it would appear as though a collection agency which does not actually purchase a creditor's accounts receivable would fall outside of this definition;

however, a factor who actually purchases accounts receivable would be embraced within this definition. Contriwise, a factor would be embraced by this definition. In contrast, 15 U.S.C. sec. 1692a(4) defines a "creditor" as any person who offers or extends credit creating a debt or to whom a debt is owed, but this does not include any person to the extent that he/she receives an assignment or transfer of the delinquent debt solely for the purpose of facilitating the collection of such debt for another. Rather, the Fair Debt Collection Act establishes a broader separate definition for a "debt collector." Particularly 15 U.S.C. sec. 1692(a)(6) defines a debt collector, in the expansive sense, as any person who uses any instrumentality of interstate commerce or the mail in any business where the principal purpose is the collection of any debts and such person regularly collects or attempts to collect, directly or indirectly, debts owed or due to be asserted to be owed to another. This definition also includes any creditor which processes the collection of its own debts, but uses a name other than the creditor which would imply or suggest that a third party is, in fact, collecting or attempting to collect the debt. There are seven statutory exclusions in the definition of debt collector, and they are as follows:

1. Any officer or employee of a creditor while, in the name of the creditor, is collecting debts for such creditor.

2. Any person, while acting as a debt collector for another person, both of whom are related by common ownership or affiliated by corporate control, if the person acting as a debt collector does so only for persons to whom it is so related or affiliated and if the principal business of such person is not the collection of debts.

3. Any officer or employee of the United States or any state to the extent that collecting or attempting to collect any debt is in the performance of his/her official duties.

4. Any person, while serving or attempting to serve legal process on any other person in connection with the judicial enforcement of any debt.

5. Any non-profit organization which, at the request of consumers, performs bona fide consumer credit counselling and assists consumers in the liquidation of their debts by receiving payments from any such consumer and distributing such amounts to any creditor.

6. Any attorney at law collecting a debt as an attorney on behalf of, and in the name of, a client and any person collecting or attempting to collect any debt owed or due or asserted to be owed or due to another to the extent that such activity is incidental to a bona fide fiduciary obligation or bona fide escrow arrangement or concerns a debt which is not originated by such persons, concerns a debt which is not in default at the time it was obtained by such person, or concerns a debt obtained by such person as a secured party in a commercial credit transaction involving the creditor.

7. Collection efforts by bona fide fiduciaries, escrow agents where the same is part of their duties and secured creditors in connection with commercial transactions.

While it appears as though there is a specific exclusion for attorneys who are collecting debts on behalf of clients, there have been at least two instances where the courts have determined that the Federal Trade Commission could investigate an attorney's practice to determine whether the law firm was acting as an attorney as defined with the exemption or otherwise. *See F.T.C. v. Schaffner*, 626 F.2d 32 (1980), and *XYZ Law Firm v. F.T.C.*, 525 F. Supp. 1235 (1891). Moreover, it is evident that the GBL includes within the purview of its provisions the in-house collection activities of a creditor while the Fair Debt Collection Act excludes in-house collection activities except where such in-house activities would give the appearance that a third party is pursuing such efforts and this is the principal activity of the collector; i.e., XYZ Corp. has a wholly owned subsidiary called "Collection Services Company" and its principal activity is the pursuit of delinquent accounts owed to XYZ Corp. The wholly owned subsidiary would presumably be included in the definition of a debt collector under the Federal Statute.

Section 601 of the GBL enumerates nine different types of activities which are proscribed. These activities, from which a principal creditor or its agent is prohibited from pursuing, are less expansive than those set forth in the Fair Debt Collection Act, as will be discussed herein. The GBL prohibits a principal creditor, or its agent, from simulating a law enforcement officer or representative of any New York State governmental agency or its political subdivision in the course of their collection efforts; it prohibits a creditor or its agent from attempting to collect or assert a right to recover any collection costs, expenses or attorney's fees unless such items are properly and legally chargeable to a debtor. The statute proscribes any threats by a principal creditor or its agent to disclose credit information regarding a debtor's reputation for credit worthiness, particularly where the creditor or its agent has reason to know that such information is false; creditors or their agents are further prohibited from communicating or threatening to communicate the nature or basis of any consumer claim to a debtor's employee at any time prior to obtaining a final judgment against a debtor. This, presumably, would be true even where an initial judgment is pending on appeal. The principal creditor or its agent, however, is authorized to communicate with a debtor's employer in order to execute a wage assignment where the same has been obtained through consent by the debtor. The principal creditor or its agent cannot threaten to disclose or actually disclose any information regarding a debt where the debt is disputed by the debtor without disclosing the fact that such debt is disputed. Communications with the debtor or the debtor's family or household members cannot be made with excessive frequency or at unusual hours or in a manner which might reasonably be expected to abuse or harass the debtor. This is particularly broad enough to encompass a telephone communication to a debtor at 11:00 in the morning where the debtor is a third-shift worker and one would expect him/her to be sleeping at that time. It is unlawful for a creditor or its agent to threaten to take any action where in the usual and ordinary course of its business it would not take such an action. For example, if a creditor were pursuing a debtor for a $50 claim and it is the policy of the creditor not to place such claims into suit due to the size of the same, but nevertheless communicates to the debtor that it will institute suit, this conduct would run afoul of this statute.

Finally, the GBL prohibits a principal creditor or its agent from using any communication which simulates, in any manner, legal or judicial processes or which might give the appearance of being authorized, issued or approved by any government or governmental agency or attorney at law when it is not. One should be particularly mindful of this provision since collection agencies or creditors sometimes request attorneys to provide them with letterheads or *pro forma* letters that the creditor, in fact, generates and sends out to debtors.

IV. THE FEDERAL FAIR DEBT COLLECTION ACT

As previously mentioned, the Fair Debt Collection Act is more detailed and broader with respect to proscribed activities. By way of general survey, the following items are covered in the applicable sections of the statute; communications in connection with debt collection, 15 U.S.C. sec. 1692c, harassment or abuse, 15 U.S.C. sec. 1692d, false or misleading representations, 15 U.S.C. sec. 1692e, and unfair practices, 15 U.S.C. sec. 1692f. A survey of the salient points of these restrictions or governing provisions, depending upon your point of view, is as follows:

A. Communications in Connection with Debt Collection, 15 U.S.C. sec. 1691

Absent prior consent of a consumer given directly to a debt collector or, alternatively, upon obtaining the expressed order of a court of competent jurisdiction, a debt collector cannot communicate with a consumer regarding the pursuit of a debt at any unusual time or place where it is known or should be known that the same would inconvenience the consumer. It is presumed that a convenient time for communicating with a consumer is between the hours of 8:00 a.m. and 9:00 p.m. at the consumer's residence. However, circumstances may dictate otherwise, but extreme caution ought to be heeded. A debt collector is prohibited from contacting a consumer if he/she knows that the consumer is represented by legal counsel with regard to the subject debt and the collector can readily ascertain the identity and address of such attorney. However, if the attorney fails to respond to the debt collector within a reasonable period of time, then a direct communication with the consumer is authorized. Moreover, a debt collector cannot contact a consumer at his/her place of employment if the debt collector knows or should know that the employer prohibits the consumer from receiving such communications.

Additionally, all communications with third parties where such third party is a person other than the consumer, his/her attorney or consumer reporting agency is strictly forbidden, except to the extent that the consumer has directly given the debt collector permission, to contact any such third parties, or the debt collector has obtained an order from a court of competent jurisdiction authorizing such contact, or such third-party communications are related to the enforcement of post-judgment judicial proceedings. However, this restriction should be considered in light of the provisions of 15 U.S.C. sec. 1692b regarding the rights of a debt collector to ascertain location information about a consumer commonly known as "skip tracing." The Fair Debt Collection Act specifically authorizes skip tracing; however, the debt collector must identify himself/herself, state that he/she is confirming or correcting location information concerning the consumer, and if requested, the debt collector must identify his/her employer. The debt collector cannot state that the consumer owes any debt and cannot communicate with any such third party more than once unless requested to do so by the third party or if the debt collector reasonably believes that the earlier response was erroneous and incomplete and that the third party has the correct or complete location information. The debt collector cannot communicate by postcard, cannot use any language or symbol which would indicate that the debt collector is in the business of collecting debts or that the communication relates to any debt collection activities. Once again, if a debt collector knows that the consumer is represented by counsel with regard to the subject debt, and can readily ascertain the identity and address of the attorney, then the debt collector cannot communicate with any party other than the attorney unless the attorney fails to respond to the debt collector's communication within a reasonable period of time.

Finally, in connection with restricted communications, a debt collector must cease all communications with the debtor and third parties where the consumer notifies the debt collector in writing that it refuses to pay the obligation or that he/she wishes for any communications to cease except that the debt collector can then advise the consumer that its further efforts will be terminated and the debt collector or the principal creditor may invoke specific remedies which are normally pursued. For the purposes of restrictions on communications, the term "consumer" is defined to include not only the principal debtor, but the debtor's spouse, parent where the consumer is minor, guardian, executor or administrator.

B. False or Misleading Representations, 15 U.S.C. sec. 1692e

Sixteen specific types of activities are statutorily deemed to be false, deceptive and/or misleading representations. A debt collector cannot represent that it is affiliated with the United States or any state or subdivision thereof by any words or symbolic expression which might result in an implication of governmental involvement. A debt collector cannot create any false inference or make any representation that he/she is an attorney or law firm or that any communication is generated from an attorney where this is not, in fact, the case. It cannot be represented that nonpayment of the debt will result in any arrest or imprisonment or the seizure of any property or garnishment of wages or other funds where such action is not permitted. A debt collector cannot threaten to take any action which legally cannot be pursued, or represent or infer that the assignment, referral or transfer of any interest in the debt shall cause the consumer to lose his/her right to assert any defenses. No representation that the consumer committed any crime or other conduct which would tend to cause the consumer to be disgraced, can be conveyed by the debt collector. Communications or threats thereof to any third person credit information where the debt collector knows or should know that the same is false is proscribed, including the failure to indicate that a debt is disputed or failing to disclose conspicuously in all communications to collect a debt or to obtain information about a consumer that the debt collector is only attempting to collect a debt and that the information obtained thereby will be used for this purpose, except to the extent that the statute authorizes innocuous communications for the purposes of skip tracing. False representations or implications that debts have been assigned to bona fide purchasers for value where the same has not occurred are prohibited. Representations that legal documents are being processed where the same is not true, is illegal and the utilization of any firm, business, company or organizational name other than the true name of the debt collector is proscribed. False representations or implications that a debt collector operates or is engaged by a consumer reporting agency is unlawful unless in fact true.

C. Unfair Practices, 15 U.S.C. sec. 1692f

The unfair debt collection practices, as set forth in 15 U.S.C. sec. 1692f, are in many respects similar to the prohibited practice as contained in GBL sec. 601. A debt collector is proscribed generally from using any unfair or unconscionable means to collect or attempt to collect any debt, including eight specific types of conduct. A debt collector cannot collect or threaten to collect any amount, including interest, attorney's fees, court costs or other charges except for the principal amount of the debt unless such additional charges are expressly authorized by an agreement wherein the debt was initially created or such charges are permitted by applicable statute. A debt collector cannot accept any post-dated check which is dated more than five days from the date of its issuance unless the maker of the check is notified in writing the debt collector intends to deposit the check, which notice must be given not more than ten or less than three days prior to such deposit. A debt collector cannot solicit any post-dated checks or other post-dated payment instrument for the purposes of threatening or instituting criminal prosecution. This, of course, is less meaningful in New York since a post-dated check cannot be used to support a criminal prosecution. *See* N.Y. Penal Law sec. 190.00 *et seq*. A debt collector cannot deposit or threaten to deposit any post-dated check or other post-dated instrument prior to the date on such instrument. The debt collector cannot cause charges to be made to any person for communications by concealing the purpose of the communication. These specifically include charges for collecting telephone calls or the like. A debt collector cannot take or threaten to take any nonjudicial action to repossess property if there is no right to repossess the property or there is no intention to repossess the property particularly where the property is exempt from such repossession. The debt collector cannot communicate with a consumer by means of a postcard. Finally, the debt collector cannot use any language or symbol other than the debt collector's address on any envelope when communicating with a consumer by use of the mails or telegram.

The Fair Debt Collection Act exceeds the scope of the GBL insofar as it contains specific provisions pertaining to the validation of debts. *See* 15 U.S.C. 1692g. The debt validation section essentially provides that a debt collector must provide to a consumer, within five days after the initial communication, unless such initial communication contains such particular information, the following items: (1) the amount of the debt, (2) the name of the creditor to whom the debt is owed, (3) a statement that unless the consumer, within thirty days after receipt of the notice, disputes the validity of the debt, any portion thereof, or the entire debt, will be assumed to be valid by the debt collector, (4) a statement that if the consumer notifies the debt collector in writing within the thirty-day period that the debt, or any portion thereof, is disputed, the debt collector will obtain verification of the debt or a copy of a judgment, if applicable, against the consumer, and a copy of such verification or judgment will be mailed to the consumer by the debt collector, and (5) a statement that upon the consumer's written request, within the thirty-day period, the debt collector will provide the consumer with the name and address of the original creditor if different from the current creditor. If a consumer notifies the debt collector in writing within thirty days, that the debt or any portion thereof is disputed, or the consumer requests the name and address of the original creditor be provided, then the debt collector must cease all collection activities until such time as the debt collector has obtained either verification of the debt, a copy of the judgment and if applicable or the identity information of the creditor and such information is then mailed to the consumer by the debt collector. Notwithstanding all of the above, the failure of a consumer to dispute the validity of any debt cannot be construed by any court as an admission of liability. Based upon the substance of the notice which the debt collector must provide to the consumer, it is evident that an intelligent consumer can stall any further collection activities by the debt collector.

There are other provisions in the Fair Debt Collection Act that also protect a consumer. 15 U.S.C. sec. 1692h requires a debt collector who receives a payment from a consumer to apply such payment to the particularly specified debt and it cannot apply the same to any disputed debt. This is of particular importance, of course, when there are multiple debts which the debt collector is handling against the same consumer. 15 U.S.C. sec. 1692i provides that any legal proceedings brought against a consumer must be commenced in a court of appropriate jurisdiction where any real property is located, if the enforcement procedures relate specifically to the real property or otherwise, in the jurisdiction where the consumer signed the contract or the consumer resides. This follows the venue provisions set forth in section 503(f) of the New York Civil Practice Law and Rules regarding the selection of venue.

Finally, 15 U.S.C. sec. 1692k sets forth the types of damages that may be awarded to an aggrieved consumer by reason of a debt collector's violations of the statute. Briefly put, the consumer can recover any actual damages together with any additional damages as the court may allow, but not exceeding $1,000. In the event of a class action, the amount of actual damages for each member of the class and such amounts as the court may also allow for other class members irrespective of the minimum individual recovery all of which is not to exceed the lesser of $500,000 or 1 percent of the debt collector's net worth and in the event of successful litigation, attorney's fees and court's costs can be awarded. However, if the court determines that an action was brought in bad faith for the purposes of harassment, the court can also award attorney's fees to the prevailing defendant which should relate to the amount of work expended and actual costs incurred.

The Court is also authorized to consider external factors, such as persistence of the debt collector's violations, frequency of noncompliance and the intent of the debt collector or other similar factors.

A debt collector, however, cannot be held liable if the debt collector shows, by a preponderance of the evidence, that a violation was not intentional and resulted from a good faith error notwithstanding the institution of procedures which were reasonably enacted by the debt collector to avoid such errors.

V. CONCLUSION

In conclusion, it is readily apparent that both the New York Legislature and the United States Congress have adopted comprehensive measures which protect consumer debtors from what were previously described as overreaching tactics by unscrupulous debt collectors or creditors. The same restrictions do not presently exist with respect to recovery of commercial or nonconsumer debts, yet unscrupulous tactics could also result in a future adoption of similar legislation. As stated at the outset, common sense probably the best guide and creditors, debt collectors and even attorneys must always be mindful of potential countersuits which seek to redress miscommunications or deceptive practices. Aggrieved parties who claim to suffer from defamation may be able to resort to the common law avenues of recovery for slander and/or lible as the case may be. It is also conceivable that remedies might be found in New York law under the *prima facie* tort concept where specific conduct cannot fit into a traditional tort category.

CHAPTER SIX

ALTERNATIVES TO LITIGATION

Raymond L. Fink, Esq.

I. INTRODUCTION

There are essentially three mechanisms in reference to the recovery of money judgment which could be considered alternatives to litigation. The first two items are similar in many respects, while the third vehicle might, in fact, be characterized, in a broad sense, as a form of litigation. Respectively, they are (1) confessions of judgment, (2) stipulations of settlement, and (3) arbitration. Both the confession of judgment and the stipulation of settlement are formats which can be utilized either pre or post litigation. The former is probably more typically used in lieu of litigation whereas the latter can be effectively utilized after the institution of suit.

II. CONFESSIONS OF JUDGMENT

Section 3218 of the New York Civil Practice Law and Rules (hereinafter referred to as the "CPLR") is the applicable provision governing judgments by confession. Subparagraph (a) of CPLR sec. 3218 articulates the substantive content of an affidavit upon which a judgment by confession is predicated. It states that no action need be commenced and that the affidavit should relate specifically to an obligation of a debtor (potential defendant) where money is either presently due or may become due to the plaintiff. The liability may either be contingent or direct in nature. In any event, the same must be embodied in an affidavit executed by the defendant which states the sum for which a judgment may be entered. The confession authorizes the entry of judgment and succinctly states the material facts creating the indebtedness and further indicates that the sum so confessed is justly due or may become due. The affidavit must also state the county where the defendant resides and if the defendant is a nonresident, the county in which the judgment may be entered. Furthermore, if the affidavit relates to a contingent or future liability of the defendant, then the particular facts upon which the contingent liability is based should also be articulated and that the amount confessed does not exceed the amount of the liability.

Subparagraph (b) of CPLR sec. 3218 sets forth pertinent information as to the entry of a judgment where such an affidavit has been obtained. The judgment based upon the affidavit must be filed within three (3) years from the date of its execution if at all. Affidavits which confess judgments will not be accepted by the judgment clerk if they are more than three (3) years old. Upon entry of the judgment, the clerk of the court shall tax costs together with any disbursements taxable in the action. Thereafter, the judgment may be docketed and enforced in the same manner and with the same effect as any other judgment. However, no judgment by confession may be entered after the defendant's death. The aforestated three-year time limit should be scrupulously adhered to particularly where it references a contingent liability or a direct liability in conjunction with an extended amortization program that exceeds a three-year period.

There are instances where the affidavit may be utilized to secure a judgment for a portion of the identified debt. If this should occur, then execution upon such judgment can only pertain to the amount which has become due. The balance of the judgment shall remain as security, to the extent that it may create a lien, for any further sums which may become due in the future. *See* CPLR sec. 3218(c). There are also provisions which provide that a joint debtor may confess a judgment for a joint debt. The obtaining of an affidavit of confession of judgment from a joint debtor does not bar the creditor from pursuing legal remedies against the non-confessing co-debtor.

Further reference must be made to CPLR sec. 3201, since this sets forth a limitation with respect to the procuring of confessions of judgment relating to certain consumer transactions. Specifically, it proscribes the entry of judgment by confession where the affidavit was executed prior to the time of a default and where the debt is for a sum of up to one thousand five hundred dollars ($1500). Moreover the debt must have been incurred from the purchasing of goods or services which are used for any purpose other than a commercial or business use. Additionally, the debt must also be payable in two or more installments. If the creditor violates this provision then the judgment is rendered null and void.

It should be noted that a judgment obtained by confession is not only attackable by the judgment debtor in the event that strict compliance is not followed, but also third-party creditors who may be prejudiced by the earlier entry of the judgment. It has been held in the case of *Baehre v. Rochester Dental Prosthetics, Inc.*, 446 N.Y.S.2d 901 (Sup. Ct., Erie Co., 1982) that two confessions of judgment obtained by a law firm against a judgment debtor which referenced that the same arose from the rendering of "legal services" was voidable by third-party creditors since the affidavit did not contain precise enough information as to the nature of the indebtedness. The mere reference to "legal services" was held to be insufficient insofar as it did not indicate when the services were rendered and why the judgment debtor was liable for these services. Another interesting variation occurred in the case of *Reliance Insurance Company v. Brown*, 399 N.Y.S.2d 286 (3d Dep't 1977). In that case, the defendants had personally guaranteed certain loans granted by the plaintiff and in connection with the same, personally executed confessions of judgment and further granted a mortgage on their residence to secure the confession of judgment. The creditor commenced a foreclosure action upon the mortgage and the defendant disputed the foreclosure action by contending that the creditor's failure to file the affidavit of confession of judgment within the three-year statutory period extinguished the indebtedness and thereby rendered the mortgage void. The Third Department held that a triable issue of fact existed as to whether the mortgage secured only the confession of judgment or also the underlying indebtedness. Apparently, the language of the mortgage referenced the obligation of the defendant to pay the indebtedness and the Appellate Court determined that this was a matter for a trier of fact to determine. This holding raises a further interesting question as to what would have happened had the affidavit of confession of judgment been recorded within the three-year period. Presumably, the creditor would have had to exhaust its remedies with respect to enforcing the judgment before it could foreclose the mortgage.

There are standard preprinted forms which can be acquired in connection with obtaining an affidavit of confession of judgment. (*See* Appendix A.)

III. STIPULATIONS OF SETTLEMENT

Insofar as stipulations of settlement are concerned, there are no standardized formats; however, if this tool is being used on a post-suit basis, it should contain the full caption of the lawsuit, together with the appropriate index number and reference that the stipulation is being executed by the defendant as a settlement to the lawsuit and in the event of a default, judgment can be entered for the amount so stipulated together with all costs, disbursements and interest. Since this is a negotiated document, there may be provisions requiring notice of default before proceeding with the filing of a judgment. This tool can also be utilized on pre-suit basis. It is advisable to formalize any amortization programs with a judgment debtor into a stipulation which provides for the immediate entry of judgment, thereby circumventing the need for time consuming and costly litigation.

IV. ARBITRATION

Finally, there is a tremendous emphasis upon alleviating the dockets of the State's court system by resolving commercial disputes through arbitration. In many instances, the parties to a contract stipulate that any differences or breaches, including nonpayment, shall be resolved by arbitration. Where there is not an expressed contractual provision establishing arbitration as a means of dispute resolution, the parties can stipulate at a subsequent point in time to resolve any such disputes through this mechanism. The local bar associations have generally adopted programs which facilitate arbitration and beyond these forums, the American Arbitration Association can also be used as a means of dispute resolution. Technically, arbitration might be considered a litigation procedure since it does envision an adversarial process and generally the parties feel that there is cause to their respective positions. It is doubtful that this sort of mechanism would be available on a post-default basis where the defendant does not possess any colorable meritorious defense.

Appendix A

X 245—Confession of Judgment. Ind. or Corp. Blank Court.

COURT

COUNTY OF

Index No.

Plaintiff(s)

against

Defendant(s)

AFFIDAVIT OF CONFESSION OF JUDGMENT

STATE OF NEW YORK, COUNTY OF *ss.:*

being duly sworn, deposes and says; that deponent is

† (the of
a corporation and is duly authorized to make this affidavit on behalf of the corporate)
defendant herein.

The defendant hereby confesses judgment herein and authorizes entry thereof against defendant in the sum of $

Defendant resides at
in the County of State of . Defendant authorizes entry of judgment in County, New York, if said residence address is not in New York State.

*This confession of judgment is for a debt justly * due to the plaintiff arising from the following facts:*

This affidavit, if made in connection with an agreement for the purchase for $1,500.00 or less of any commodities for any use other than a commercial or business use upon any plan of deferred payments whereby the price or cost is payable in two or more installments, was executed subsequent to the time a default occurred in the payment of an installment thereunder.

Sworn to before me this
day of *19*

....
The name signed must be printed beneath

† Strike out matter in parenthesis if defendant is individual.
* Insert words "to become" if debt is not yet due.
** If in a city court, insert name of court, UCCA §1403.

COURT
COUNTY OF

Index No.
Address of Plaintiff:

Plaintiff(s)

against

Defendant(s)

JUDGMENT BY CONFESSION

Amount Confessed	$	
Interest		$
Costs by Statute		
Transcript		
Fees on Execution		
Satisfaction		
Filing Fee		
	Total	$

STATE OF NEW YORK, COUNTY OF

ATTORNEY'S AFFIRMATION

The undersigned, attorney at law of the State of New York, affirms that he is

attorney(s) of record for the plaintiff herein and states that the disbursements above specified are correct and true and have been or will necessarily be made or incurred herein and are reasonable in amount and affirms this statement to be true under the penalties of perjury.

Dated:

Print Name Beneath Signature

JUDGMENT *entered the day of 19 .*

On filing the foregoing affidavit of Confession of Judgment made by the defendant herein, sworn to the day of 19 ,

NOW, ON MOTION OF

attorney(s) for plaintiff it is

ADJUDGED *that* *plaintiff*

residing at
do recover of *defendant*

residing at
the sum of $ *with interest of $* *making a total of $*
together with $ *costs and disbursements, amounting in all to the sum of $*
and that the plaintiff *have execution therefor.*

....*Clerk*

Index No.

COURT
COUNTY OF

Plaintiff(s)

against

Defendant(s)

Affidavit and Judgment by Confession

Attorney(s) for Plaintiff
Office and Post Office Address

CHAPTER SEVEN

INSTITUTING SUIT

Bradley E. Rock, Esq.
Richard A. Nicoll, Esq.

I. CHOICE OF COURT

We will not here examine the jurisdiction of the various courts on a court by court basis. Because such analyses are available elsewhere,[1] and because this book is intended to be a practical guide to lawyers with collection matters, we will instead analyze how to choose the appropriate court by treating the questions that the lawyer should ask himself/herself when making the decision.

A. What Relief is Sought?

Since our concern is with collection actions, the answer to this question will almost always be "money damages." This dramatically uncomplicates this phase of the decision making process because all courts of original jursdiction in New York State have subject matter jursidiction of claims for money damages.

Actions for replevin or to foreclose a lien on personal property are not "collection" actions in the strictest sense because they do not seek money damages. For the purposes of this discussion and the discussion which follows in subsection B on jurisdictional limits, however, what is true for money damage claims is usually true for the occasionally related claims of replevin or to foreclose a lien on personal property.[2]

For lawyers in New York City, there are two courts which may be used for collection claims, the Supreme Court and the Civil Court of the City of New York. In Nassau County and in western Suffolk on Long Island,[3] collection actions may be brought in the Supreme Court or the District Court. Throughout the rest of the state, including eastern Suffolk and all of the upstate counties, there are four possible forums: the Supreme Court, a county court, a city court or a justice court. The Supreme Court and county courts are available, of course, throughout this part of the state, but city courts and the justice courts established by town and village ordinances may or may not be available depending upon the lawyer's proximity to such municipalities.

While there are at least two possible forums for a collection action anywhere in the state, that does not necessarily mean that the lawyer always has a choice. There is a policy embodied in a number of statutes and rules designed to encourage that a case be brought "in the lowest court with jurisdiction sufficient to entertain it."[4] These statutes and rules include provisions for the transfer of actions to a lower court,[5] and provisions for costs penalties in actions where the amount eventually recovered indicates that the action should have been brought in a lower court.[6]

So, a lawyer should commence the action in the lowest court which has subject matter jurisdiction of the claim (and in which he/she can obtain personal jurisdiction of the defendant, a matter discussed in subsection C below). Therefore, we must examine the jurisdictional limits of each of the courts available, and the lawyer must ask himself/herself: "What is the amount in controversy in this action?"

B. What is the Amount in Controversy?

1. Jurisdictional Limits

The Supreme Court, available for the commencement of a collection action anywhere in the state, is a court of general jurisdiction. There is no limit on the amount of damages which can be claimed in the Supreme Court.

In New York City, where the choice is between the Supreme Court and the Civil Court, actions where the amount in controversy is $25,000 or less should be commenced in the Civil Court.[7] (This choice may, of course, be subject to revision depending upon the lawyer's answers to the remaining questions listed in this section on choice of court.)

In those areas on Long Island which have a district court, actions for $15,000 or less should be brought there.[8]

Throughout the rest of the state, there may be more choices available. All of the county courts now hear cases involving claims for $25,000 or less.[9] The lawyer may, however, also have the option of bringing the action in a city court or a justice court if one is available locally. Each of the state's 61 cities outside the City of New York has a city court, but local laws fix the monetary jurisdiction. In no event can the monetary jurisdiction of a city court exceed $15,000.[10] Similarly, the justice courts are established by local laws, and can exercise monetary jurisdiction up to $3,000.[11]

2. Aggregating Claims

Suppose that an action is brought in a city court that exercises jurisdiction of money damage claims up to $6,000. The complaint pleads three causes of action, each for $5,000. Is such an action within the subject matter jurisdiction of the city court? Yes. Section 211 of each of the four lower court acts provides: "Where several causes of action are asserted in the complaint, and each of them would be within the jurisdiction of the court if sued upon separately, the court shall have jurisdiction of the action." Each of the statutes further provides that, in such a case, the court may award a judgment in excess of its monetary jurisdiction if the excess results from the joinder of multiple causes of action in a single complaint.

The rule is not so clear, however, in a county court. There is no separate court act governing practice in the county courts, and there is no provision in the CPLR which corresponds to section 211 of the lower court acts. A literal reading of the constitutional and statutory provisions governing the jurisdiction of a county court points in a direction completely at odds with section 211. The Constitution says that the court has jurisdiction of an action "where the amount sought to be recovered" does not exceed the monetary limit,[12] and the statute similarly grants jurisdiction "where the complaint in such action demands judgment for a sum of money" not exceeding the monetary limit.[13] Measuring this language against the example of a case with three causes of action for $20,000 each, it is clear that the "amount sought to be recovered" is $60,000, and that "the complaint. . . demands judgment" for a sum exceeding the monetary limit of $25,000. Therefore, the current weight of authority tips in this direction, forbidding the aggregation of claims, especially in the Second Department.[14]

There are, however, some well-reasoned cases which permit the aggregation of claims in a county court, and follow a rule similar to that set forth in section 211.[15] These courts have reasoned that the language of the Constitution and the Judiciary Law is somewhat ambiguous, while section 211 evidences a clear legislative intent (expressed four times) on how this problem should be treated in the lower courts. There is also some force to the argument that a plaintiff could serve a separate complaint for each cause of action to fall within the permissible limits, and that this sort of nonsense ought to be avoided to conserve legal and judicial effort.

In any event, until such time as the answer may be clarified by an amendment of the Judiciary Law, and to the extent that the answer remains unclear in the Third and Fourth Departments, the lawyer should probably choose to commence the action in the Supreme Court over the county court whenever this question arises. Only the most compelling of other considerations should cause the lawyer to opt for county court, where he/she may well be met with a motion to dismiss and subsequent appeals concerning this unsettled point of law.

Even in the four courts governed by their own separate court acts, there is some difficulty in the application of section 211. Such difficulty is inevitable with any rule that requires defining what constitutes a single "cause of action." To avoid miring ourselves in the confusion that has often been engendered by understandably difficult efforts to define a "cause of action," let us state one definition which has been commonly used, and review the two most often encountered practical consequences of that definition.

It has been said a "cause of action" is "a set of operative facts which gives rise to a separate and distinct legal right and to a right to seek separate and distinct redress for a violation of that legal right."[16]

This means, first, if a particular act may give rise to a recovery on more than one legal theory (for example, theories of negligence, breach of warranty and strict liability), and the complaint pleads each legal theory of recovery as a separate "cause of action," nonetheless, all three will be treated as a single cause of action because they arise from a single set of operative facts. Note also that if the plaintiff sought to recover $20,000 on each of the three legal theories, and the plaintiff was completely successful, he/she would recover only $20,000.

Secondly, if a single act caused various kinds of damage (say, both general and consequential), or if the act caused damage to several of plaintiff's properties (such as a single fire which caused damage to the plaintiff's house, shed and car), then the complaint will be deemed to plead but one cause of action, even if it labels each item of damage as a separate cause of action.[17] Note, of course, that if the plaintiff were to plead three causes of action for $20,000 each for damage to his/her house, shed and car, respectively, and the plaintiff were to be completely successful, the plaintiff would recover $60,000. Therefore, such an action would be beyond the subject matter jurisdiction of a court with a $25,000 monetary limit for any cause of action.

C. Where Can the Defendant be Served? Where Did the Cause of Action Arise?

The answers to these questions will help the lawyer decide which courts may acquire personal jurisdiction of the defendant. The questions are grouped together because they are related, and because the lawyer need not always ask himself/herself both of the questions in every case. Sometimes the answer to one of the questions may end the inquiry. For example, where the defendant can be served by personal delivery of the summons within a certain geographic area, the court will have personal jurisdiction of the defendant, with no further inquiry being necessary.

The Supreme Court has personal jurisdiction of the defendant if: (1) the summons is personally delivered to the defendant in New York State, regardless of where the defendant resides; (2) the defendant either resides in New York or does business in New York, and is properly served by some method authorized by statutue;[18] or (3) a nonresident defendant is subject to "long-arm" jurisdiction under CLPR sec. 302 on the basis of acts performed within the state, and, again, if such a defendant is properly served. A thorough discussion of the nature and extent "long-arm" jurisdiction is impossible here, and for more information on that subject, the lawyer may consult any number of fine commentaries.[19] Let it suffice for our purposes to say that a nonresident will be subject to the personal jurisdiction of the Supreme Court if the cause of action asserted arose from a transaction of business done or a tortious act committed within New York State by the nonresident, or if the nonresident owns, uses or possesses any real property located in the state.[20]

All of the other courts to be discussed exercise more limited personal jurisdiction. In this respect, as with subject matter jurisdiction, the Supreme Court is residual in character. That is, if a case would be appropriate in a lower court, but the lower cannot exercise personal jurisdiction of all the necessary defendants, then the action should be commenced in the Supreme Court. For example, if a $5,000 cause of action is to be asserted against two individual defendants in an upstate county, but the county court cannot exercise personal jurisdiction of both defendants because one of them does not reside in the county, then the action must be commenced in the Supreme Court.

In a county court, the action must be supported by one of the jurisdictional bases listed above for the Supreme Court, but there are additional requirements which must be met. A county court may only exercise jurisdiction where the defendant, or if there are two or more defendants, where all of them, at the time of the commencement of the action: (1) reside in the county; (2) where the defendant has an office for the transaction of business in the county and the cause of action arose in the county; or (3) where the defendant is a foreign corporation that is doing business in the county and the cause of action arose in the county.[21] Interestingly, though these statutory requirements appear to place limitations on the subject matter jurisdiction of the court, they are treated as going to personal jurisdiction, which means they can be waived by the defendants if not raised in the answer or by a motion to dismiss.[22]

The Civil Court and the district courts exercise personal jurisdiction in a manner quite similar to the Supreme Court, with one important geographic difference. All three of these courts exercise personal jurisdiction over anyone served within its geographic boundary. For the

Supreme Court, this geographic boundary is New York State, but for the Civil Court and the district courts, respectively, the boundaries are New York City[23] and the county in which the district court is organized.[24] Similarly, for "long-arm" purposes, the relevant geographic boundaries are New York State, New York City and the county of organization, for the Supreme Court, Civil Court and district courts, respectively.[25]

For city courts, the relevant geographic boundary is the *county* in which the city is located, both for purposes of summons service[26] and for long-arm purposes.[27] But there are further limitations set forth in UCCA section 213, requiring that the parties have certain contacts with the city. Though these additional limitations are not jurisdictional and may be waived by either party, the plaintiff's lawyer should commence an action in a city court only if the requirements are met in order to avoid dismissal of the case at the urging of the defendant or upon the court's own initiative.[28]

Finally, the justice courts have the most limited jurisdictional reach. Service must be made within the county,[29] and there is no applicable long-arm provision. And, as in city courts, there are additional, non-jurisdictional requirements that the parties have certain contacts with the municipality in which the justice court is organized.[30]

D. Other Considerations

There are too many variations from one locality to another to discuss all of the possible choices of court with which a lawyer may be faced, and to suggest guidelines or answers to each question that may be raised. The point to be remembered, however, is simply this: Where the answers to questions concerning subject matter jurisdiction and personal jurisdiction leave the lawyer with a choice of courts in which to commence the action, the lawyer should consider the impact on his/her case of the procedural and practical differences between the alternative courts. Several examples should illustrate the point.

Suppose the lawyer's client has a claim against someone for $2,500. Both the plaintiff and defendant reside in a village upstate which has a justice court exercising monetary jurisdiction of civil claims up to $3,000. The lawyer has a choice between commencing the action in the county court or the justice court.

If the lawyer anticipates that the defendant will appear to defend, and the case involves factual issues, the lawyer should probably commence the action in the justice court. By doing so, the lawyer's client will benefit from the relatively simplified procedures often employed in a justice court (e.g., the "indorsed complaint" permitted by UJCA section 902(a)(1)), and, more importantly, from an early trial date, which in some localities may be as little as four to six weeks from the date the summons is served (similar to a "small claims" procedure).

Suppose, however, that the same lawyer with the same $2,500 case anticipates that the defendant will default. The defendant is a person who has recently encountered numerous financial difficulties, and the lawyer knows or suspects that the defendant is simultaneously being pursued by other creditors. The lawyer also knows that the defendant owns real property in the village.

In this second example, the lawyer's main concern is collecting upon the default judgment he/she anticipates. If the plaintiff recovers a default judgment in the justice court, that judgment will not become a lien on the defendant's real property when it is entered. The lawyer will have to take the additional steps of securing a transcript of the judgment from the clerk of the justice court, and, then, of filing the transcript with the county clerk.[31] By the time the process of "transcripting" the judgment is completed, other judgments may have become liens against the property before the plaintiff's, reducing the plaintiff's chances for recovery. So, the lawyer in these circumstances should probably commence the action in the county court. A judgment in a county court becomes a lien on real property owned by the defendant in the county as soon as it is entered.[32]

As a final example, suppose that the same lawyer with the same $2,500 case knows that the defendant also has a claim against the plaintiff for $4,000. If the only alternative were county court, the lawyer might well advise his/her client to "let sleeping dogs lie" because as soon as the plaintiff commences a $2,500 action in county court, the defendant is sure to counterclaim for $4,000. But remember, this lawyer has the alternative of going to the justice court, and if he/she commences the action there, he/she may gain an advantage for his/her client.

The justice court only has jurisdiction of counterclaims up to $3,000.[33] If the defendant interposes a counterclaim for more money, the counterclaim is deemed waived as to the excess above $3,000.[34] So, if the $2,500 claim is brought in the justice court, the defendant or his/her lawyer may either mistep or be placed in quandary. If the $4,000 counterclaim is interposed in the justice court action, it is waived to the extent of $1,000. On the other hand, if the defendant chooses not to interpose the counterclaim, but instead, to sue separately on the $4,000 claim in county court, he/she will multiply his/her own litigation expenses and will likely have a judgment rendered against him/her much sooner than he/she will be able to secure a judgment against the plaintiff. These problems are the stuff of which favorable settlements are made. Assuming that both the plaintiff and defendant have good claims for $2,500 and $4,000, respectively, the plaintiff's lawyer may have just saved his/her client $1,000 or more simply by choosing the right court.

Here is a brief, nonexclusive list of some of the procedural and practical points that a lawyer should consider when choosing between alternative courts in which to commence a collection action:

1. Early Trial

In many localities, a plaintiff can secure a much earlier trial by selecting the lower court. This fact is important in a case with factual issues and where the defendant is expected to appear. If the lawyer does not know the state of the alternative court calendars or the local practice in setting a matter down for trial (which is often the case where a justice court is being considered as an alternative), the lawyer should simply call the clerks of the alternative courts and ask. Such inquiries are not frowned upon.

2. Legal Skill and Character of Judge

While we suppose these are factors one is not supposed to mention in a book, every good lawyer weighs the legal skill and/or character of the judge he/she is before at every step of the action, and the time of commencement is no exception. In many of the lower courts throughout the state, there is only one judge assigned to the court, so the lawyer can be almost certain that the case will be decided by that judge if commenced there. Therefore, if the only anticipated defense is a heart rending tale and the only county court judge in the area is a "tough old bird," you go to county court. Similarly, if the success of the plaintiff's case depends upon adherance to a little known or often misunderstood legal principal, the lawyer should not choose a court where the only judge has little legal skill, as may well be the case in a justice court, where the judge need not be a lawyer.[35]

3. Need for Motion Practice

If the lawyer anticipates that either he/she or his/her adversary will make a particular motion, the lawyer should try to avoid, if possible, a court where such a motion would be unfamiliar to the judge and court personnel (which will probably mean selecting the higher of the alternative courts). Because time is always a factor for the plaintiff in a collection action, the lawyer should also consider the return dates available for motions in the alternative courts and the usual time it takes to get a decision on a motion in each court. With regard to the return dates, the variance can be substantial. In some courts, motions can be made returnable on any business day, while in others, the available dates may be as much as a month apart. The lawyer should consult any published rules on the subject, or the respective clerks. As for the time it takes to receive a decision on a motion, this is much more difficult to assess. Experience (your own or that of others) is the only real guide. Unfortunately, in some courts in some areas, it can take as long as six months to receive a decision on a motion. If time is crucial to your recovery, you cannot lightly regard the factor of "decision time." Exercise what control you can over this factor by anticipating the likelihood of motions in advance, and by considering your assessment in selecting a court.

4. Simplified Pleadings and Procedure

In some courts, certain simplified procedures are followed, such as the "indorsed complaint" permitted by some court acts,[36] which is discussed in more detail in a later section.[37]

5. Availability of Enforcement Devices

A property execution or an income execution may issue out of any of the six courts of original jurisdiction which we have discussed, with one exception. To serve a property execution against realty in an action in the Civil Court, a district court, a city court or a justice court, the lawyer must first file a transcript of the judgment with the county clerk and proceed in the Supreme Court.[38] The so-called "supplementary proceedings" (such as a restraining notice),[39] however, are available only in the Supreme Court,[40] a county court,[41] the Civil Court,[42] a district court[43] and 19 of the city courts.[44] Supplementary proceedings cannot be initiated in most city courts nor any justice court. But in some instances, this restriction may be of little import, for the lawyer enforcing a judgment of one of these two lower courts may need to do nothing more than caption his/her papers differently subsequent to the judgment. If the enforcement device chosen does not require court approval (such as a restraining notice or a subpoena), and there is no other reason either to file the judgment or a transcript of the judgment with the county clerk, the lawyer may simply, for example, proceed by simply captioning the restraining notice in the Supreme Court. So, while it may often be wise to file a judgment or transcript of judgment of a lower court with the court clerk, the CPLR does not necessarily require such steps to be taken before initiating supplementary proceedings to enforce the lower court judgment.

6. Judgment as a Lien on Real Property

Only a judgment entered in the Supreme Court or a county court automatically becomes a lien on real property.[45] For judgments secured in other courts to become a lien a realty, a transcript of the judgment must be filed with the county clerk.

7. Limitation on Counterclaims in Justice Courts

Section 208 of the UJCA only permits the interposition of counterclaims up to $3,000. If a counterclaim of more than $3,000 is interposed in a justice court, the claim is deemed waived to the extent it exceeds $3,000.

II. VENUE

Venue signifies the geographical subdivision in which an action may be commenced. The Supreme Court, for example, has statewide jurisdiction, but a suit for money damages cannot be brought in any county merely at the plaintiff's whim. The venue rules determine which of the counties is proper for a particular Supreme Court action.[46]

When discussing venue, we assume that the court already has both subject matter and personal jurisdiction because an absence of either would warrant dismissal and render the venue questions academic.

A defective venue is not a dismissal ground in New York practice as it is in federal practice. Generally, unless a defendant acts to change the venue, it will remain the place designated by the plaintiff.

A. Courts with Territorial Subdivisions

Venue rules are required only for courts with territorial subdivisions, such as the Supreme Court, New York City Civil Court and District Court. Each county court is an independent entity and whether or not suit can properly be brought in a particular county court, therefore, is a question of jurisdiction, not venue.

The New York City Civil Court[47] consists of the five New York City counties while the District Court[48] has districts into which the counties of Nassau and western Suffolk are divided.

B. General Rule as to Place of Trial

The general rule concerning venue is that the place of trial shall be in a county in which one of the parties resided when it was commenced; or, if none of the parties then resided in the state, in any county designated by the plaintiff. A party resident in more than one county shall be deemed a resident of each such county.[49]

C. Consumer Credit Transactions

To remedy certain abuses in consumer credit transactions, CPLR sec. 503(f) requires that in an action arising out of a consumer credit transaction[50] where a purchaser, borrower or debtor is a defendant, the place of trial shall be the residence of a defendant, if one resided within the state, or the county where the transaction took place, if it is within the state, or, in other cases, as set forth in CPLR sec. 503(a).

The purpose of CPLR sec. 503(f) is to make it easier for consumers to defend by compelling plaintiffs to sue consumers in the county where they reside or where the transaction took place.

Whether a particular transaction constitutes a consumer credit transaction may raise a question of fact. To the extent that a practitioner faces any doubt in this regard at the outset of the case, he/she should avoid trouble and potential delay by giving the defendant the benefit of any doubt, treating the transaction as a consumer credit transaction, and suing where the defendant resides or where the transaction took place.

III. PREPARATION OF PROCESS AND PLEADINGS

Once the lawyer has decided where he/she is going to commence the action, the lawyer must prepare the papers to be served. A lawyer commencing a collection action can have as many as four different choices available to him/her in determining the form of his/her papers. The lawyer can prepare and serve: (1) a summons containing a default notice, or as it is commonly called, a "summons with notice"; (2) a summons with an indorsed complaint; (3) a summons and formal complaint; or (4) a summons and papers in support of a motion for summary judgment in lieu of complaint. In the subsections that follow, we will discuss each of these alternatives except the last. We will treat a motion for summary judgment in lieu of complaint in a separate section because of its unique substantive and procedural trappings.

A. Content and Form of Summons

In the Supreme Court and county courts, the content and form of the summons are governed more by past practice and case law than by statute or rule.[51]

The summons should include the name of the court, the venue, the basis of the venue,[52] the full names of all parties, the word "Summons," the time to answer, a statement that judgment will be taken in the event of a default, and the name, address and telephone number of plaintiff's attorney.[53] An official form is available for the guidance of practitioners.[54]

CPLR sec. 305(a) sets forth a few special requirements. If the venue designated is based upon the residence of the plaintiff, the summons must specify the plaintiff's address. The rule also requires that in an action arising out of a consumer credit transaction, the summons shall: (1) prominently display the words "consumer credit transaction" at the top of the summons, and (2) where a purchaser, borrower or debtor is a defendant (which will almost always be the case), specify (a) the county of residence of a defendant if one resides within the state, and (b) the county where the consumer credit transaction took place, if it is within the state.

In the Civil Court, district courts and city courts, the content and form of the summons are dictated entirely by court rules.[55] The requirements are very specific, and in some instances, vary significantly from area to area (*e.g.*, as in New York City, where certain statements must be set forth in Spanish).[56] Therefore, even if the lawyer uses a printed form of summons, the form should be compared to the local rule to be sure that the form is appropriate and up to date.

B. Summons with Notice

In the Supreme Court or a county court, an action may be commenced by service of a summons alone, if the summons contains (or has attached thereto) a notice stating "the nature of the action and the relief sought, and . . . the sum of money for which judgment may be taken in case of default."[57]This procedure may not be followed, however, in the Civil Court, a district court, a city court or a justice court. In each of those courts, the plaintiff must service either a summons with an indorsed complaint, or a summons and a formal complaint together.[58] A "summons with notice" alone will not suffice.

Where a summons with notice may be used, it is enough to include on the face of the summons a fairly simple statement containing the three required items of information. In a typical collection action, the notice might provide: "This is an action to recover money damages for breach of contract, and if you fail to appear, judgment will be taken against you by default for the sum of $15,000 with interest from November 1, 1983, plus the costs and disbursements of this action."[59] This statement is similar to the one contained in the official form of summons with notice adopted pursuant to CPLR sec. 107,[60] but the reader should note that the offical form was devised before a 1978 amendment to CPLR sec. 305(b), which changed the statutory language slightly.[61]

A summons missing all three of the required items of information is void, and the action may be dismissed for want of personal jurisdiction.[62] Furthermore, because the summons is a nullity, no action is commenced by serving it, and a second attempt to commence the action will not qualify for the six-month extension of the statute of limitations sometimes afforded by CPLR sec. 205.[63]

On the other hand, if the summons gives notice of the nature of the action and the relief sought, but fails to specify the amount of a possible default judgment, the summons is not jurisdictionally defective. The omission is merely an irregularity correctable pursuant to CPLR sec. 305(c).[64]

Finally, we must weigh the practical advantages and disadvantages of using a summons with notice. The obvious advantage is, again, we suppose, something which ought not be mentioned in a book, that is, less work for the lawyer and/or his/her secretary. In a law office which does a heavy volume of collections, or in a situation where speed is of the utmost importance, this may be a valid consideration. But there are practical disadvantages, too. First, the sufficiency of a particular notice may be open to some small doubt, and no lawyer should want to be the one who makes law in this area for the guidance of the rest of us. More importantly, if the defendant decides to defend, he/she will serve a notice of appearance or a demand for a complaint.[65] This procedure slows down the action somewhat,[66] and in collection actions, speed is often an important consideration.

In sum, the lawyer probably should use a summons with notice only when he/she feels compelled to do so by extremely urgent circumstances. In all other cases, the small amount of extra time required for the preparation of a complaint should be expended to insure a swifter, more risk-free prosection of the action.

C. Summons with Indorsed Complaint

1. When is Indorsement Permitted?

In the Civil Court, district courts, city courts and justice courts, if plaintiff's cause of action is for money only, "the complaint may be set forth by indorsement upon the summons."[67]

In the Civil Court and the justice courts, there are no other limitations on the use of this simplified pleading device.

In the district courts and city courts, however, there are further limitations. Some of those limitations are provided by statute, and others by local court rule.

The statutory limitations concern the place and method of service. In district court, an indorsed complaint may be used only where the defendant is served within the county.[68] In the city courts, not only must service be made within the county, but service must also be made by personal delivery.[69]

Some local court rules impose severe restrictions upon the use of an indorsed complaint. In the district courts[70] and some city courts,[71] local rules prohibit the use of an indorsed complaint in a long list of enumerated actions, including any where the amount claimed is more than $1,000. This restriction virtually eliminates the legislatively granted right to proceed by indorsed complaint, but both the Uniform District Court Act and the Uniform City Court Act permit such a limitation to be imposed by court rule.[72]

2. What Constitutes a Sufficient Indorsement?

In most of the courts which permit an indorsement upon the summons, the basic content and form of the summons itself is prescribed by court rule.[73] The only question remaining for the lawyer who chooses this route, then, is what words should be written on the summons to constitute a sufficient "indorsement"?

The respective court acts advise only that the indorsement "shall consist of a statement of the nature and substance of the action." This is very little indeed. Note that even the amount of money damages sought need not be included as part of the indorsement (though it must be included as part of the summons itself).[74] To emphasize the desire to achieve simplicity, each of the court acts admonishes: "The requirements of this act or of the CPLR applicable to a formal pleading shall not be applicable to an indorsement pleading."[75]

In practice, one sees everything from a phrase such as "goods sold and delivered," to three or four numbered paragraphs in the nature of a short formal complaint written upon the summons. One respected commentator suggests that the mere phrase, "goods sold and delivered" should suffice in a collection action.[76] While this may be so, we suggest that the practitioner link more description or factual information to his/her legal theory to insure that the defendant has notice of the subject transaction. For example, the following indorsement might be used in a typical collection action: "For damages of $2,450 for breach of a contract dated December 5, 1984, for the sale of snow removal equipment." A defendant could hardly contend that such a statement does not give him/her fair notice of what he/she is being sued for, and, on the other hand, to require anything more would contradict the legislative intention that something less than a formal pleading should suffice.

D. Complaint

In most instances, the plaintiff's attorney should prepare a complaint to accompany the summons. Though it is sometimes referred to as a "formal complaint" in collection practice, this is done simply to distinguish it from an indorsed complaint. The modifier "formal" should not be taken to imply either that the complaint must be long or that it must meet many technical requirements. It need not. In fact, there are only two points that a lawyer drafting a complaint in a collection matter need keep in mind, and one of them is to keep the allegations as short and plain as possible. The other concerns the need for verification.

1. Style

When drafting a complaint in a collection action, a lawyer should, even more than in other actions, heed the mandate of CPLR sec. 3014 that: "Each paragraph shall contain, as far as practicable, a single allegation." Let us add to that fine rule the suggestion that the allegations contain as few characterizations of the facts as possible.

Following these rules will do more than bring your complaint into compliance with the CPLR. The practice can produce strategic advantages. If the complaint contains concise, plain factual statements, denial of those allegations may show the answer to be a sham, or, at the very least, help to clearly frame the issues for the court. For example, one often sees a paragraph like this: "Defendant has failed and refused to pay the sums owing though plaintiff has duly demanded same." The same facts would be better pleaded: "Plaintiff demanded payment in full on August 24, 1984." "Defendant has not made any payment on this claim."

If the defendant denies either of these last two statements, later on, when the plaintiff seeks judgment, the denials can be used to attack the defendant's credibility. Suppose, for example, at trial the defendant emphasizes an affirmative defense, and offers no proof of any payment. This earlier denial in the pleading (often made under oath) can be used to cast doubt upon the testimony underlying his/her affirmative defense. Any collection practictioner who has been met with general denials by rote should appreciate a technique that can be used to turn such an answer back against the defendant.

2. Verification

The CPLR generally leaves verification of the complaint to the option of the pleader. In two intances sometimes encountered by collection attorneys, the complaint must be verified. First, if the lawyer chooses to particularize the items of his/her claim in the complaint as permitted by CPLR sec. 306(f), then that same rule requires that the complaint be verified. Secondly, the complaint must also be verified in a subsequent action against a joint obligor who was not summoned in the original action against his/her co-obligor.[77]

Some court rules, however, supply a good reason for most complaints in collection cases to be verified. In some of the lower courts where collection cases are most often brought, to obtain a judgment by default, you must present to the clerk an affidavit of the plaintiff (or other person having knowledge of the facts) setting forth the facts constituting the cause of action.[78] But if the complaint is verified, no separate affidavit is necessary.[79] Preparing a verified complaint in the first instance, therefore, will eliminate a need to prepare a second paper and to have the client sign it before judgment can be entered. This can be an important practical consideration when speed is a factor, where a particular law office does a heavy volume of collections, or where other factors make it difficult or inefficient to have the client sign such an affidavit.

IV. MOTION FOR SUMMARY JUDGMENT IN LIEU OF COMPLAINT

Some claims need not be prosecuted by a plenary action. Where the claim is based upon an "instrument for the payment of money only" or upon a judgment, the plaintiff's attorney has an alternative. Simultaneously with commencing the action, plaintiff may move for summary judgment. In a case where a meritorious claim is contested, this abbreviated procedure is likely to bring the case to a successful conclusion much more quickly than an ordinary action because the pleading and discovery stages of an action are eliminated.

This special procedure, authorized by CPLR sec. 3213, probably is not used as much as it should be because its unique procedural trappings are unfamiliar or uncomfortable to many lawyers. We will examine the procedural features of the device first. Then we will discuss the most frequently litigated question in this area, namely, what qualifies as an "instrument for the payment of money only."

A. Procedure

The papers to be prepared and served are a summons, a notice of motion, and an affidavit in support of the motion, signed by the plaintiff or other person with personal knowledge of the facts. The papers should be bound together in a legal back, in that order, with the instrument or judgment included as an exhibit to the affidavit. The standards of proof generally applicable to any other motion for summary judgment apply here as well. A sample set of papers is included in the Appendix.

With respect to time periods, CPLR sec. 3213 provides:

> The summons served with such motion papers shall require the defendant to submit answering papers on the motion within the time provided in the notice of motion. The minimum time such motion shall be noticed to be heard shall be as provided by subdivision (a) of rule 320 for making an appearance, depending upon the method of service. If the plaintiff sets the hearing date of the motion later than the minimum time therefor, he may require the defendant to serve a copy of his answering papers upon him within such extended period of time, not exceeding ten days, prior to such hearing date.

Sometimes the lawyer's uncertainty of the date and method of service at the time he/she is preparing the papers may discourage him/her from using this device. The overall time savings in some contested matters, however, should encourage the lawyer to try to use the device by allowing for the uncertainty. For example, suppose that the plaintiff's attorney can be sure that the defendant will be served by personal delivery within 10 days after the attorney delivers the papers to the process server. The attorney could safely schedule the return date for the motion 37 days from the date papers are delivered to the process server. Such a schedule allows 10 days for service to be made, 20 days for the defendant to answer, and 6 days for the plaintiff's attorney to reply (recalling that the reply papers must be served at least one day before the last day, the return date, pursuant to CPLR sec. 2214(b)). Similar time schedules can be worked out to accommodate the attorney's own needs by reading together the time periods continued in CPLR secs. 3213, 320(a) and 2214(b).

Two further procedural points bear brief mention. With respect to counterclaims, the rule may be generally stated that if the counterclaim arose from a transaction unrelated to the main claim, the allegations of the counterclaim will not defeat the the motion for summary judgment. If the counterclaim did arise from some transaction, it may, but does not necessarily, defect the motion.[80] In the event the motion is denied for any reason, the action is converted into an ordinary action. Either the moving and answering affidavits will be deemed the complaint and answer, or the court will direct that pleadings be served, and in either event, the case will proceed like any other. Only the motion, not the action, is "dismissed."

B. "Instrument for the Payment of Money Only"

The most frequently litigated question under CPLR sec. 3213 is whether particular writing constitutes an "instrument for the payment of money only," thereby qualifying for use of this special procedure.

In a recent opinion, Justice Kassal of the Appellate Division, First Department, did a splendid job of collecting and summarizing the law on this subject.[81] The court held that to qualify for CPLR sec. 3213 treatment, the plaintiff must prove a *prima facie* case by proving the instrument and a failure to make the payments called for by its terms.[82] Where proof outside the instrument is necessary to establish the underlying obligation, the CPLR sec. 3213 procedure is not available.[83]

Applying these standards, the courts have permitted the accelerated procedure in cases involving a promissory note,[84] an unconditional guaranty,[85] an accepted sight draft,[86] a letter of credit,[87] a nonnegotiable note,[88] a letter evidencing a debt obligation for a fixed period at a stated rate of interest,[89] and a letter acknowledging a debt in an amount set forth in an account stated.[90] In probably one of the most liberal applications of the rule, a court permitted the procedure to be used by a bank to recover on overdrafts where the bank presented the relevant bank statement and a corporate resolution executed by the defendant wherein the defendant agreed to be bound by the bank statements unless it notified the bank of any errors within 30 days.[91]

"On the other hand, resort to this expedited procedure has been denied, where the action was founded upon documents which, although calling for the payment of a sum of money, also required some other condition or performance, thus leading to the conclusion that the instrument from the face of the document was not one for the payment of money *only*."[92] Courts have denied CPLR sec. 3213 treatment to an unsigned statement of account,[93] a separation agreement,[94] a contract to provide services,[95] an action on a forged check,[96] a bill of lading,[97] a bond and mortgage,[98] and a savings account passbook.[99]

V. SERVICE OF PROCESS

Jurisdiction in personam is the power of the court over the person of a party defendant. It is the power a court has to adjudicate that a plaintiff is entitled to money damages from a defendant and is entitled to enforce payment from the defendant's assets.

A court does not take jurisdiction in a collection action on its own initiative. Jurisdiction is given to the court by the plaintiff and defendant. The plaintiff submits to a court's jurisdiction when he/she initiates legal action. Other parties must be brought within the court's jurisdiction by proper service.

The purpose and function of the service of process, in addition to giving the court power over the parties, is to give the defendant notice of the commencement of the action.

A. Service of a Summons Upon a Natural Person

Personal service of a summons upon a natural person can be made by any one of the five following methods:

1. Personal Delivery

The first alternative is to deliver the summons within the state to the person to be served.[100]

Personal delivery of the summons is the most desirable method of giving notice of a claim because it provides a defendant with first-hand knowledge. From the plaintiff's point of view, personal delivery is most desirable because it minimizes the risk of judgment being set aside.[101]

Personal delivery also requires the defendant to appear sooner. A defendant served by personal delivery has 20 days to appear.[102] A defendant served by other methods has until 30 days after service "is complete,"[103] and service is complete 10 days after the affidavit of service is filed.[104] Taking into account the time it takes the plaintiff's attorney to get the affidavit of service from his/her process server and into the hands of the clerk, the difference in the times to appear can amount to a month. Such a difference can be significant in collection matters, where time is often an important factor.

Service of a summons will, in some cases, be considered valid personal delivery even though process is not handed to the defendant. This is so, for example, where a defendant resists service of process by force or deceit or a refusal to accept service.[105]

2. Delivery and Mailing

The second alternative is to deliver the summons within the state to a person of suitable age and discretion at the actual place of business, dwelling place or usual place of abode of the defendant, to mail the summons to the defendant at his/her last known residence.[106]

This method can be used without any prior effort to make personal delivery. Delivery and mailing are both essential in order for a court to obtain jurisdiction over the defendant.

The person of suitable age and discretion need not be an adult. A teenager will suffice if it appears with reasonable certainty that he/she will advise the defendant of the service of process.[107]

A court may also consider fluency in English as a factor in determining whether the individual served was of suitable age and discretion, especially when the plaintiff, plaintiff's counsel or the process server is on notice that such person is not fluent in English.[108]

What constitutes a dwelling place or "usual place of abode" is a question which can be answered only by examining the facts of each case. The court will examine the circumstances to determine whether the delivery was reasonably calculated to give the defendant notice of the action.

Generally, where a defendant resides in a multiple dwelling, the dwelling place or usual place of abode is the apartment of the defendant. The summons may nonetheless be delivered to a person living in another apartment in the same building, or, in some cases, to the doorman at the entrance to the lobby.[109] The court will examine the size of the apartment house, proximity of the place of delivery to the apartment of the defendant, and other factors. Courts have also applied a similar approach in determining the "actual place of business" of the defendant.[110]

Proof of such service must be filed within twenty days thereafter with the clerk of the court designated in the summons. The proof of service must identify the person of suitable age and discretion, and the date, time and place of service. Service is complete ten days after filing.[111]

3. Agent for Service

A third alternative is to deliver the summons within the state to the agent designated by the defendant for service of process.[112] This method is rarely used in collection practice, however, because a defendant will generally do little to cooperate with a plaintiff.

4. "Nailing" and Mailing

If service under CPLR secs. 308(1) and (2) should fail, efforts to achieve service may be made by affixing the summons either to the door of the actual place of business, dwelling place or usual place of abode within the state of the person to be served, *and* mailing the summons to him/her at his/her last known address. Proof of service must be filed within twenty days, and service is complete ten days after filing.[113]

Service is not complete until both acts of affixing and mailing are done, and the expiration of a statute of limitations will not be averted by affixing within the statutory time if the mailing is not also accomplished within the same period. Using registered or certified mail, return receipt requested, may avoid a possible claim that actual notice of the action was never received. On the other hand, defendants sometimes refuse registered or certified mail, and using ordinary mail raises a presumption of receipt. The attorney must judge for himself/herself which to use by considering all the circumstances of the particular case.

Because of the "due diligence" requirement built into the statute, service under this paragraph requires a more detailed affidavit of service which must indicate the efforts made to achieve service under the other provisions.[114] Generally, a single visit to the premises when no one is home will not suffice. On the other hand, several visits at different times to the defendant's residence and place of business probably does constitute the requisite diligence. Again, the determination turns on the particular circumstances.

5. Court Directed Service

The final alternative is offered by CPLR sec. 308(5). The statute permits service to be made "in such manner as the court, upon motion without notice, directs if service is impracticable" under subdivisions (1), (2) and (4) of CPLR sec. 308.

This section is intended for use in unpredictable circumstances where a plaintiff is unable to follow the usual methods of service, and the situation requires more flexibility. The Court of Appeals has held that in order for a plaintiff to use this section, he/she need only establish that the methods of service set forth in CPLR secs. 308(1), (2) and (4) cannot be met.[115]

B. "Additional Notice" Required in Some Cases

Effective January 1, 1978, CPLR sec. 308 was amended by the addition of an unnumbered paragraph which requires that a natural person is entitled to an "additional notice" of the commencement of any action based upon the nonpayment of a contractual obligation. CPLR sec. 3215(e) was similarly amended to require proof of such additional notice upon the entry of a default judgment. Therefore, it may be prudent for the plaintiff's attorney to make this additional mailing in every applicable case at the outset. If the plaintiff waits for a default in appearance appearance by the defendant, and then makes the additional mailing, his/her application for entry of a judgment will have to wait 20 more days.

The additional notice provision requires that the plaintiff or his/her attorney, at least twenty (20) days prior to the entry of judgment, serve an additional copy of the summons upon the defendant by forwarding it by first class mail to the defendant at his/her last known residence address. If, prior to the entry of judgment, the summons is returned by the post office as undeliverable, or the home address of the defendant is not known, then a copy of the summons should be mailed to the defendant's place of business, if known, in an envelope marked "personal and confidential" and not indicating that it is from an attorney.

C. Personal Service Upon a Corporation

Personal service upon a domestic or foreign corporation shall be made by delivering the summons to an officer, director, managing or general agent, or cashier or assistant cashier, or to any other agent authorized by appointment or by law to receive service.[116]

Generally, delivery of a summons to a low level clerical employee who possesses no supervisory or administrative duties, and who tells the process server that he/she is unauthorized to accept service, is not good service upon the corporation.[117]

An issue sometimes litigated is the question of who qualifies as a "managing or general agent." Generally, if there are a handful of employees at a corporate office, the person who appears to be in charge qualifies as a managing agent for service, and this person needs no formal title indicating a high position.

D. Personal Service Upon a Partnership

Personal service upon persons conducting a business as a partnership may be made by personally serving the summons within the state upon any one of the partners.[118] For any partner who is not personally served, however, only his/her partnership interest may be reached by the judgment creditor.[119]

E. Personal Service Outside New York

Service of process outside the state gives personal jurisdiction if the defendant is a domiciliary of the state or has committed acts which meet the requirements of CPLR sec. 302.[120]

The time to answer a summons served outside the state is thirty days from the time service is complete rather than the twenty days available where service is made by personal delivery within the state.[121]

F. Proof of Service and Filing

The requirements of proof of service are set forth in detail in CPLR sec. 306. These requirements should be closely followed if the practitioner expects to enter a default judgment without any unnecessary delay.

The filing of proof of service is not mandatory in New York at the outset of the case, when service is made by personal delivery to the defendant or to a CPLR sec. 318 agent, but it is mandatory when service is made under CPLR secs. 308(2) and 308(4). In such cases, proof of service must be filed with the clerk within twenty days after service is made and service is complete ten days after such filing.

Footnotes

[1] For an excellent analysis of the subject matter jurisdiction of the various New York courts on a court by court basis, *see* Siegel, *New York Practice* sections 12-22 (1978).

[2] *See* CCA sec. 202; UDCA sec. 20; UCCA sec. 202; UJCA sec. 202 (which excludes, however, actions to foreclose liens on personal property).

[3] The towns of Babylon, Brookhaven, Huntington, Islip and Smithtown are part of the District Court of Suffolk County.

[4] Siegel, *New York Practice* sec. 12, at 15 (1978).

[5] CPLR sec. 325(d); 22 NYCRR sec. 660.21; 22 NYCRR sec. 861.17; 22 NYCRR sec. 1024.20.

[6] CPLR sec. 8102.

[7] CCA sec. 202.

[8] UDCA sec. 202.

[9] Judiciary Law sec. 190(3).

[10] N.Y. Const. Art. VI, secs. 17(a), 16(d).

[11] UJCA sec. 202.

[12] N.Y. Const. Art. VI, sec. 11(a).

[13] Judiciary Law sec. 190(3).

[14] *Mandel v. Kent*, 70 A.D.2d 903, 417 N.Y.S.2d 306 (2d Dep't 1979); *Peoples National Bank of Rockland County v. Yodowitz*, 99 Misc. 2d 978, 417 N.Y.S.2d 849 (County Ct., Rockland Co. 1979); *J.A. Mennella Foods Corp. v. Neptune's Nuggets, Inc.*, 74 Misc. 2d 839, 346 N.Y.S.2d 43 (County Ct., Suffolk Co. 1973).

[15] *Benson v. Cohoes School Board*, 98 Misc. 2d 110, 413 N.Y.S.2d 600 (County Ct., Albany Co. 1979); *Weber v. Kowalski*, 85 Misc. 2d 349, 358, 376 N.Y.S.2d 996, 1007 (Sup. Ct., Dutchess Co. 1975).

[16] *See, e.g., Benson v. Cohoes School Board*, 98 Misc. 2d 110, 113, 413 N.Y.S.2d 600, 602 (County Co., Albany Co. 1979).

[17] *See, e.g., Kemper v. Transamerica Insurance Co.*, 61 Misc. 2d 7, 304 N.Y.S.2d 515 (Civil Ct. 1969).

[18] How to make proper service on various kinds of defendants is discussed in subsection 5 of the chapter, *infra*.

[19] *See, e.g.*, Siegel, *New York Practice* sec. 84, *et seq.* 1978); *McKinney's Consolidated Laws of New York Annotated*, Practice Commentary, CPLR sec. 302.

[20] For a complete explanation of "long-arm" jurisdiction, the reader should consult the sources cited in footnote 19, *supra*, and CPLR sec. 302 itself, especially subdivision (a)(3) thereof, to which no allusion is made in the text because it plays no role in an ordinary collection action.

[21] Judiciary Law sec. 190(3). Note that the numbering and punctuation which appears in the text is not part of the statute. The statute itself does not make clear whether all three of the alternative requirements must be met by *all* of the defendants, nor does it make clear whether the office and "doing business" requirements are to be tested as of the time of commencement of the action. Nor does the published case law clarify the point. Nonetheless, we have so framed the rule in the text because we feel that is what was intended, and because any reading of the statute which does not apply the initital "all of them" and "time of commencement" modifiers equally to the residence, office and "doing business" requirements would result in inconsistent applications of the rule.

[22] *See, e.g., Meyers v. American Locomotive Co.*, 201 N.Y. 163, 94 N.E. 605 (1911).

[23] CCA sec. 403.

[24] UDCA sec. 403.

[25] Compare CPLR sec. 302, CCA sec. 404 and UDCA sec. 404.

[26] UCCA sec. 403.

[27] UCCA sec. 404.

[28] UCCA sec. 213(d).

[29] UJCA sec. 403.

[30] UJCA sec. 213.

[31] For a more complete description of the transcripting process, *see New York Practice* sec. 422 (1978).

[32] CPLR secs. 5018, 5203.

[33] UJCA sec. 208.

[34] *Id.*

[35] N.Y. Const. Art. VI, sec. 20.

[36] *See* CCA sec. 902; UDCA sec. 902 (*but see* 22 NYCRR sec. 3840.5(a) and 22 NYCRR sec. 3935.5(a)); UCCA sec. 902; UJCA sec. 902.

[37] Sec. 3, *infra*.

[38] CCA sec. 1505, UDCA sec. 1505; UCCA sec. 1505; UJCA sec. 1505.

[39] A restraining notice, CPLR sec. 5222, disclosure in aid of enforcement, CPLR sec. 5223-24, a motion for a turnover order CPLR secs. 5225, 5227, a motion for an installment payment order, CPLR sec. 5226, a motion for a receivership, CPLR sec. 5528 and a motion for an order of contempt, CPLR sec. 5251, are generally referred to as "supplementary proceedings." *See generally,* Siegel, *New York Practice* sec. 492 (1978).

[40] CPLR sec. 5221(a)(4).

[41] CPLR sec. 5221(a)(4).

[42] CPLR sec. 5221(a)(3).

[43] CPLR sec. 5221(a)(2).

[44] CPLR sec. 5221(a)(1).

[45] CPLR secs. 5018, 5203.

[46] CPLR Article 5.

[47] CCA Article 3.

[48] UDCA Article 3.

[49] CPLR sec. 503(a).

[50] CPLR sec. 105(f).

[51] Cases concerning the content and form of a summons are collected at 1 Weinstein, Korn & Miller, *New York Civil Practice*, pars. 305.02 to 305.10.

[52] CPLR sec. 305(a).

[53] CPLR sec. 2101(d).

[54] Official Form No. 1, which is available, among other places, in 1 *Bender's Forms for the Civil Practice*, Form No. 305:1A.

55 For the Civil Court, *see* 22 NYCRR sec. 2900.2; for the district courts, *see* 22 NYCRR sec. 3840.3 (Nassau) and 22 NYCRR sec. 3935.3 (Suffolk); and for city courts outside New York City, *see* 22 NYCRR sec. 3000.3 (2d Dep't), 22 NYCRR sec. 3200.5 (3d Dep't), and 22 NYCRR sec. 3400.11 (4th Dep't).

56 22 NYCRR sec. 2900.2.

57 CPLR sec. 305(b).

58 CCA sec. 902(b); UDCL sec. 902(b); UCCA sec. 902(b); UJCA sec. 902(b).

59 A sample form of summons with notice is included in the Appendix.

60 Official Form No. 3, which is available, among other places, in 1 *Bender's Forms for the Civil Practice*, Form No. 305:5A.

61 Laws of New York, 1978, c. 528.

62 *Ciaschi v. Town of Enfield,* 86 A.D.2d 903, 448 N.Y.S.2d 267 (3d Dep't 1982).

63 *Id.*

64 *Premo v. Cornell,* 71 A.D.2d 223, 423 N.Y.S.2d 64 (3d Dep't 1979).

65 CPLR sec. 3012(b).

66 Twenty days are allowed for service of the notice of appearance or demand for a complaint, twenty more for service of the complaint, and twenty more for service of the answer. CPLR secs. 320(a), 3012(b).

67 CCA sec. 902(a)(1); UDCA sec. 902(a)(1); UCCA sec. 902(a)(1); UJCA sec. 902(a)(1).

68 UDCA sec. 902(a)(1). Interestingly, the district court rules for both Nassau and Suffolk counties suggest that, to use an indorsed complaint, service must not only be made within the county, but it must also be made by personal delivery. *See* 22 NYCRR sec. 3840.3(b), 22 NYCRR sec. 3935.3(b). That suggestion does not conform to the statutory language. *Compare* UDCA sec. 902(a)(1) with UCCA sec. 902(a)(1).

69 UCCA sec. 902(a)(1).

70 22 NYCRR sec. 3840.5(a) [Nassau County]; 22 NYCRR sec. 3935.5(a) [Suffolk County].

71 *See, e.g.*, 22 NYCRR sec. 3020.5(a) [City of Glen Cove].

72 UDCA sec. 902(d); UCCA sec. 902(d).

[73] For the Civil Court, *see* 22 NYCRR sec. 2900.2(b); for the district courts, *see* 22 NYCRR sec. 3840.3(b) [Nassau County] and 22 NYCRR sec. 3935.3(b) [Suffolk]; and for city courts outside New York City, *see* 22 NYCRR sec. 3003.3(b) (2d Dep't), 22 NYCRR sec. 3200.5(b) (3d Dep't) and 22 NYCRR sec. 3400.11 (a) (4th Dep't). In some city courts, a local rule may prescribe a form supplementing the one set forth in the "uniform rules" for city courts within that department. *See, e.g.*, 22 NYCRR sec. 3020.3(b) [City of Glen Cove].

[74] *See, e.g.*, CCA sec. 902(a)(1).

[75] CCA sec. 903, UDCA sec. 903, UCCA sec. 903, UJCA sec. 903.

[76] *McKinney's Consolidated Laws of New York Annotated*, Practice Commentary, CCA sec. 903 (1984 supp.).

[77] CPLR sec. 1502.

[78] *See, e.g.*, 22 NYCRR sec. 2900.18(a) [Civil Court]; 22 NYCRR sec. 3840.15(a) [District Court, Nassau County]; 22 NYCRR sec. 3935.15(a) [District Court, Suffolk County]; 22 NYCRR sec. 3030.10(a) [City Court, Long Beach]. Other local court rules should be consulted for similar provisions.

[79] *Id.*

[80] *See, e.g., Logan v. Williamson & Co.*, 64 A.D.2d 466, 469-70, 409 N.Y.S.2d 883, 885 (4th Dep't 1978), *appeal dismissed*, 46 N.Y.2d 996, 416 N.Y.S.2d 242 (1979); *Diversified Industries, Inc. v. Casa del Tesoro Corp.*, 79 A.D.2d 534, 433 N.Y.S.2d 465, 466 (1st Dep't 1980).

[81] *Maglich v. Saxe, Bacon & Bolan, P.C.*, 97 A.D.2d 19, 468 N.Y.S.2d 618 (1st Dep't 1983).

[82] *Id.* at 21, 468 N.Y.S.2d at 620.

[83] *Id.*

[84] *Seaman-Andwall Corp. v. Wright Machine Corp.*, 31 A.D.2d 136, 295 N.Y.S.2d 752 (1st Dep't 1968), *aff'd*, 29 N.Y.2d 617, 324 N.Y.S.2d 410 (1971).

[85] *Rhodia, Inc. v. Steel*, 32 A.D.2d 753, 300 N.Y.S.2d 1005 (1st Dep't 1969).

[86] *Banco Portugues Do Atlantico v. Fonda Mfg. Corp.*, 31 A.D.2d 122, 295 N.Y.S.2d 701 (1st Dep't 1968), *aff'd*, 26 N.Y.2d 642, 307 N.Y.S.2d 668 (1970).

[87] *Banco Tornquist, S.A. v. American Bank & Trust Co.*, 71 Misc. 2d 874, 337 N.Y.S.2d 489 (S.Ct. N.Y.Co. 1972).

[88] *Louis Sherry Ice Cream Co. v. Kroggel*, 42 Misc. 2d 21, 245 N.Y.S.2d 755 (S.Ct. N.Y.Co. 1963).

[89] *Baker v. Gundermann*, 52 Misc. 2d 639, 276 N.Y.S.2d 495 (S.Ct. Nassau Co. 1966).

[90] *Ace Office Cleaning Corp. v. Brodsky, Hopf & Adler, P.C.*, 81 Misc. 2d 170, 364 N.Y.S.2d 737 (Civil Ct. 1975).

[91] *Bank Hapoalim v. Madison Carpet Corp.*, 103 Misc. 2d 522, 426 N.Y.S.2d 211 (S.Ct. N.Y.Co. 1980).

[92] *Maglich v. Saxe, Bacon & Bolan, P.C.*, 97 A.D.2d 19, 22, 468 N.Y.S.2d 618, 620 (1st Dep't 1983).

[93] *Interman Industrial Products Ltd. v. R.S.M. Electron Power*, 37 N.Y.2d 151, 371 N.Y.S.2d 675 (1975).

[94] *Wagner v. Cornblum*, 36 A.D.2d 427, 321 N.Y.S.2d 156 (4th Dep't 1971).

[95] *Mike Nasti Sand Co. v. Alman Landscaping Corp.*, 34 A.D.2d 554, 309 N.Y.S.2d 697 (2d Dep't 1970).

[96] *Signal Plan, Inc. v. Chase Manhattan Bank*, 23 A.D.2d 636, 256 N.Y.S.2d 866 (1st Dep't 1965).

[97] *Hellenic Lines Limited v. Crown Cork & Seal Co.*, 70 A.D.2d 567, 417 N.Y.S.2d 61 (1st Dep't 1979).

[98] *New York Conference Ass'n of Seventh Day Adventists of Syracuse v. 915 James St. Ass'n*, 63 Misc. 2d 38, 310 N.Y.S.2d 742 (S.Ct. Onondaga Co. 1970).

[99] *Stern v. Chemical Bank*, 83 Misc. 2d 508, 372 N.Y.S.2d 913 (Civil Ct. 1975).

[100] CPLR sec. 308(1).

[101] *See* CPLR sec. 317.

[102] CPLR sec. 320(a).

[103] CPLR sec. 320(a).

[104] CPLR secs. 308(2) and 308(4).

[105] *See, e.g., Estate of Turecamo*, 96 Misc. 2d 120, 121, 408 N.Y.S.2d 930, 931 (Sur. Ct., Nassau Co. 1978)(where the defendant refused to open the door to accept service).

[106] CPLR sec. 308(2).

[107] *See, e.g., Room Additions, Inc. v. Howard*, 124 Misc. 2d 19, 475 N.Y.S.2d 310 (Civil Ct. 1984).

[108] *Nuez v. Diaz*, 110 Misc. 2d 399, 421 N.Y.S.2d 770 (S.Ct., Monroe Co. 1979).

[109] *F.I. DuPont, Glore Forgan & Co. v. Chen*, 41 N.Y.2d 794, 396 N.Y.S.2d 343 (1977); *Braun v. St. Vincent's Hospital*, 57 N.Y.2d 909, 456 N.Y.S.2d 763 (1982).

[110] *DiGiuseppe v. DiGiuseppe*, 70 Misc. 2d 188, 333 N.Y.S.2d 245 (Civil Ct. 1972).

[111] CPLR sec. 308(2).

[112] CPLR sec. 308(3); CPLR sec. 318.

[113] CPLR sec. 308(4).

[114] CPLR sec. 306(c).

[115] *Dobkin v. Chapman*, 21 N.Y.2d 490, 289 N.Y.S.2d 161 (1968).

[116] CPLR sec. 311(1).

[117] *Arce v. Sybron Corp.*, 82 A.D.2d 308, 441 N.Y.S.2d 498 (2d Dep't 1981).

[118] CPLR sec. 310.

[119] CPLR sec. 5201(b).

[120] CPLR sec. 313.

[121] CPLR sec. 320(a).

CHAPTER EIGHT

COMMENCING LAWSUIT

Marvin Krumholz, Esq.
Sennet & Krumholz

I. TYPE OF CLAIM

We shall focus our attention on some fundamental principles that simultaneously come into play in the preparation and issuance of a summons and complaint. At the outset it is important, in debt collection practice, to determine the type of claim that is involved. Primarily, the collection attorney will be handling two distinct types of claims, the retail or consumer claim as opposed to the commerical or business claim.

A consumer claim is defined as a transaction wherein credit is extended to an individual and the money, property or service which is the subject of the transaction is primarily for personal, family or household purposes. CPLR sec. 105(F). A commercial claim is defined as a claim which arises from an obligation to pay for goods sold or leased, services rendered, or monies loaned for use in the conduct of a business or profession. Definition as stated in the Commercial Law League Rules.

Although the rates or commissions earned between an attorney and his/her client are confidential and usually subject to an agreement or retainer, certain premises concerning such rates are common knowledge with the collection attorney, however, and are normally contingent upon collection. If no recovery is made, no fee is earned.

Pursuant to the Rules of the Commercial Law League, the rates on commercial claims are as follows:

20% on the first $300 collected
18% on the excess of $300 to $2000 collected
13% on the excess of $2000

These sliding scale rates are prevailing in commercial claims, however, they can be varied by special agreement which will include a "suit fee." The suit fee is additional compensation paid by the client to the attorney for extra work on a complex case, not ordinarily anticipated at the outset. As an illustration, a trial lasting several days, or one in which the law is unique and requires several days of research, or voluminous motion practice or discovery which entails deposing several witnesses, are instances in which a suit fee is justified. It is important to remember when entering into an agreement of retainer to include these contingencies for a suit fee to be earned or requested.

In consumer credit transactions (retail claims) the rates or commissions are likewise subject to an agreement of retainer and are confidential. However, they can vary between 25 percent to 33⅓ percent depending on the volume of cases assigned to the attorney, the area of litigation, such as suits within the City of New York as opposed to suits outside the City, and the complexity of the issues involved in the claims.

A word of caution to the attorney starting a collection practice is that the client must always bear the cost expense of litigation. In extreme cases for reasons of expediency, if the attorney advances court costs and starts a lawsuit, the costs must be subject to reimbursement. The Canons of Ethics and The Code of Professional Responsibility prohibit an attorney to advance costs for suit, without reimbursement at some point during litigation, either during or at the termination thereof.

The rates or commissions charged for a commercial claim are usually lower than the rates charged for a consumer claim. The reason for this is that the claim is more substantial in amount and is governed by Commerical Law League rates, which are always incorporated in every retainer agreement. Although consumer claims such as department store or bank credit card accounts and loans usually have a higher volume of referrals, the dollar amount of the claims are less and consequently the fee earned after recovery is greater. These are rates in consumer credit transactions which are prevailing among collection attorneys but each attorney should negotiate for the best possible retainer.

Suit fees in consumer claims are virtually nonexistent. These are instances in which an attorney can request and charge a suit fee which is based on a fixed or flat fee, or on a time basis at a fixed hourly rate. In the event a counterclaim is asserted by the defendant, by their attorney or in person, report such counterclaim promptly to the client and give them the option to retain outside counsel or their house counsel or allow the collection attorney to defend the counterclaim. If your firm is prosecuting the underlying claim, and defending the counterclaim, additional compensation is justified and a request for same should made.

It should be noted that when you are defending a counterclaim you must act promptly to determine the wishes of your client, as a reply might be necesary. Therefore, the better practice would be to obtain additional time to reply from your adversary, while the client decides who will defend the counterclaim. In the Supreme Court, where the monetary jurisdiction is now in excess of $25,000, a reply is necessary to an asserted counterclaim. CPLR sec. 3012 (a). In the Civil Court of the City of New York, which has city-wide jurisdiction, a reply to a counterclaim is not required, as the allegations of the counterclaim are automatically deemed controverted and denied. N.Y.C.C.A. sec. 907(a). Similarly, under the Uniform District Court Act, which governs the various District Courts in Nassau and Suffolk Counties, counterclaims are deemed denied, and no reply is necessary, except by court order. Uniform District Court Act sec. 907(a).

II. VENUE

An important consideration, sometimes overlooked, is venue (place of trial) in the preparation and issuance of a summons and complaint in consumer credit transactions. Venue in such transactions is governed by CPLR sec. 503(F), which states that the place of trial shall be the residence of defendant, if within the state, or the county in which the consumer transaction took place, if within the state. There does not appear to be any priority in the use of either residence or transaction, inherent in this statute, which is strictly adhered to by the courts. The Clerk of the Court has the absolute right and authority not to accept a summons and complaint for filing, when it appears on its face that venue is improper and properly belongs in a different county. CPLR sec. 513(a). Section 513 (b) of the CPLR requires the Clerk to maintain a register and enter the date of a rejected summons, and the county where the summons should properly be filed.

Venue in a commerical or business claim is more liberal in scope, and is based upon the residence of the parties (either party) at the time of commencement of the action. If none of the parties reside in the state at the time of commencement of the action, then plaintiff can designate the place of trial, subject to objection and change by the court, pursuant to CPLR sec. 510. A demand to change the place of trial based on improper county shall be served prior to or simultaneously with the answer. A demand to change venue on other grounds specified in CPLR sec. 510 can be made within a reasonable time after commencement of the action.

Venue based on residence in commercial claims, pursuant to CPLR sec. 503(c): Corporation, domestic or foreign authorized to conduct business in this state, shall be deemed a resident of the county in which its principal office is located, except that a railroad or common carrier shall be deemed a resident of the county where the cause of action arose. CPLR sec. 503(d): Unincorporated association, partnership or individually owned business—venue is deemed where the association has its principal office as well as the county where the president or treasurer resides; partnership or individually owned business, venue is placed where its principal office is located, as well as the county in which the partner or individual owner suing or being sued resides.

A further consideration that should be given special attention in the preparation of a summons and complaint in a consumer credit transaction is that compliance must be made with CPLR sec. 305 (a), which states in part that the words CONSUMER CREDIT TRANSACTION shall be prominently displayed at the top of the summons, and shall specify the county of residence of defendant, and where the consumer credit transaction took place.

In the Civil Court of the City of New York, rule provides 2900.2 (b), provides that in addition to the above requirements in a summons in a consumer credit case, there also be a Spanish translation equivalent to the mandates stated in English, and a caveat or notice to the defendant, in English and Spanish, as to the steps to be taken upon receipt of a summons and complaint. Annexed hereto and referred to as Appendix A is a sample copy of a summons and complaint for goods sold and delivered in a consumer credit transaction case. There are no similar requirements in the various district courts for notice or Spanish provisions.

After evaluating the nature of the claim, the proper party defendant to be sued, and the type of summons to be issued, you can then turn your attention to your client's precise cause of action and the probability of success. You should make every effort to have a frank discussion with your client, at the outset of litigation, to evaluate the debtor's possible defenses to the action, or any counterclaims that could be asserted against your client.

In collection practice you will probably handle cases involving the following causes of action:

1. goods sold and delivered;
2. services rendered and unpaid;
3. promissory notes in commerical cases, and installment loan notes in consumer credit cases;
4. bank and department store credit cards;
5. individual guarantees of a primary obligors of joint and several obligors;
6. breach of agreement.

If an agreement or credit application is available, it should be reviewed to determine if attorneys' fees are to be included in the action, or if accrued interest is to be added, and any liquidated damage clause in the event of a breach of agreement.

In discussing the case with your client, it is good practice to ascertain any possible defenses that the debtor might have available, such as:

1. damaged or defective goods or merchandise;
2. goods or services that do not conform to sample or warranty;
3. Statute of Limitations;
4. Statute of Frauds;
5. usurious rates of interest;
6. improper party defendant.

The attorney representing the creditor might be faced with a defense that does not challenge the substance of the claim, such as lack of jurisdiction over the person of the defendant. This defense is frequently interposed in an answer in collection cases. Whether such defense is credible or not, it could delay the case being noticed for trial. Such a defense can be pleaded prior to or simultaneously with answer, and is waived if not raised in a responsive pleading. CPLR sec. 3211(e). After a default judgment, lack of jurisdiction could be asserted at any time pursuant to CPLR sec. 5015 (4), subject to the provisions of CPLR sec. 317, which states that such a motion can be made within one year after notice of entry of the judgment, but not more than five years after such entry.

Another issue to be discussed with the client is the possibility of a counterclaim being made, especially in consumer credit cases, by irate debtors. In most cases the counterclaims can be mutually worked out between the parties, and are spurious in the majority of cases. These are instances when counterclaims are serious and should be promptly reported to the client. Some of the most common counterclaims faced by the creditor's attorney are as follows:

1. injury from unworkmanlike performance of a service;
2. injury from defective goods;
3. loss of business or profits as a result of untimely delivery of goods;
4. damages to credit rating or reputation as a result of a groundless lawsuit.

Properly evaluating your client's claim and anticipating potential defenses and counterclaims at the pre-litigation stage is an integral part of becoming a successful collection attorney, and most of all in the successful resolution of the case.

III. DETERMINING PROPER PARTY DEFENDANT

Whether the claim assigned to the collection attorney is a commercial or consumer claim, you must determine and identify the proper party defendant. Without the proper name of the defendant in the lawsuit, the eventual judgment and execution will be extremely difficult, if not impossible, to collect. In such instance a motion to amend will have to be made, and ordinarily should be granted unless prejudice to the defendant can be shown.

In this regard it should be noted that where a change in substance in a judgment is sought, the remedy is not amendment. *Goldspinner v. Goldspinner*, 52 A.D.2d 837 (1976); *Bankers Trust Co. v. Jackson*, 99 Misc. 2d 225 (1979). If the attorney has caused process to be issued against an entity with a name different from the proper named entity, and proceeds to judgment, he/she may not complain of his/her neglect if an amendment is not granted. *First National City Bank v. Elsky*, 62 Misc. 2d 880 (1970). The effect of this would be to add a party not originally served.

Clerical errors or a mistake in the entry of the judgment or the omission of a right of relief to which a party is entitled as a matter of course, may alone be corrected by the court through amendment. *Herpe v. Herpe*, 225 N.Y. 323 (1919); *First National City Bank v. Elsky, supra.*

The defendant in a lawsuit can be either an individual, an individual operating under an assumed name, a partnership or a corporation. It is as important to determine the proper name of the defendant as it is to determine the proper party defendant. State laws require individuals operating under an assumed name and partners conducting business under a partnership entity to file a Certificate of Doing Business with the County Clerk where the principal office is located. Likewise, under the General Business Law, a Certificate of Incorporation must be filed in Albany, which routinely files a copy of such certificate in the county where the principal office is located.

In the event such filing is not done and the creditor does not obtain complete information as to the name of the person or entity he is doing business with, and the creditor's file or application is not complete, the attorney can discover such assumed names, partnership identities and corporate designations by checking the following places:

1. Secretary of State in Albany;
2. County Clerk's Office;
3. credit reporting agencies, but your client must be a subscriber to obtain such information, and a nominal fee is required;

4. client's file to review correspondence such as letterheads, debtor's checks, applications, signed agreements or any other instruments that might shed light on the proper entity responsible.

It should be kept in mind that other individuals could be responsible and liable for the same debt upon different causes of action and should be included in your suit, other than primary obligors, comakers and guarantors. To illustrate:

1. Parent-child relationship: Items to be considered in determining whether both are responsible is the contracting age and ability and emancipation of the child, and the type of debt involved.

2. Husband-wife relationship: If both parties contracted or signed an agreement to purchase goods or services, they are both responsible and can be joined in one lawsuit. Where the spouses are living together, the husband has a duty to support his wife, and failing that the wife may contract for goods or services as her husband's agent. In light of the decision in *Orr v. Orr*, 440 U.S. 268 (1979), New York's support and matrimonial statutes were amended to conform to gender-neutral requirements. Statutory support obligations are now mutual and dependant upon the parties' needs and ability to pay. *Nelson v. State*, 105 Misc. 2d 107 (1980). A husband is completely discharged of responsibility if he made reasonable and adequate provisions for the wife's necessaries, which depends on the circumstances of the parties, and the accustomed manner of living.

There is an implied agency authorizing the wife to pledge the husband credit, when the parties are living together. *R H Macy, Inc. v. Hershkowitz*, 56 Misc. 2d 847 (1968).

Where the spouses are not living together, or separated, a wife can bind her husband's credit for necessaries, but the creditor must prove that the husband failed to provide the necessaries or an allowance with which to acquire them. These doctrines are to be considered when a suit is to be started against husband or wife separately or jointly. A separation agreement or divorce requiring one spouse to pay the debt due your client from the other spouse does not affect your client's rights to collect that debt from the contracting spouse. At most, you will be faced with an impleaded third-party action.

3. Credit card holder-user relationship: It is routine for a bank or department store, or other companies issuing credit cards, to issue the card in only one name, notwithstanding the fact that the Retail Installment Credit Agreement was executed by two individuals, such as husband and wife. Upon reviewing the credit agreement, if both husband and wife executed the agreement, proceed against both despite the issuance in one name only.

In a situation where one spouse has executed the Retail Installment Credit Agreement, and the non-executing spouse is an authorized user only, proceed against the executing spouse as contractually liable as there is a reasonable expectation that the goods or services are chargeable solely to the account holders in whose name the card was issued. The wife in this situation should not be named or sued for such purchases made on the account of her husband.

In a situation where the non-executing spouse uses the credit card without authorization, after the account holder cancels same or notifies the issuer to deny credit to the wife, you can proceed against the wife and not the account holder as the sale should have been rejected. You can proceed against the unauthorized user for goods sold and delivered or unjust enrichment. You cannot sue the unauthorized under the terms of the Retail Installment Credit Agreement so as to request attorney's fees.

A comaker is liable on a note to the same extent as the maker. Uniform Commerical Code sec. 3-401(1). Even a comaker who alleges accommodation only and received no proceeds is liable in the capacity in which he signed. You can proceed against either or both.

A guarantor, whether it be a guarantor of payment or a guarantor of collection, is responsible to the same extent as the primary obligor. You can proceed against the primary obligor and the guarantor at the outset, where the guaranty is one of payment. Where the guaranty is one of collection, you must proceed against the maker first and exhaust your remedies to judgment and execution. If the execution has been returned unsatisfied, you now have a viable cause of action against the guarantor of collection. In order to defeat the defense of lack of notice, it would be good practice to give the guarantor of collection notice at the time suit is commenced against the guarantor of payment.

At the outset, the collection attorney should determine whether a summons and complaint is to be served as opposed to the summons with notice. The writer suggests a summons and verified complaint be served as it expedites litigation and requires the defendant to answer within a prescribed period of time and swear to the contents of the answer.

The verification of an answer by an attorney is not to be encouraged. The main reason for the party to verify the pleading is two-fold: to determine the accuracy of the amount in dispute at time of verification, and correct any factual allegations that might be misquoted so as to avoid unnecessary motion practice at a later time to amend the pleading.

The verification of an answer is usually made by the party in interest, a domestic corporation by an officer thereof. CPLR sec. 3020(d)1. Under certain circumstances the attorney can verify the answer of foreign corporation, or a party not within the county where the attorney maintains his/her law office, or where the action or defense is founded upon a written instrument for the payment of money only which is in the attorney's possession. CPLR sec. 3020(d)3. If the verification is made by the attorney, he/she must set forth the grounds of his belief as to all matters not stated upon his/her knowledge, and the reason why the verification is not made by the party. CPLR sec. 3021.

An important consideration in having the complaint verified is that in an action for goods sold and delivered, or labor, services or materials furnished, an itemization attached to the complaint of reasonable value or agreed price of each item compels defendant to indicate under oath in his/her answer items in dispute, whether delivery, performance, reasonable value or agreed price. CPLR sec. 3016(F). In a verified complaint based upon a promissory note, it is a good practice to attach the complete instrument to the complaint, which in turn requires the defendant to swear to the authenticity of his signature to the note. The signature on a note is deemed admitted, unless specifically denied. CPLR sec. 3015(d).

The advantage of a summons and complaint as opposed to a summons with notice is readily apparent. The use of a summons with notice is allowed pursuant to CPLR sec. 305(b), but it delays the action as it provides the defendant additional time to answer. The only requirement for a summons with notice is that the notice portion state briefly the nature of the action and the relief sought, and the amount for which judgment could be entered in case of default, except such summons cannot be used in medical malpractice actions for obvious reasons.

Another important reason to discourage the use of a summons with notice is that plaintiff's attorney may serve and file a late complaint in response to a notice of appearance and demand for complaint. The court, upon motion, may dismiss the action pursuant to CPLR sec. 3012(b) if the complaint is not made in accordance with the rules for an appearance to be made. CPLR sec. 320. There have been a series of significant cases to discourage this practice of serving a summons with notice, especially if the delay in serving the complaint is founded solely upon "law office failure." The Court of Appeals case that started this consternation was the case of *Barasch v. Mincussi*, 49 N.Y.2d 594 (1980).

IV. DILEMMA CAUSED BY *BARASCH/EATON* RULE

Barasch v. Mincussi, stated that "law office failures" are no excuse for plaintiff's failure to serve a complaint within the prescribed period of time, as it was an abuse of discretion to decline to grant a default judgment against plaintiff five months later in serving a complaint under CPLR sec. 3012(b). *Eaton v. Equitable Life Assurance Society*, 56 N.Y.2d 900 (1982), extended the *Barasch* rationale caused by attorney neglect in serving an answer several weeks late despite a meritorious defense. An obvious trend was started by permitting opening of default based solely upon failure of counsel to serve complaint or answer within specific time limits.

The Court of Appeals in *Barasch/Eaton* found the non-defaulting party was not prejudiced by the delay but suggested in *Eaton* that prejudice was inherent in the failure to observe relevant time limits.

The Court of Appeals maintained this trend and reversed the Appellate Division in *Q.P.I. Restaurants Ltd. v. Slevin*, 60 N.Y.2d 676 (1983) stating that the Appellate Division abused its discretion as a matter of law in vacating default judgment against defendant who failed to answer for more than one year with law office failure as the only excuse despite a 10 percent penalty imposed against defendant, but not counsel.

First, Second and Fourth Departments of the Appellate Division maintain that discretion still existed to excuse a default of short duration, *Weinstein v. Nat'l Committee for Jewish Education*, 105 A.D.2d 674 (1984) which vacated two-day default, *Harris v. Schiller*, 90 A.D.2d 822 (1982) which vacated twelve-day default caused by non-party insurer, *Semler v. County of Monroe*, 90 A.D.2d 689 (1982) which vacated a default judgment of approximately seven days.

In June 1983, the legislature responded by enacting CPLR secs. 2005 and 3012(b) to ameliorate the harsh consequences of the *Barasch/Eaton* rule. These sections in essence give the Court discretion in the interests of justice to excuse delay or default resulting solely from "law office failures" upon a showing of reasonable excuse for delay or default and affidavit of merit.

In *Garcia v. City of New York*, NYLJ, February 16, 1984, the Court used its discretion in not dismissing a complaint not timely served caused by the attorney's neglect, but penalized the attorney and not the litigant. Could this case start a new trend in penalizing attorneys for "law office failures"?

V. SERVICE OF PROCESS

The service of process is as important as the form and content of the summons and complaint. You could draft an artful and sufficient complaint, but if the summons and complaint is not served in accordance with statute, it will not withstand a jurisdictional attack and the case will be delayed before it gets off the ground.

The first step is to obtain the services of a well-known and reputable process server or process serving agency. Remember, the process server is not your agent, but is an independent contractor working for a fee. Usually the process server bills the attorney for the costs of service. However, the client is responsible and must bear the cost of litigation. A process server and the agency are required to maintain and retain records of each and every service made for the prior two years. G.B.L. sec. 89.

In collection practice the process server could be an invaluable source of information for the recovery of a debt or judgment. The process server routinely talks with neighbors or relatives to obtain a nonmilitary service affidavit required by Federal Law, 50 U.S.C. sec. 520, and always should make an attempt to obtain the defendant's place of employment. You should never instruct the process server on the method or means to serve the defendant so as to form a principal and agent relationship. This theory could conceivably make the attorney responsible for any tortious conduct or injury to the debtor at the hands of the process server. The process server must be licensed if he serves five or more summonses in any given year.

These are three methods of making service upon a natural person:

1. Delivery of the summons within the state to the person to be served, CPLR sec. 308(1)., referred to as personal service;

2. Delivery of the summons within the state to a person of suitable age and disrection, at the *actual* place of business, dwelling place or usual place of abode, and by mailing the summons to defendant's last known residence, CPLR sec. 308(2)., referred to as "leave and mail" method and is the equivalent of personal service;

3. If service of either number 1 or 2 above cannot be made with due diligence, by affixing the summons to the door of either the *actual* place of business, dwelling place or usual place of abode within the state of the person to be served, and by mailing the summons to such person at his last known residence, CPLR sec. 308 4., referred to as "affix and mail" service.

Where personal service is made pursuant to CPLR secs. 308(1) or (2), the process server is required to include a description of the person served. CPLR sec. 306(b). CPLR sec. 3215(F), formerly CPLR sec. 308(5), requires a notice of the summons and complaint to be mailed to the defendant 20 days prior to the entry of judgment. This notice should be sent immediately upon receipt of the affidavit of service. This requirement applies to a natural person based upon nonpayment of a contractual obligation. This twenty-day notice requirement many vary in an action commenced in the Supreme Court, where the directives would indicate that such notice should not be mailed until after the defendant's time to answer expires. It is important to consult the Rules promulgated by each court.

In a lower case, *Bankers Trust New York Corp. v. Greenberger*, 120 Misc. 2d 957 (1983), the court held that where plaintiff was aware of defendant's business and residence addresses, due diligence required an attempt to serve at the place of business, before serving by substituted service.

In the case of *Barnes v. City of New York*, 70 A.D.2d 580 (1979), the Appellate Division, Second Department, held that when it appeared that defendant was a working person, service pursuant to CPLR secs. 308(1) or (2), must be attempted during nonworking hours, at a time when it would be most likely that the defendant would be at home. These cases stand for the premise that when the plaintiff is aware of and knows the residence or business address of defendant, due diligence requires service to be made at either addresses, prior to service under CPLR sec. 308(4), the "affix and mail" service.

In a 1979 Court of Appeals case, the Court held that two (2) visits to the premises resulting in unsuccessful attempts to deliver the summons to a person of suitable age and discretion is a legally sufficient predicate for serving process under CPLR sec. 308(4). This case also stated that when jurisdiction is sought to be obtained through substituted service, there must be strict and scrupulous compliance with the statutory requirements. This case also held that the summons must be affixed to the place where the defendant *actually* resides; the "last known residence" to which a summons may be mailed is not synonymous with the actual dwelling place requirement. *Feinstein v. Bergner*, 48 N.Y.2d 234, 422 N.Y.S.2d 356 (1979).

Service of process upon a partnership may be made by personally serving the summons within the state upon any of the partners. CPLR sec. 310.

Service upon a corporation may be made by delivering the summons to an officer, director, cashier or managing agent. CPLR sec. 311. If there is difficulty in serving the corporation, promptly serve the Secretary of State in Albany, who mails a copy of the summons and complaint to the office of the corporation as stated in its cerificate.

VI. ALTERNATIVES TO LITIGATION

There are several alternatives to litigation, which is costly and time consuming. Since payment in full upon demand is a rare occurence, these are the alternative methods to handle a collection matter:

1. Attempt to work with the debtor and arrange for installment payments, under a letter agreement prior to litigation, or a stipulation of settlement, subsequent to litigation. In the former situation, if the debtor acknowledges the debt and promises to pay a certain sum in installments, and signs the agreement, it could be used later in the event of suit as an admission of the debt on a motion for summary judgment.

2. Stipulation of Settlement, after suit is authorized pursuant to CPLR sec. 3215(h). This is used in the majority of consumer collection cases.

The stipulation must be signed or executed by the party to be bound thereby, and is usually entered into by the parties and their attorneys.

The purpose of a stipulation settlement is to provide reasonable and convenient terms of repayment. If there is a default in payment, the stipulation should provide for the entry judgment, after notice to debtor to cure the default, and without notice to the court for its entry, with interest and costs. There are stipulations of settlement that contain an admission of the debt, withdrawal of the answer, and consent to *in personam* jurisdiction. The stipulation of settlement should not be drafted to appear to be a confession of judgment, which is statutory and must be in strict compliance with CPLR sec. 3218. A copy of such stipulation is annexed hereto as Exhibit B.

3. Compromise or settlement of the claim or action is a viable and often used method of settling collection cases with the authorization of client, after full knowledge of all the facts. The client should be made aware of the fact that the claim or action may involve lengthy litigation which will include defenses and counterclaims. The client should also be made aware of the debtor's inability to pay and other obligations, whether legal or moral, which would impede recovery.

4. Confession of Judgment. CPLR sec. 3218. If the situation presents itself, and other alternatives are not viable to the debtor who realized that he cannot prevent a creditor from taking a judgment, a Confession of Judgment, although rare in collection cases, is a useful device.

There must be strict compliance with CPLR secs. 3201 and 3218 for a Confession of Judgment to be valid. It must be executed by the defendant and is valid for three years and cannot be entered after the death of defendant. CPLR sec. 3218(b). The debtor can confer judgment for money due or to become due, and must state the facts out of which the debt arose. This device can be used as an alternative to formal litigation, either prior to or subsequent to service to a lawsuit.

There is no requirement that a Confession of Judgment be filed and entered promptly after the debtor executes the instrument, as long as it is entered within three years after the date of execution and the debtor is still alive. A Confession of Judgment can be used in conjunction with a repayment arrangement and entered only when the debtor fails to meet or make the payments required. In consumer credit cases, there is a reluctance on the part of the debtor to sign a Confession of Judgment, which can be immediately entered without notice and execution issued, because there appear to be several other options available to the debtor in litigation. A compromise and settlement of the claim, a convenient stipulation of settlement, and even defending the litigation with a more favorable award or decision, may be better alternatives than the Confession of Judgment.

Selecting the court is also an important consideration and should be given special attention by plaintiff's counsel in the pre-litigation stage. In the first instance plaintiff's attorney would want to select the best possible forum wherein his client can obtain the desired results in the shortest possible time, keeping in mind the strict requirements of venue. The Civil Court of the City of New York, with its five branches in each borough of the City of New York has city-wide jurisdiction, is considered one court of record with a monetary jurisdiction of $25,000 (formerly $10,000). The monetary jurisdiction was increased effective February 21, 1984. Chapter 11 of the Laws of 1984, amending Article 2 of the New York City Civil Court Act, specifically section 201 of the Civil Court Act.

The Civil Court of the City of New York has subject matter jurisdiction over landlord-tenant proceedings (residential and commercial) of property located within its jurisdiction and for summary proceedings to recover real property, and other civil causes of action to recover money or property within the monetary jurisdiction of the court. The Civil Court does not have jurisdiction over equity matters as the New York State Constitution did not confer or grant the Civil Court with the powers of a court of equity.

The Civil Court can obtain personal jurisdiction over nonresidents if the cause of action arose out of any transaction of business, or tortious conduct, or use of real property in the City of New York, commonly referred to as the "long arm statute." N.Y.C.C.A. sec. 404(a).

The various District Courts that comprise the counties of Nassau and Suffolk now have monetary jurisdiction of $15,000 (formerly $6,000), which became effective February 21, 1985. These courts have similar subject matter jurisdiction as the Civil Court.

The Supreme Court of the State of New York, which has state-wide jurisdiction, has monetary jurisdiction over $25,000, is a court of record with equity jurisdicton. If there is a choice of courts where speed is a consideration, the lower courts are preferred.

VII. ARBITRATION PROCEDURES (22 NYCRR Part 28)

The primary purpose of compulsory arbitration is the resolution of cases heard by qualified attorneys assigned to the Arbitration Program. It has reduced the civil case backload, thereby relieving judges to speed up or reduce the criminal calendars and other cases outside the jurisdiction of this program, referred to as The Compulsory Arbitration Program. The following are some of the more important provisions in the Arbitration Rules:

1. If amount sued is under $6,000, it falls within the Compulsory Arbitration Program and is first assigned to a Compulsory Arbitration Calendar for settlement, limiting the issues or marked for arbitration trial.

2. If amount sued for is $2,000 or less, it is assigned to one arbitrator for a hearing on all issues for disposition; over $2,000, panel of three arbitrators.

3. Fees—chairman of panel receives $45 per case heard or settled, and panelists receive $35 per case heard or settled.

4. If adverse award, must move within 30 days (if not in default) from filing of the award with Arbitration Commissioner for Trial de Novo and pay the appropriate fees payable to the Court covering panel fees. Arbitration Rules 28.12.

5. The Arbitration Program and Rules do not provide for jury demands, unless demand for Trial de Novo is filed.

6. Under Arbitration Rules 28.13 any party who has not demanded Trial de Novo may move within 30 days after award is filed to vacate the award only on the following grounds:

a. Fraud, corruption, misconduct.

b. Panel exceeded its power.

c. Failure to follow the Arbitration Rule; if motion granted case restored to Compulsory Arbitration Calendar.

7. In the event that after Trial de Novo, the result is the same or less favorable to the party who requested Trial de Novo, such party is to pay statutory costs and disbursements to the other party and shall not recover interest or costs. Arbitration Rules 28.12(e).

The Rules of Arbitration are attached hereto as Appendix C.

The following comments should be made concerning the Compulsory Arbitration Program. Although the arbitrator or panel has discretion to adjourn an arbitration trial, it is rarely granted unless an affidavit is submitted in advance of actual engagement or other legal excuse, or sudden emergencies. This appears to be consistent with the purpose of the program.

Secondly, Rule 28.8(b) states in part, "The panel shall have the general powers of a court . . . . This also means that the panel shall have the responsibilities of a court and litigants and the legal profession must be given the same opportunities for a fair hearing before an arbitrator as they would expect at a trial before a judge of the court.

Most importantly, if the arbitrator or panelist assigned to hear your case is a present adversary in pending unresolved matters with your office, request that he/she promptly disqualify himself/herself. In the event the arbitrator fails to remove himself, write to the Commissioner of Arbitration and inform him that you believe a fair and impartial hearing cannot be had. I am certain that the Commissioner of Arbitration will replace that arbitrator. The Compulsory Arbitration Program is a good program and its continuance as part of our judicial system in civil cases should be encouraged by the legal profession.

Appendix B

CIVIL COURT OF THE CITY OF NEW YORK
COUNTY OF
---x

Plaintiff,

-against-   Index No. ______________

Defendant.
---x

IT IS HEREBY STIPULATED AND AGREED, by and between the undersigned parties, that the above entitled action be settled upon the following terms and conditions, and upon payment by the undersigned defendant to plaintiff of the sum of $ representing principal amount of claim, plus disbursements of $25.00, and the sum of $ representing attorneys fees which are agreed between the undersigned parties, making the total stipulated sum due of $ payable in the following manner:

1. Defendant agrees to and will pay the sum of $______________
on 19 and the balance of $______________
in successive equal instalments of $______________
commencing on or before the day of
197 and thereafter, until the aforesaid
stipulated sum is fully paid, and

CHAPTER NINE

PROCEDURES DURING LITIGATION

Marvin Krumholz, Esq.
Sennet & Krumholz

After the service of the summons and complaint, answer and reply if required, referred to as joining of issue, the litigants and their attorneys plan their strategy. The objective of plaintiff's attorney is to respond, as diligently as possible, to any discovery devices used by his/her adversary and notice the case for trial as soon as legally permissible. It is hoped this will lead to a resolution of the issues at either Compulsory Arbitration or Pre-Trial and compromise and settlement of the case at that stage; failing that, obtaining a trial date and moving ahead and preparing for trial with plaintiff's witness for a judgment in his/her client's favor. The sooner a judgment is entered, the sooner enforcement proceedings can be commenced to recover the judgment.

The objective of defendant's attorney is to prolong the case so that ultimately plaintiff will reluctantly consent to a settlement. There are several methods by which defendant's attorney can delay the case, and put plaintiff to its burden of proving his/her case. The attorney for defendant can move prior to answer for dismissal under CPLR sec. 3211 upon numerous grounds, some of which are lack of jurisdiction over the person or subject matter, discharge in bankruptcy, statute of limitations or statute of frauds. These affirmative defenses can also be pleaded in defendant's answer. The defendant's attorney in alleging lack of jurisdiction over the person may be successful at a hearing on the issue of service, and force plaintiff to reserve process. If defendant has knowledge that plaintiff is extremely busy at his/her business or profession, and it would be a hardship to appear in court, an examination before trial may be the remedy to force a favorable settlement at a fraction of what the claim actually is worth. Consequently, the object of plaintiff's attorney is to proceed with forceful prosecution of his/her client's case towards a judgment and eventual recovery, whereas the object of defendant's attorney is to use dilatory tactics, if permitted, so as to obtain the best settlement for his/her client, or a judgment of dismissal on the merits.

A judgment is a legal determination that one party is entitled to recover a certain amount from the other party, or that the losing party must do, or refrain from doing, a specific act. A judgment is often the ending of litigation that represents much work, time and expense by attorney and client alike. In consumer credit cases, the majority of judgments entered in the Civil Court and District Courts are by default. The reason for this overwhelming default rate is that there is no legal dispute and the claim is actually due and owing. An answer interposed by an attorney in a consumer credit case, in the absence of a legal dispute, is usually to avoid a default judgment and to obtain a favorable repayment of his/her client's debt.

Although the entry of a judgment is the end of litigation in favor of the successful party, it is not the only way litigation is terminated. Settlement of an action, especially a favorable settlement skillfully negotiated by the attorney, is also an end to litigation. It should be noted that a representation made by an attorney in settlement of a case, when approved, accepted and confirmed by the other party, is binding to constitute an enforceable settlement. It is presumed that the attorney making the representation of settlement has the authority of his/her client. Therefore, it is always good practice and a safeguard to the attorney to obtain his/her authority to settle a claim in writing from his/her client, so he/she cannot be held responsible if the client later reneges or disavows the settlement. In the case of *Robinson v. Hall Cab Corp.*, 81 Misc. 2d 569 (1974), the court stated that settlement is the end of litigation, and not an intermediate step, and awarded discretionary costs to plaintiff's attorney for the failure of defendant to honor a settlement negotiated in good faith by defendant's attorney.

I. ENTRY OF DEFAULT JUDGMENTS

A. By Clerk

The Clerk of the Court (Judgment Clerk) can enter a default judgment when the defendant has failed to appear, plead or proceed to trial within one year from the date of default. The clerk can enter a default judgment upon submission of the following papers: summons and verified complaint or affidavit of merit by the plaintiff if the complaint is not verified; affidavit of nonmilitary service which is usually the process server's affidavit and a statement in the judgment by the attorney incorporating by reference the allegation on nonmilitary service; the 20-day notice, which is an additional copy of the summons and complaint mailed by regular mail to the defendant, formerly CPLR sec. 308(5) now relocated under CPLR sec. 3215, which does not extend the time to answer; the judgment roll containing the amount in the complaint which must be a sum certain, statutory costs and actual disbursements.

If the default judgment is not entered within one year from the date of the default, the attorney must apply to the court, by notice of motion served upon the defaulting party in the same manner as in the service of a summons and complaint, for leave to enter judgment. CPLR sec. 3215(c). The application must contain a good and sufficient reason for not proceeding timely, and should include an affidavit of merit by the party.

B. By Court

In all other circumstances, such as when the amount demanded in the complaint is not for a sum certain (liquidated amount) or when damages are to be assessed by the court or when the court directs a reference as to a specific issue to be determined by a referee, the court can enter a default judgment. CPLR sec. 3215(b). In the event multiple defendants are named, the judgment roll should contain an order of severence as to defendants not served, or non-judgment parties.

There are other types of default judgments such as when a defendant answers but fails to appear at an Arbitration or Pre-Trial conference call. Although this type of judgment is technically not a default judgment, as defendant has approved and answered, it is referred to as an inquest before the clerk if the amount demanded in the ad damnum is for a sum certain which can be entered by the clerk. At an arbitration trial before an arbitrator or panel, if the amount demanded is not for a sum certain, the arbitrator having the same powers as a judge can hear the proof as to damages and award judgment.

II. OPENING DEFAULT JUDGMENTS

It is the writer's experience that our courts are inclined to open default judgments of pro se defendants without the strict requirements necessary for such relief. Is this a trend or do the courts have a special duty to place the pro se defendant in a status quo position to have his/her day in court and adjudicate his, issues? Courts are equipped to assist pro se defendants with required forms of show cause orders and assorted motions for their relief.

Procedure, pursuant to CPLR sec. 5015:

1. By order to show cause, with stay of enforcement proceedings, if execution has been issued.

2. By motion, refer to CPLR sec. 2214(b) for time of service of papers.

3. By stipulation between parties or counsel, on consent, usually approved by ex parte order to restore to calendar or permit answer within a prescribed period of time.

4. Both (1) and (2) above must be supported by a detailed affidavit of person having knowledge of the facts (affidavit of merit) and a legal and sufficient reason for the failure to answer or appear. Documentation is helpful to show a bona fide dispute or inability to answer. Motions under CPLR sec. 5015 are discretionary, and are usually granted upon a showing of the necessary requirements. *See Cappell v. BKO*, 60 A.D.2d 936 (1978).

Necessary allegations:

1. Excusable default, made within one year after service of copy of judgment or order, with notice of entry.

2. Meritorious defense, must be a clear showing that a real dispute exists as opposed to self-serving statements that raise no triable issues.

3. Copy of proposed answer.

4. Additional Grounds:

a. newly discovered evidence;

b. fraud and misrepresentation, or other misconduct;

c. lack of jurisdiction of person or subject matter;

d. CPLR sec. 5015(c), formerly Judiciary Law, sec. 217(a) Judiciary Law, by application of an Administrative Judge, by formal notice to all the parties. This procedure is invoked when the issue presented affects a multitude of parties and cases, rather than an individual case:

(1) must be a clear and proper showing that default judgments were obtained by fraud, misrepresentation, illegality, unconscionability, lack of due service or other illegalities;

(2) court weighs the number of judgments obtained by the above grounds, and whether a number of defendants were deprived of their rights to answer before proceeding in this manner; *see Thompson v. Chemical Bank*, 84 Misc. 2d 721 (1975);

(3) apparent differences between proceedings commenced under CPLR sec. 5015(c) and Class Actions under CPLR sec. 901, *see Wasserbauer v. Marine Midland*, 92 Misc. 2d 388 (1977), although results could be similar.

Procedure to oppose motion to open default:

1. By consent of parties or counsel to vacate judgment and permit answer within specific time.

2. Opposing counsel should request judgment and/or execution remain as security pending final outcome of the case.

3. In the majority of cases, lack of jurisdiction over person is raised and opposing counsel should attempt to waive such defense in answer, in consideration of consent to vacate, in order to avoid traverse, which is time consuming and not productive.

4. Request stay not be continued beyond hearing date of motion.

Opening default judgment when not personally served:

1. May move to open default judgment within one year and defend the action, after notice of entry of judgment or order.

2. If a defendant was not personally served nor appeared therein, may move to open default up to a maximum of five years under CPLR sec. 317, after notice of entry of judgment—with a clear demonstration of a meritorious defense and a finding by the court that defendant was not personally served.

III. ATTORNEYS' FEES

A sometimes complex issue that might delay a prompt resolution of the case is the inclusion of attorneys' fees in the summons and complaint. Attorneys and litigants alike find attorneys' fees unconscionable and against public policy, feeling that the attorney for plaintiff is compensated according to his/her retainer, upon recovery. Consumer debtors usually balk at the thought of paying attorneys' fees, and would rather litigate the matter in the hope that the court or the arbitration might persuade plaintiff's attorney to waive such fees in consideration of a settlement.

Attorneys' fees may be allowed and permitted to be pleaded in the complaint if the agreement or statute allows it, and the defendant-obligator has executed the agreement with such provision. There has been an evolution in the manner in which the courts have handled the issue of attorneys' fees.

The Banking Law sec. 108 sub. 4(C)111, 5(E)111, enacted in 1937, allows attorneys' fees in consumer loans, revolving credit agreements and checking account overdraft loans. Usually these agreements provide for 15 percent of unpaid balance due. The Personal Property Law sec. 413(5), enacted in 1957, allows attorneys' fees of up to 20 percent in retail installment credit agreements if there was a default and the matter was referred to an attorney who was not a salaried employee of the seller. The Legislature gave some indication that the statute would compensate vendors and be the equivalent of a service charge for investigating and making the installment credit agreement.

There are many cases that hold for the proposition that a provision in the agreement or contract, or note, that calls for attorneys' fees is valid. *Roe v. Smyth*, 278 N.Y. 364 (1938); *Wayman v. Williamson*, 256 N.Y. 117 (1931); *Equitable Lumber Corp. v. IRA Land Development Corp.*, 38 N.Y.2d 516, (1976); *Franklin National Bank v. Wall Street Commercial Corp.*, 40 Misc. 2d 1003 (1963), *aff'd*, 21 A.D.2d 878 (1964).

Prior practice, or prior to 1975, attorneys' fees were granted by the clerk on a fixed basis of either 15 percent or 20 percent, depending on the type of agreement, and based on the percentage of amount in suit. *National Bank of Westchester v. Pisani*, 58 A.D.2d 597 (1977).

Since 1975 there have been many changes in the formula used for determing attorneys' fees. The present trend is to limit attorneys' fees in consumer cases. The Civil Court of the City of New York has promulgated a Directive number 441 (*see* Appendix A) where attorneys' fees are granted on a quantum meruit basis. In the District Courts, the case of *First National Bank of East Islip v. Brower*, 42 N.Y.2d 471 (1977) and the case of *Thompson v. Chemical Bank*, 84 Misc. 2d 721 (1975) reiterated the premise that attorneys' fees are to be controlled by the courts on a quantum meruit basis.

The legal rationale for this theory was that attorneys' fees were unliquidated in amount and should be reasonable in accordance with the legal work performed. *Wasserbauer v. Marine Midland*, 92 Misc. 2d 388 (1977).

The case of *Broadstreets Inc. v. Parlin*, 75 Misc. 2d 662 (1973), held that attorneys' fees are not a fixed amount, but an escalating amount up to the percentage specified, and further that attorneys' fees cannot be contracted at the outset. Further, the court has the right to review and supervise attorneys' fees for legal remedies. *Gair v. Peck*, 6 N.Y.2d 972 983 (1959); *First National Bank v. Brower, supra.*

The present basis for granting and fixing attorneys' fees are based on the following factors:

1. Refer to local administrative rules of the particular court.

2. Limit on amount of fees fixed by court based upon proof by affidavit showing all activity and work done and time spent from receipt of claim to date of submission of affidavit. *See* Blumberg form T-360.

3. The court, pursuant to Civil Court Directive 441 and other local administrative rules, can request an inquest before the court if the amount of attorneys' fees requested exceed a specified amount, usually determined by the judge sitting at the ex parte part.

4. Court fixes attorneys' fees on a quantum meruit basis which is not uniform in all courts, and depends upon custom of courts and the formula used by the judge for awarding attorneys' fees.

IV. INTEREST RATES

Effective July 6, 1981, the rate of interest was increased from 6 percent to 9 percent per annum, with interest to be computed from the earliest possible ascertainable time cause of action existed. CPLR sec. 5001(b).

Post judgment rate of interest is 9 percent per annum as of July 6, 1981, CPLR sec. 5004, which prior to above date was 6 percent per annum.

Post maturity rate of interest in consumer loans or other consumer transactions depends on the rate of the contract or agreement, or the rate provided for in a disclosure statement. This rate of interest, if higher than the statutory rate, can be assessed and computed to the date of entry of judgment.

In the event the contract, agreement or disclosure statement is silent as to the rate of interest to be used, you may assess 9 percent from July 6, 1981, and 6 percent prior thereto.

Interest is not an automatic right, or even discretionary, but it is a right that belongs to the successful party in the action. In the event interest is not included in a decision, or Referee's report, the successful party may move to reform the decision to include interest. Every money judgment shall bear interest from the date of its entry. Every order directing the payment of money, which has been docketed as a judgment, shall bear interest from the date of such docketing.

V. TRANSCRIBING JUDGMENTS

The entry of judgment occurs when the judgment clerk affixes the name of the Clerk of the Court and the date to the judgment roll. It is important that plaintiff's attorney makes certain that all taxable costs, disbursements and accrued interest to the date of entry are included in the judgment. In most courts it is not necessary for the judgment to be entered in the judgment book to be official and valid as a judgment as that is only an administration function for the permanency of the court's records.

After the entry of judgment in the lower courts, such as the Civil Court of the City of New York or the District Courts, it is necessary to transcribe the judgment with the County Clerk within the jurisdiction where the judgment was entered. A judgment of the Supreme Court does not require docketing with the County Clerk of the court of entry, as it is automatically deemed docketed in that county. CPLR sec. 5018.

As a practical matter, the judgment should be filed or transcribed in any county where defendant owns or has an interest in realty, and where defendant resides. A judgment of a City Court should be promptly filed within the county of that court.

The effect of filing or transcribing a judgment with the County Clerk is to create a lien on the defendant's realty interest, which is in force for a period of ten years, CPLR sec. 5203, or longer extended by motion. CPLR sec. 5203(b).

The ultimate result of creating a lien on the judgment-debtor's real property is to execute by foreclosure and sale. This is an expensive, time-consuming remedy so that plaintiff's attorney, in conjunction with his client, will use his professional judgment to determine if such a procedure is economically feasible. Not all of the realty owned by a judgment-debtor is subject to execution and sale, as CPLR sec. 5206 covers a multitude of exemptions, as homes under $10,000 are exempt from execution.

In advance of proceeding against the debtor's real property, you must consider the amount of the judgment as opposed to the fees involved by the sheriff for the advertising and sale. The procedure in real property executions consists of petitioning the court to permit a sale of a judgment-debtor's home, where the value exceeds $10,000 over liens and other encumbrances. There is a trend that courts are reluctant to sell the real property of a judgment-debtor if it happens to be his/her principal residence and the amount of the judgment is nominal. The court can invoke a protective order and require that other remedies be first exhausted. *Gilchrist v. Commercial Credit Corp.*, 66 Misc. 2d 791, 322 N.Y.S.2d 200 (1971).

Shares in a cooperative apartment are technically not considered real property, but are treated as such for the purpose of the homestead exemption under CPLR sec. 5206. The condominium apartment is treated as realty for all purposes.

The homestead exemption of $10,000 over liens and encumbrances remains in effect for one year after payment to the judgment-debtor. If the judgment-debtor receives money as a result of a surplus after a mortgage foreclosure, there is no exemption as the surplus becomes personalty subject to execution.

There is a fee to obtain and file transcripts of judgments, and the local courts should be contacted to determine the fees which are nominal in each instance.

VI. FOREIGN JUDGMENTS

Foreign judgments entered in any court of the United States, or its territories, which is final and conclusive where entered, is entitled to full faith and credit in New York.

It is fundamental that a state must give the final judgment of a sister state the same force and effect as it is entitled to in the state in which it is rendered. U.S. Const. Art. IV, sec. 1. The full faith and credit clause in the U.S. Constitution directs that "full faith and credit shall be given in each state to the public acts, records and judicial proceedings of every other state." The U.S. Supreme Court has recognized that in order to fulfill this constitutional mandate, the judgment of a state court should have the same credit, validity, and effect, in every other court of the United States, which it had in the state where it was pronounced. *Underwriters Assurance Co. v. N.C. Guaranty Ass'n.*, 455 U.S. 691 (1982); *City of Philadelphia v. Bauer*, 97 N.J. 372 (1984). The Supreme Court further states that "a judgment of a court in one state is conclusive upon the merits in a court of another state only if the court in the first state had power to pass on the merits—had jurisdiction to render the judgment." *Durfee v. Duke*, 375 U.S. 106 (1963). Moreover, "a judgment presumes jurisdiction over the subject matter and over the persons." *Cook v. Cook*, 342 U.S. 126 (1951). In light of the above discussion, there can be no doubt that a judgment entered in one state will receive full faith and credit in this state.

Under CPLR sec. 5304 this state can refuse to recognize a foreign country judgment if it is found that the foreign court did not have personal and subject matter jurisdiction, lack of notice by defendant, fraud in obtaining the judgment, or if the judgment is against public policy of New York. These issues can be raised in New York in challenging the foreign judgment. New York courts have discretion to recognize foreign country judgments where it is proven that the defendant was properly and personally served, or appeared in the foreign state. CPLR sec. 5305.

A judgment obtained by default or by confession of judgment is not entitled to full faith and credit in this state. CPLR sec. 5401. Foreign judgments, final and conclusive where entered, can be enforced in the same manner as a Supreme Court judgment of this state by following and complying with CPLR sec. 5402, which states as follows:

1. Foreign judgments must be authenticated and filed within 90 days with any county clerk of the state together with an affidavit stating that the judgment was not obtained by default or by confession of judgment, and remains unpaid and has not been stayed.

2. Within 30 days after filing of the judgment and affidavit, the judgment creditor shall mail notice of the filing of the foreign judgment to the judgment debtor at his/her last known address. In the event the foreign judgment cannot be filed, then suit is to be instituted upon the judgment, or a motion for summary judgment in lieu of complaint, under CPLR sec. 5406.

VII. ANSWERS

After a summons and complaint, or summons with notice is served, and the defendant does not default, the plaintiff's attorney will be served with an answer by a defendant, appearing by himself (pro se) or by an attorney. The receipt of an answer without any jurisdictional defenses pleaded, such as non-service of the summons and complaint on the defendant, gives the court in personam jurisdiction of the parties.

When a defendant appears in person in the Civil Court, the clerk places the case on the Compulsory Arbitration Calendar within fifteen days from date of answer. Plaintiff's attorney has practically no time to conduct discovery proceedings, especially if affirmative defenses are pleaded. It is good practice to promptly issue a deposition of defendant for a date of examination subsequent to the arbitration date, together with a letter to the defendant informing him/her that you will make an application to conduct discovery, and request an adjournment at the Compulsory Arbitration Calendar call. If you fail to take such procedures to inform the court that you intend to examine the defendant or serve him/her with interrogatories, the court can set the matter down for arbitration if the dispute cannot be resolved at the conference. The procedures are similar in the various District courts when a defendant appears in person, but the calendar call is referred to as Pre-Trial Arbitration. If the cases on the conference calendar cannot be resolved or settled, they are assigned to Trial by Arbitration if the ad damnum is under $6,000.

If plaintiff's attorney fails to take these necessary steps to inform the court of his/her desire to conduct discovery, and the case is marked arbitration, you will then be required to make a motion on notice to the defendant for leave to conduct discovery. The notice of motion is required to have a legend at the top of the notice whether the case has or has not been assigned to a Conference or Assignment Part. If the case has been assigned, it should also contain the number of the Trial Part and the date the case will appear on the calendar pursuant to Civil Court Directive issued March 12, 1979, and which is strictly followed by the courts.

Upon receipt of an answer by an attorney, it is important, especially in consumer credit cases, to contact defendant's attorney to determine if the case can be promptly settled. If the dispute is minor, or the answer was interposed to avoid a default judgment, there is a very good chance that the case could be settled. If the answer was interposed solely because of the defendant's inability to pay, make every effort to arrange a repayment schedule that is suitable and convenient for the defendant, taking into consideration the repayment guidelines of your client.

The plaintiff's attorney should carefully analyze the answer to determine if there are any special defenses or counterclaims that require immediate attention. If a counterclaim is asserted in a Supreme Court action, you must reply, but in the Civil Court and District Courts the counterclaim is deemed denied and no reply is necessary, unless by court order.

If plaintiff's cause of action is one for goods sold and delivered, and the answer alleges a merchandise dispute, you should promptly contact the client to determine if there is any record or correspondence by the defendant complaining of the merchandise, its quality or defective condition, or failure of delivery. If your client confirms that the dispute has merit, you should make an attempt to adjust the dispute with defendant's attorney. The adjustment could be in the form of a discount or deduction in the purchase price, or repairs of the defective items, or the return of the defective item to your client for full credit. This approach, at the outset of litigation, if successful can save both the attorney and client time and expenses of further litigation. It should be encouraged.

Regardless of the nature of the answer, plaintiff's attorney should make every effort by the use of discovery or motion practice to limit and narrow the issues between the litigants. You must determine who has the burden of proof on each issue in dispute, and select the most appropriate discovery technique to properly elicit the information necessary to assist the attorney to prosecute the claim or defend the action.

VIII. DISCOVERY DEVICES

Article 31 of the CPLR governs discovery or disclosure practice, and the litigating attorney should make every effort to familiarize himself/herself with the more frequent discovery techniques available. Under CPLR sec. 3101, full disclosure of all evidence, *material and necessary* in the prosecution or defense of an action, regardless of the burden of proof is allowed. The key to this Section is that the information sought must be material and relevant to the issues. Under sec. CPLR sec. 3102 there are several disclosure devices, which are not exclusive of each other, that the attorney can use to limit and narrow the issues for purposes of trial, such as: examinations before trial, interrogatories, demands for names of witnesses and addresses, notice of discovery and inspection and notice to admit.

If the attorney for either plaintiff or defendant is served with one or more of the above disclosure devices, he/she can move, on notice, under CPLR sec. 3103 for a protective order if in his/her opinion the disclosure is oppressive or burdensome, not material or necessary, or germane to the issues. The making of the motion stays or suspends the particular disclosure in dispute, until the court either denies, limits, conditions or regulates the items in dispute, or denies in its entirety the disclosure sought. The only restriction in using one or more of the disclosure devices is that written interrogatories, a very useful device, cannot be served or utilized when that party has already made a written demand of a bill of particulars. CPLR sec. 3130.

It should be noted that a bill of particulars is not a discovery device, as it is governed under Article 30 for the CPLR relating to pleadings, as opposed to the above discovery techniques which are governed by Article 31 of the CPLR relating to disclosure. A bill of particulars is actually an extension of the pleadings as it limits the proof to be offered on the theory of amplifying, explaining and making more definite the allegations set forth in the pleadings. Where there is a variance between the bill of particulars and any other document, even the pleading amplified, it is the bill of particulars which must govern.

The bill of particulars is a very useful device and should be utilized by defendant's attorney when an answer is interposed. This tactic will give the party making the demand additional information of plaintiff's claim, but will also delay the case from being noticed for trial. If defendant's answer contains affirmative defenses, plaintiff is entitled to a bill of particulars concerning such defenses.

It is well established law that the function of a bill of particulars is to limit the evidence which may be introduced at the trial, and the theory of recovery. *Estate of Friedman*, 51 A.D.2d 1018, 381 N.Y.S.2d 302 (1976). A bill of particulars is limited to the issues or matters on which the party upon whom demand is made has the burden of proof. *Zummo v. Campbell*, 27 Misc.2d 607 (1961). Accordingly, such issues as lack of personal jurisdiction, wrong party defendant and payment cannot be obtained through the medium of a bill of particulars. In essence, the purpose of a bill of particulars is to advise the adversary of what the pleader is *claiming*, not of what the facts actually are, so that the adversary may not be surprised at the trial. The sanctions for failing to serve a bill of particulars, or for serving a defective bill, are preclusion of the evidence required, or a conditional preclusion. CPLR sec. 3042. The sanctions for failing to comply with disclosure can be dismissal of the complaint.

An examination before trial is a very useful disclosure device because it usually gives the litigants an opportunity to face each other before trial, thereby opening dialogue for a possible settlement of the case. There are instances in which a litigant fails to appear for a deposition because of the time spent and the cost involved, thereby making that party more amenable to a settlement of the case, in lieu of its dismissal. Depositions can now be taken by a recording device instead of a court reporter, but to be allowed the deposition must state that fact so that the person upon whom the notice is served can move to object to this device which is controlled and in the custody of the examining party. A deposition of a party or witness can be used for many purposes such as impeachment of the testimony of the party or witness at trial, perpetuate the testimony if the witness or party is dead, infirm and unable to appear at trial or the party or witness cannot be found after due diligence to locate that party for trial. In serving a deposition upon your adversary, it is essential that you name and identify the party or witness to be deposed. Failing that the noticed party has the option to select the witness to be produced and examined, provided the witness has knowledge of the facts.

The use of a Notice to Admit is another useful disclosure device that should be employed whenever and wherever permissable. CPLR sec. 3123. It should be noted that practice commentaries of CPLR sec. 3123 are clear in cautioning counsel that despite the language of such statute permitting service of the Notice to Admit up to twenty days before trial, the rules of the court by virtue of CPLR sec. 3401 take precedence. Consequently, absent a motion based on unanticipated conditions, the filing of a Note or Issue or Notice of Trial, with its statement of readiness, curtails the right to further disclosure, including the right to serve a Notice to Admit. New York City Court Rules sec. 2900.16(d).

The purpose of a Notice to Admit is supposed to elicit an admission of something to which the seeking party "reasonably believes there can be no substantial dispute" which is within the knowledge of the other party, or ascertainable "upon reasonable inquiry." It is dubious whether the party seeking the admission can obtain an admission of something which is at the core of the dispute. As an illustration, it is doubtful whether a Notice to Admit would be successful if served upon a defendant to admit that he agreed to pay a disputed amount, or admission of the genuineness of copies of the party's own documents.

The use of interrogatories is extremely important if the party serving such interrogatories does not want to incur the expense or time wasted at an examination before trial. There can be a first and second set of interrogatories, if the questions are germane, material and relevant, and not duplicative or oppressive or burdensome. Interrogatories area a device whereby questions relating to the substance and merit of the advisary's claim are elicited, including all evidentiary matter, regardless of the burden of proof.

The answers to interrogatories must be under oath and served within fifteen days, CPLR sec. 3134(b), unless objection is made to the whole or part of the interrogatories. By the use of interrogatories the party serving them may require the answering party to furnish papers or documents relating to the answers given. The sanctions for failing to answer interrogatories is dismissal of the complaint.

IX. MOTION PRACTICE

Motions made under CPLR secs. 3211(a)(b) and 3212 are extremely valuable techniques to be frequently used by the attorney for either plaintiff or defendant. Plaintiff's attorney could utilize either of the above motions to strike affirmative defenses and counterclaims asserted by defendant. The making of one motion under sec. 3211 does not preclude moving for summary judgment under sec. 3212.

Motion for summary judgment under CPLR 3212, in some instances, has the same effect and can elicit the same information and evidence from the adversary as would discovery devices, but in different form. Discovery devices are questions propounded to your adversary that call for specific answers, whereas responses to a motion for summary judgment are narrative in form contained in an affidavit by the party or witness having personal knowledge of the facts. A motion of summary judgment has other important functions, such as limiting the issues for trial, granting partial summary judgment, if warranted, and proceeding to trial on the other issues not already resolved; if damages are in issue and summary judgment is granted, the court will order an immediate assessment of damages for a date certain selected by the court.

In view of its importance in the collection attorney's arsenal, the following premises and cases cited appear to be noteworthy:

It has been held that on a motion for summary judgment issue finding, rather than issue-determination, is the key to the procedure. Where there is any significant doubt whether there is a triable issue of fact or whether the material issue of fact is arguable, summary judgment must be denied. *Moyer v. Briggs*, 47 A.D.2d 64 (1975). Before summary judgment is granted, the court must be completely satisfied that no material issue and triable issue of fact are presented. *Stillman v. Twentieth Century-Fox Film Corp.*, 3 N.Y.2d 395 (1957)

Summary judgment is a drastic remedy and should not be granted when there is any doubt as to the existence of a triable issue. *Moskowitz v. Garlock*, 23 A.D.2d 943 (1965). Only the existence of a bona fide issue raised by evidentiary facts and not based on conclusory or irrelevant allegations will suffice to defeat summary judgment. *Mullad Constr. Corp. v. County Federal Savings & Loan Ass'n.*, 32 N.Y.2d 285 (1973); *Rosenberg v. Del Mar Div. Champion Int. Corp.*, 56 A.D.2d 576 (1977)

In a lower Civil Court case, plaintiff moved for summary judgment to recover for reimbursement of student loan proceeds made to defendant while attending college. The answer consisted of several affirmative defenses such as lack of proper service of the summons and complaint, disputed amount and statue of limitations. The affidavit submitted in opposition to plaintiff's motion was made and signed by defendant's attorney, without any opposing affidavit by the named defendant. The court granted summary judgment for plaintiff and directed the entry of judgment stating that the affidavit of the attorney is insufficient to defeat summary judgment as it is not based on personal knowledge of the facts, nor does it indicate why defendant did not submit his/her affidavit in opposition. The attorney's affidavit was deficient of any factual content, but consisted merely of conclusory allegations. *Shaw v. Time-Life Records*, 38 N.Y.2d 201 (1974).

An affidavit which is required to oppose or support a motion for summary judgment *must* be by a person having knowledge of the facts and *must* recite all material facts. CPLR sec. 3212(b). Conclusory or hearsay statements are not sufficient, nor is the requirement of "knowledge" met if the affidavit merely alleges facts upon information and belief and no statement is made as to the source of the information or grounds of belief.

A party's attorney may properly submit an opposing affidavit where he/she states he/she is familiar with the facts and circumstances of the action, and which affidavit sets forth facts which amply support such contention of familiarity. An affidavit by a party's attorney which fails to allege personal knowledge of the facts averred is insufficient and should be disregarded since it has no probative value. *DiSabato v. Soffes*, 9 A.D.2d 297 (1959); *Israelson v. Rubin*, 20 A.D.2d 668 (1964) *aff'd*, 14 N.Y.2d 887 (1964).

A defense may not be considered where the opposing affidavit is that of the defendant's attorney, who does not indicate why defendant did not execute it, and upon what basis his/her own knowledge of the facts is founded. *Louis Sherry Ice Cream Co. v. Kroggel*, 42 Misc. 2d 21, 25 N.Y.S.2d 755 (1963).

Lastly, it should be remembered that a motion for summary judgment is the equivalent of a trial on paper, without witnesses. Such a motion is the procedural equivalent of a trial. *Falk v. Goodman*, 7 N.Y.2d 87 (1959). It is incumbent upon a party who opposes a motion for summary judgment to assemble, lay bare and reveal its proof to establish a genuine issue of fact for trial. Moreover, to defeat such a motion, defendant must present evidentiary facts sufficient to raise a triable issue of fact. *Oppenheimer v. Dresdues Bank A.G.*, 50 A.D.2d 434 (1975), *aff'd*, 41 N.Y.2d 949 (1977); *DiSabato v. Soffes, supra.*

Motion under CPLR sec. 3211 is likewise a very valuable tool in the collection attorney's arsenal of procedural devices to expedite the resolution of a case. It should be clear to the other side that upon receipt of a motion to dismiss a cause of action or defense under this section, that the attorney-movant means business and will engage in forceful litigation to either force a settlement or obtain a judgment in his/her client's favor. Under CPLR sec. 3211(c) this motion is treated as a motion for summary judgment and any and all material evidence should be used, as upon a motion for summary judgment. The advantages of proceeding under sec. 3211 is that it can be made before joining of issue, and the court can order an immediate trial of the issues raised on the motion or order a continuance for further affidavits and even order disclosure, if warranted. CPLR sec. 3211(d).

This section is frequently used to allege the jurisdictional defense of lack of jurisdiction over the person of defendant, prior to answer, which extends the time to serve a responsive pleading until ten days after service of notice of entry of the order disposing of the motion. This defense, if not raised prior to joinder of issue, can be raised in defendant's answer. CPLR 3211(e).

The courts generally order a traverse hearing on the issue of service, when a motion is made to dismiss for lack of jurisdiction over the person, or upon the service of an order to show cause upon a default, and pending the traverse hearing the motion or show cause is held in abeyance.

If the traverse hearing is sustained, it is good practice to have a process server available and ready to serve a new summons and complaint, but outside the courthouse in order to avoid any judicial impropriety.

We have commented on the fact that where there is a triable issue of fact, or whether the material issue of fact is arguable, summary judgment must be denied. *Moyer v. Briggs*, 47 A.D.2d 64 (1975). When lack of jurisdiction over the person of defendant is pleaded as a defense, there becomes a triable issue of fact, and the burden shifts to the plaintiff to show proper service. It has been held that the affidavit of service is not conclusive of proper and correct service. In the case of *Ralloway v. National Services Industries*, 93 A.D.2d 734 (1983) the court stated that: CPLR secs. 320(b) and 3211(e) permit a defendant who objects to jurisdiction the right to preserve such objections by asserting an affirmative defense to that effect in the answer. The practical effect of asserting the defense by answer rather than by motion is to put off resolution of the objection until the trial.

It is plaintiff's responsibility to seek a hearing on the matter if an earlier determination than trial is sought. Clearly, a motion for summary judgment will not be granted when the answer asserts lack of jurisdiction over the person as a defense, as there is a traible issue of fact.

This was made clear in the case of *The Greenpoint Savings Bank v. Taylor*, 92 A.D. 910(1983) which stated, in part: The sworn denial by the appellant that she had been served requires a hearing to determine whether she was in fact served. "The affidavit of service is not conclusive once there has been a sworn denial of receipt." *Empire Nat'l Bank v. Judal Const. of N.Y.*, 61 A.D.2d 789, (1978). The burden of proving jurisdiction is upon the party asserting it and when challenged that party must sustain that burden by preponderating evidence. *Jacobs v. Zurick Ins. Co.*, 53 A.D.2d 524 (1976).

This leads us to an important consideration when this defense is raised on the issue of statute of limitations. When the statute is not a problem, it is good practice to move for a traverse hearing so the issue of service can be resolved, and a new summons served immediately thereafter if the traverse is sustained. Conversely, if the statute of limitations is a problem and has expired or will expire shortly, CPLR sec. 205(a) is the savior section to correct this situation.

When an action is timely commenced but is later dismissed, sec. 205(a) provides that a new action may be commenced within six months, even if the statute of limitations has or will run, if the dismissal was not because of a voluntary discontinuance, neglect to prosecute or final judgment on the merits.

However, the courts have determined that an action will not be deemed commenced until the defendant has been properly served by the method prescribed by CPLR sec. 308. Accordingly, where the prior action was dismissed for lack of sufficient service, CPLR sec. 205(a) will not apply because the action was never commenced.

The Court of Appeals, in *Euson v. May*, 236 N.Y. 412 (1923), stated that if there was not proper service on the defendant, the action was not validly commenced and hence would not fall under the provisions of CPLR sec. 205(a). This view seems to be upheld by the courts in *Markoff v. South Nassau Community Hospital*, 61 N.Y.2d 283 (1984), wherein the Court of Appeals stated the requisite predicate for application of CPLR sec. 205(a) is that the terminated action must have been timely commenced. An action is commenced within the meaning of any statute governing limitation, including CPLR sec. 205(a), when there has been service of a summons. Service is only effective when it is made pursuant to the appropriate method authorized by the CPLR.

Actual notice alone will not sustain the service or subject a person to the court's jurisdiction when there has not been compliance with prescribed conditions of service. *Parker v. Mark*, 61 N.Y.2d 114 (1984).

It would appear that the purpose of CPLR sec. 205(a) is to give a party an additional six-month period to commence a new action, if the prior terminated action was dismissed, but the case law above-cited holds otherwise. The writer does not prescribe to this case application view, and recommends further research on this point, otherwise the purpose and intent of this important statute is defeated.

X. DEBT COLLECTION RESTRICTIONS

The attorney whose practice is concentrated in collection law should familiarize himself/herself with the Federal Fair Debt Collection Practices Act, the City of New York Consumer Protection Law and the provisions relating to prohibited practices under the General Business Law of the State of New York. The Penal Law of the State of New York sec. 190.50 contains illegal and unlawful collection practices. Under the circumstances, the novice attorney who is entering the field of collection law with his/her first collection case, and the veteran attorney, should carefully abide by the above collection statutes to avoid sanctions.

The Fair Debt Collection Practices Act, Title VIII of the Consumer Credit Protection Act, does not apply to attorneys. As consequence, the City of New York enacted the Consumer Protection Law, which specifically applies to attorneys and in reality is a codification of the Federal statute.

The persons who are subject to this Act are third-party debt collectors, who regularly collect debts for others, other than a finance company seeking to collect a debt assigned to it before a consumer's default; separate entities established by a creditor whose principal purpose is to collect debts; creditor, who in collecting own debts, uses other than own name, which would indicate that a third person is collecting or attempting to collect such debt; entities whose principal business is the enforcement of security interests.

Debt collectors does not include officer or employees of the creditor collecting debts for and in the name of the creditor; governmental officer or employee collecting a debt in the performance of his official duties; process servers non-profit bona fide consumer credit counselling service and an attorney collecting a debt as an attorney on behalf and in the name of a client. An attorney could be considered a debt collector where for a flat fee he composes standard collection letters which client completes and which attorney signs and mails, but the attorney has no authority to take further action. Is it possible for an attorney to collect a debt as a debt collector and not as an attorney under the Act? There has been some commentary that an attorney could be subject to the restrictions of the Act if he only proceeds as a debt collector would in the pre-litigation collection stage of letter writing and telephone communicating, and does not proceed in the normal and usual manner as an attorney would.

The basic restrictions of the Act are as follows:

1. Improper communication with the consumer or third parties, except to acquire location information.

2. Improper communication with the consumer, after the consumer's refusal to pay the debt and refuses to communicate further with the debt collector.

3. Harrassment or abuse of any person in connection with collection of the debt. Such conduct includes, but is not limited to, use or threat of violence, criminal means to harm persons, property or reputation, use of obscene or abusive language, the publication of "shame lists" except to persons permitted to receive such information, pursuant to the Fair Credit Reporting Act. Illustrations of the above: form letters requesting employer to discuss debt with employee-debtor constitutes harrassment; threat to send agent personally to recover credit cards is a threat of violence; repeated calls to neighbors is harrassment.

4. False or misleading representations made in connection with collection of the debt. Illustrations of the above: as to the identity of the debt collector; as to the amount or status of the debt, or fees; as to the legal ramifications of a failure to pay the debt; as to the communication of false credit information; as to the nature of any written communication; as to the nature of any written communication (form letters laid out like legal document); as to the purpose for which information will be used, a letter form which threatens suit within three days violates Act unless such proceedings are instituted within that time. A form letter should not imply that legal action *may* be taken unless suit is ordinary response to nonpayment, or action taken more than half the time.

5. Unfair or unconscionable means of collection of the debt. Such practices include the collection of fees not expressly authorized by the agreement creating the debt; solicitation of postdated checks for purposes of instituting criminal prosecution, or the deposit of postdated checks prior to payment date; causing persons to incur charges for the communications by concealing the true purpose thereof.

The Act for the first time requires that within five days after the initial communication with the consumer the debt collector must send the consumer a written notice containing the amount of debt, the name of the creditor, a statement that if the consumer fails to dispute the validity of the debt, or any portion thereof, within 30 days the debt will be presumed valid (failure to dispute validity by consumer cannot be construed as an admission of the debt by court), a statement that upon written notice of dispute from the consumer within 30 days, the collector will verify the debt to the consumer.

It is obvious that the validation requirements are extremely useful in attempting to settle disputed matters prior to actual suit. The vendor might have a billing error, payments not credited to the consumer's account, defective or undelivered merchandise, which may come to light upon the consumer giving notice, which otherwise might not be noticed until a costly lawsuit is commenced.

The sanctions for not complying with the Act, or any of its provisions, can result in civil liability for compensatory damages plus an additional amount up to $1,000. Class action recovery is also provided for by way of actual damages, plus an additional amount for each named plaintiff up to $1,000, but the total class recovery may not exceed the lesser of $500,000 or 1 percent of the collector's net worth. Attorneys' fees can also be recovered by the consumer if the court finds that the debt collector acted in bad faith. It is especially important for debt collectors to set up reasonable procedures to avoid errors of conduct by its personnel.

The State of New York, under General Business Law sec. 601, contains many prohibitions of debt collection practices. The attorney who is engaged in this type of practice should throughly familiarize himself/herself with this statute to avoid any impropriety or unlawful conduct. The Attorney General, under General Business Law sec. 602, can bring an action to enjoin such conduct, which if found guilty thereof constitutes a misdemeanor.

The violations and penalties of sloppy, careless and negligent debt collection practice should be emphasized, as follows:

General Business Law—Section 602
Violations and Penalties

1. Except as otherwise provided by law, any person who shall violate the terms of this article shall be guilty of a misdemeanor, and each such violation shall be deemed a separate offense.

2. The attorney general or the district attorney of any county may bring an action in the name of the people of the state to restrain or prevent any violation of this article or any continuance of any such violation.

Penal Law—Section 190.50
Unlawful Collection Practices

A person is guilty of unlawful collection practices when, with intent to enforce a claim or judgment for money or property, he knowingly sends, mails or delivers to another person a notice, document or other instrument which has no judicial or official sanction and which in its format or appearance, simulates a summons, complaint, court order or process, or an insignia, seal or printed form of a federal, state or local government or an instrumentality thereof, or is otherwise calculated to induce a belief that such notice, document or instrument has a judicial or official sanction. Unlawful collection practices is a class B misdemeanor.

The Consumer Protection Law applies to attorneys and basically contains the same or similar provisions of the Fair Debt Collection Practices Act. The Department of Consumer Affairs monitors this local law.

If the attorney has a set of guidelines or procedures for its nonprofessional staff to deal fairly and in good faith with consumer debtors, there should not be a problem with debt collection procedures in the pre-litigation or litigation stage. One last word of caution to the novice attorney, who is handling his/her first collection case, is that your adversary might not be an attorney, but a defendant in person. Under such circumstances, it is good and sound practice to make certain that your legal procedures and remedies are ethical, necessary, warranted and in the best interests of you and your client to resolve the dispute amicably and speedily. Although your primary objective is to obtain recovery or a judgment for your client, however, your procedures should not be dilatory or unnecessary. The majority of collection cases will be resolved prior to trial.

Appendix A

CIVIL COURT OF THE CITY NEW YORK
COUNTY OF

INDEX NO.:

AFFIRMATION IN SUPPORT OF CLAIM FOR ATTORNEY'S FEES PURSUANT TO DIRECTIVE 441.

Plaintiff,

—against—

Defendant(s),

STATE OF NEW YORK, COUNTY OF NEW YORK ss.:

The undersigned, an attorney at Law and partner/associate of SENNET & KRUMHOLZ attorneys for Plaintiff herein affirms the following to be true under the penalities of perjury:

1. I respectfully submit this affidavit in support of the amount claimed in the complaint for attorney's fees. Neither I nor any partner or associates of this firm are salaried employees of plaintiff. I am familiar with the facts hereinafter stated. The claim reflected by this lawsuit was referred to this firm by plaintiff on as a result of the default by defendant(s) under the terms of:
RETAIL INSTALLMENT CREDIT CARD AGREEMENT, A COPY OF WHICH, EXECUTED BY FINANCING AGENCY, WAS ON INFORMATION AND BELIEF MAILED TO THE DEFENDANT(S), BY PLAINTIFF PURSUANT TO THE REQUIREMENTS OF PERSONAL PROPERTY LAW, SECTION 413 (11) (e).

2. This firm specializes in and devotes a substantial part of its legal practice to lawsuits concerning, and collection of, consumer credit obligations.
3. I am familiar with the professional services furnished by me and this firm in this matter.
4. Legal and non-legal personnel in this firm rendered the following services under a lawyer's direct supervision in the within matter:
   (a) Documentation of claim furnished by plaintiff and reviewed for legal sufficiency: opened file showing name and address of debtor, amount in suit, referral date and determination made as to legal procedures for collection, jurisdiction and venue.
   (b) Contacted or attempted to contact debtor to amicably adjust claim, demand letter sent to debtor for confirmation of home address and place of business; asset and credit checking to

determine feasibility of suit and work and control records prepared for litigation.

(c) Summons and Complaint prepared and reviewed for correctness as to proper parties and issued for service after obtaining verification where appropriate; process served and filed with this Court obtaining information as to date of service, index number and file diaried for further action.

(d) Additional notice as required by law mailed to defendant(s) together with further letter informing defendant of pending lawsuit; caused judgment on default to be prepared after interest and costs computed; caused to be prepared an affidavit of merit, where appropriate and submitted judgment and within affirmation for attorney's fees after review of facts.

(e) Anticipated and possible post-judgment proceedings: verification of defendant(s) home address, place of business or assets for either income or property execution to be issued to Marshal or Sheriff; where appropriate, restraining notice to judgment debtor or garnishee and/or information subpoena; where appropriate, issuance and filing of transcripts of judgment; collection and remittance of funds to plaintiff and periodic review of file and status reports.

5. The services rendered by legal personnel in this law firm directly attributable to this matter involved approximately ½ HOUR and non-legal personnel in this law firm rendered approximately ONE HOUR of services in this matter.

6. The affidavit of service indicates that the defendant(s) was/were served on . The defendant(s) failed to appear or answer and is/are now in default.

7. The principal unpaid amount as shown in the summons and complaint is , (which includes accrued interest). The agreement between the parties provide, in accordance with:

SECTION 413 SUB 5 OF THE PERSONAL PROPERTY LAW, FOR THE PAYMENT OF ATTORNEY FEES OF UP TO 20%.

The attorneys' fees sought on this application are , which does not exceed the specified limit.

8. The attorneys' fees which plaintiff is obligated to pay this firm in connection with this matter is a contingent fee, by retainer agreement at present equal to or in excess of of each dollar recovered from the defendant(s) which would total in excess of if the principal is recovered. It is my opinion and belief, based upon my years of legal practice in the State of New York and experience in litigation involving consumer credit obligations, that the amount of represents the fair and reasonable value of the attorneys' services and is equal to or less than usual fee charged by attorneys for comparable services in New York City.

WHEREFORE, I respectfully request that this Court both fix and allow attorneys' fees in the sum of

Dated:

____

APPROVED: __________________________

J.C.C.

CHAPTER TEN

THE CONSTITUTIONAL CHALLENGE TO CPLR ARTICLE 52

Professor Barry Zaretsky

I. PREJUDGMENT RIGHTS AND REMEDIES

A. Types of Creditor Remedies

The New York CPLR provides several remedies for judgment creditors seeking to collect their claims. Among these remedies are the restraining notice,[1] which may be served on either the judgment debtor or a third party and which operates as an injunction against the transfer or other disposition of the debtors, property, and the execution,[2] which directs the sheriff to levy on the debtor's property, wherever it is located. These remedies have come under increased scrutiny as courts have attempted to protect debtor's due process rights in their property.

B. Development of Debtor Protection Due Process Rights

1. Prior Notice and Hearing Requirements

The seminal debtor protection due process case was *Sniadach v. Family Finance Corp.*[3] In that case, the creditor sought to garnish the debtor's wages at the outset of a lawsuit, prior to any judgment. The Wisconsin procedure at issue did not require notice or an opportunity for a hearing prior to the garnishment. The Supreme Court held that the procedure violated the debtor's due process rights because it permitted a deprivation of the use of the debtor's wages prior to any judicial determination that the garnishment was proper. The Court was particularly concerned about the importance of wages to individual debtors and the enormous burden that would be imposed by mistaken or improper garnishments.

Several years later, the Court extended the *Sniadach* requirement of prior notice and hearing to replevin actions. In *Fuentes v. Shevin*,[4] It held that a debtor could not be deprived of possession of property without prior notice and hearing even when a secured creditor claimed an interest in the same property. Again, the Court was concerned with the enormous burden that would be imposed upon debtors by mistaken or improper deprivations.

2. When Prior Notice and Hearing Not Required—Replevin

The Court drew back some from its broad *Fuentes* holding in *Mitchell v. W.T. Grant Co.*[5] In that case, the Court upheld a replevin procedure which did not require notice or an opportunity for a hearing prior to the seizure but which required notice and a hearing immediately after the seizure. The Court held that since both the debtor and the creditor claimed interests in the same property, the provision for an immediate post-seizure hearing, coupled with other statutory protections for the debtor,[6] was sufficient to satisfy the dictates of due process. The Court seemed particularly impressed with the argument that the property did not belong solely to the debtor and that the creditor's interest in the property could be adversely affected if the debtor was to receive notice and a hearing prior to the creditor's opportunity to seize the property. It noted that most replevin actions involve fairly simple fact situations in which the creditor's property interest and the debtor's default can be easily proven. The risk of mistaken deprivations is therefore not great. Moreover, the immediate post-seizure hearing would decrease the length of the deprivation.

3. Garnishment

The Court once again tackled the due process issues in *North Georgia Finishing, Inc. v. Di-Chem, Inc.*[7] It reviewed the Georgia garnishment procedure in a case between two commercial parties and found that the procedure, which provided neither prior nor immediate post-seizure notice and hearing, violated the debtor's due process rights. The Court seemed to resurrect in part the *Fuentes* case by citing it favorably in its discussion of the due process violation. Some commentators have suggested that the reference to *Fuentes* was intended to indicate that the due process protections must be stronger in a garnishment case, in which the creditor has no prior interest in the garnished property, than in a replevin case, in which the creditor has a specific, prior interest in the property concerned.[8]

C. Prejudgment Amendments Under New York Law

All of the Supreme Court cases involved prejudgment "provisional" remedies. The New York Legislature responded to these cases by amending many of the provisions in the CPLR that concerned prejudgment remedies.[9] The amendments generally provide opportunities for debtors to contest seizures of their property in a meaningful manner. Other litigation[10] induced the Legislature to amend the Lien Law[11] to provide for notice and hearing even when the deprivation does not directly involve the court system.

II. POST-JUDGMENT RIGHTS AND REMEDIES UNDER CPLR ARTICLE 52

A. Exempt Property

In recent years, litigation has raised a question concerning the constitutionality of post-judgment remedies in Article 52 of the CPLR. For even with a valid judgment, questions arise in the post-judgment setting over attempts to execute on or restrain property of the debtor which might qualify for an exemption. In *Cole v. Goldberger, Pedersen & Hochron,*[12] creditors levied on funds which plaintiffs claimed were social security and veteran's benefits entitled to a statutory exemption. The court found that the provisions of Article 52 of the CPLR concerning restraining notices and execution were unconstitutional to the extent that they affected a debtor's exempt assets in the hands of third parties without providing for service of notice on the debtor. The court noted that the existence of the judgment itself may be sufficient notice to the debtor of possible action with respect to nonexempt property.[13] The Legislature has clearly provided, however, that a debtor's exempt property is not subject to seizure to satisfy a judgment and the judgment itself gives no notice of such a seizure.

The creditor argued that while prior notice to the debtor would permit the debtor to prevent erroneous seizures of exempt assets in a post-judgment action, it would also give the debtor an opportunity to dissipate the asset. The creditor would thus be unable to assure that property would be available to satisfy the judgment. The court agreed, noting that the state, debtor and creditor all share an interest in the prompt and efficient enforcement of money judgments as it tends to "increase the availability and reduce the cost of consumer credit." It then balanced the debtor's interest in protecting exempt assets with the creditor's interest in payment. Comparing these interests with the Supreme Court's decisions in the prejudgment line of cases, the court found that although the creditor's right to payment is much stronger in the post-judgment setting, the creditor has absolutely no property right in the debtor's exempt assets. The court held, therefore, that notice of a restraining notice or execution must be given to the debtor simultaneously with or soon after service upon a third party in possession of the debtor's exempt assets. This would protect the creditor against a dishonest debtor while assuring a minimal deprivation when exempt property is involved.

The court stated that if timely and adequate notice is given to the debtor, the procedure in CPLR sec. 5240 for contesting an enforcement procedure or asserting an exemption is sufficient. It noted that the burden of claiming and proving an exemption is on the debtor and that this is reasonable since the debtor possesses the facts necessary to prove his/her exemption. The *Cole* case was decided by the Broome County Supreme Court and seems to have had a direct immediate effect only in that County. Apparently informal provisions for notice to debtors were worked out by the Bar in that county and further litigation was avoided.[14]

B. Adequacy of Notice

A broader challenge to CPLR post-judgment collection procedures occurred in *Deary v. Guardian Loan Co., Inc.*[15] In that case, the debtors argued that the procedures for restraint and execution under sections 5222, 5230, and 5232 violated the due process and supremacy clauses of the United States Constitution by failing to provide the judgment debtor with notice of, or an opportunity to be heard on, the restraint or execution.

Section 5222 permitted a creditor's attorney to issue a restraining notice and serve it upon any person other than the judgment debtor's employer. The creditor could tie up the debtor's assets held by third parties to the extent of twice the amount of the judgment. There was no provision for notice to the debtor, nor was there any specific procedure for challenging the restraint.

Section 5232 permitted the creditor's attorney or the Clerk of the Court to issue an execution which would be levied by the sheriff or marshal upon property of the debtor. As with section 5222, there was no provision for notifying the debtor of the levy nor was there any specific provision for contesting the levy.

A debtor was not left without any remedy for wrongful restraints or executions. Section 5239 did and does permit "any interested person" to commence a special proceeding contesting a levy or a sheriff's sale and section 5240 permits the court on its own initiative or on motion to "make an order denying, limiting, conditioning, regulating, extending or modifying the use of any enforcement procedure."

1. Debtor's Arguments

Of course, without notice of the restraint or execution a debtor would be unable, as a practical matter, to contest wrongful creditor actions. The debtors argued, therefore, that the right in sections 5239 and 5240 to contest a restraint or execution is an empty right if the debtor has no notice. Although a debtor would eventually learn about a restraint or execution on property held by a third party, and although some garnishees might voluntarily inform debtors of actions taken with respect to debtors, property, these are not sufficient to satisfy due process requirements. Moreover, the debtors argued that although the judgment itself gives notice of an impending restraint or execution, such notice does not enable a debtor to protect exempt property from erroneous seizure because the debtor does not know exactly when a seizure will occur or what property will be seized.

2. Creditor's Arguments

The creditors noted that the Supreme Court in *Endicott-Johnson Corp v. Encyclopedia Press*[16] held that due process does not require notice prior to a post-judgment garnishment of wages because the judgment is sufficient to put the debtor on notice of impending enforcement procedures. They claimed that *Endicott-Johnson* is still good law since the subsequent due process creditor's rights cases involved only prejudgment provisional remedies. Moreover, even the more recent Supreme Court decisions suggest that due process requires a balancing of the creditor's and debtor's interest which, in the post-judgment enforcement situation, weighs more heavily towards the creditor's interest since there has been a court determination of the creditor's right to payment.

3. Holding

The court held that the New York enforcement procedures violated due process requirements by "failing to afford the judgment debtor adequate protection against erroneous restraint or execution" and granted declaratory and injunctive relief. It noted that a debtor would be unable to protect his/her interest in exempt property if the debtor had no notice of a restraint or execution. While a judgment creditor's interest is stronger after judgment than before, the judgment does not itself authorize the use of particular property to satisfy the claim. Since exemptions are designed to protect a debtor's basic survival, the debtor's interest in protecting exempt property is stronger than even the post-judgment creditor's interest in collection. Moreover, since the exempt property involved in this case and in many of these cases is money, the creditor will often have difficulty in determining its exempt character. The court also noted the substantial increase in possible exemptions since the time *Endicott-Johnson* was decided, in particular, the "enormous expansion of public welfare and pension statutes with attendant exemption rights." Thus, the debtor has an even stronger interest in an adequate opportunity to learn of and dispute an erroneous seizure.

4. What Constitutes Adequate Notice

Based on this reasoning, the court held that a debtor must be given adequate notice of a restraint or execution.[17] It defined adequate notice to include information concerning exemptions and procedures for challenging the restraint or execution. The notice would enable even unsophisticated debtors to protect their rights. While the court found the post-judgment procedures inadequate because of the lack of notice, it took no position on the procedures for contesting erroneous restraints or seizures. It noted that debtors are entitled to a prompt procedure for challenging erroneous actions and found that the New York procedure could be constitutional if applied to provide prompt hearings. Since there was no evidence about the practical application of these procedures, the court made no finding.

5. Legislative Reaction

While the court's holding was limited to the class of judgment debtors who receive exempt income and hold accounts at the banks which were defendants in the action, the decision did not go unnoticed by the State Legislature. That body took prompt action to amend Article 52 to eliminate the constitutional objections. The amendments, effective September 1, 1982, added language to sections 5222, 5232, and 5234 which in general requires that adequate notice of a restraint or execution, of a right to exemptions, and of the procedure for contesting exemptions be provided to judgment debtors.

Section 5222 provides that the Clerk of the Court or the judgment creditor's attorney may issue a restraining notice and serve it upon any person other than the debtor's employer. The notice restrains a third party who has property of the debtor, or owes money to the debtor, from doing anything with the property or debt other than transferring it to the sheriff according to the sheriff's direction or pursuant to a court order. The 1982 amendment requires that notice must be given to the judgment debtor within a year before service of a restraining notice or must be mailed to a judgment debtor who is a natural person within four days of the service of a restraining notice. The statute sets out a particular form to be used as the notice[18] and a particular procedure for service which is designed to assure that the debtor receives the notice and that appropriate confidentiality is maintained.[19]

6. Remaining Questions

a. Time of Notice

Several things are unclear in this amendment. If notice was not given within a year before service of the restraining notice, must it be given four days before or four days after service of the restraining notice? Presumably the Legislature intended that notice be given after service since prior notice would be subsumed by the service within a year provision. With respect to notice given within a year before service of a restraining notice, it is unclear how the debtor will learn when a restraining notice is actually served. Thus, a debtor's bank account may be tied up for a period of time until the debtor attempts to withdraw money and learns that a restraining notice was served. If the fact of a judgment is insufficient to put the debtor on notice of the likelihood of post-judgment remedies, a notice that a restraining notice may be served any time within the next year is not much more useful. Thus it is unclear whether this new procedure will be constitutionally acceptable. While creditors might argue that a requirement that a separate notice be given to the debtor each time a restraining notice is served places too great a burden on them, the balance of interests would seem to favor the debtor's need to know quickly that a restraining notice has been served.

b. Type of Notice and Allocation of Burden

The notice itself is also not particularly clear. For example, the notice states that if a debtor thinks exempt property was taken, the debtor "may contact the person sending this notice." When the creditor's attorney sends the notice, it seems appropriate to suggest that the debtor contact him/her. It does not state, however, whether the creditor's attorney has any duty when contact is made. Since no burden is explicitly placed on the creditor, the burden of contesting a restraining notice presumably remains on the debtor. If that is so, the creditor's obligation would seem to be simply to listen to the debtor's objection, possibly release the restraining notice if the creditor is convinced the debtor is correct, and otherwise to suggest that the debtor consult an attorney.[20] While some courts have considered the allocation of the burden of acting to be an important part of the balance between the debtor's and creditor's rights,[21] placement of the burden on the debtor in this situation may not be inappropriate.

The creditor has already received a judicial determination that a debt is owed. He/she has presumably given prompt notice of any restraining notice to the debtor. If the debtor does contest the restraint, *Deary* suggests that the Court must, under secs. 5239 and 5240, provide a prompt procedure for resolving such disputes. To read into the statute a requirement that the creditor seek court confirmation of his/her restraining notice would seem to place too great a burden on creditors. Moreover, since the creditor may be liable for wrongful restraint[22] if his/her restraining order covers exempt property, it is in the creditor's interest to listen carefully to the debtor's objection and to take action where appropriate. Nevertheless it has been suggested that the allocation of the burden of acting may have purposely been left vague in order to permit courts to interpret the statute in whatever way would make it constitutional.[23]

c. Procedure for Determining Exemption Claims

The notice also informs the debtor that an attorney may be consulted and that a procedure exists for determining exemption claims. It does not, however, explain the procedure or suggest to the debtor any action other than contacting the sender or consulting an attorney. Thus the unsophisticated debtor may not receive much benefit from this notice.

7. Levy of Judgment

The 1982 amendment also added a paragraph to section 5232. That section sets out a procedure for levying on a judgment debtor's property. Levy may be by service of a copy of the execution or by seizure of tangible personal property. The addition to section 5232, denominated subsection (c), requires that the debtor be given a notice of execution similar to the notice required in section 5222 for restraining notices. Section 5232(c) requires either that the execution state that notice was served on the judgment debtor within a year or that the sheriff mail or personally deliver the notice to a judgment debtor who is a natural person, together with a copy of the execution, within four days of service of the execution upon any garnishee. The sheriff's notice must specify the name and address of the judgment creditor or his/her attorney.

As in section 5222, a blanket notice may be served once a year. In the event such notice has not been served, the burden is on the sheriff to serve the notice after the execution. Interestingly, the notice is required only when the execution is served upon a garnishee, a third party in possession of the debtor's property or who owes a debt to the debtor. When the sheriff executes on property in the debtor's possession, the debtor will obviously know of the execution. He/she will not, however, necessarily know about his right to exemptions and there is no provision for notifying the debtor of this right. Since most of the executions against individual debtors will be on bank accounts and the like, this should not be a major problem. A creditor who wants to be safe will, however, mail the blanket notice to be assured that the debtor is aware of the right to exemptions.

If the sheriff serves the notice the debtor may, following the notice's direction, contact the sheriff as the person who sent it. While there is probably little that the sheriff can do, he/she can and probably should refer the debtor to the creditor's attorney.

8. Distribution of Proceeds

The final amendment in the 1982 package was to section 5234 of the CPLR. That section orders the sheriff to distribute the proceeds of personal property or a debt acquired in the course of enforcing a judgment. The proceeds are used to pay fees, expenses and taxes, and then the judgment creditor, with any remainder going to the judgment debtor. The 1982 Amendment adds a sentence which states, "No distribution of proceeds shall be made until 15 days after service of the execution except upon order of the court." This 15-day period is intended to permit the debtor to contest an execution and protect exempt property before the property leaves the sheriff's hands.

a. Commencement of Waiting Period

It is unclear in this amendment exactly when the 15-day waiting period begins. The provision orders the sheriff to wait "until 15 days after service of the execution." Under section 5232 levy may be made by service of the execution upon a garnishee or by physical seizure of tangible personal property. With respect to the first method, presumably the sheriff will wait 15 days after the execution is served on a garnishee. This does not mean, however, that the debtor will have 15 days to contest the execution. The debtor may have received his/her 5222(e) notice within a year prior to the execution, in which case he/she may not learn of the execution until after the 15-day period has run, or he/she may receive his/her notice within four days after the execution in which case the debtor will have less than two weeks to contest the execution before a sheriff's sale. With respect to execution by seizure, the sheriff may physically seize the property and then "shall forthwith serve a copy of the execution . . . upon the person from whose possession or custody the property was taken." If the property was seized from the debtor, the execution will be served on him/her "forthwith" and he/she will presumably have most of the 15-day period to contest the levy. If the levy by seizure is on property held by a third party, the service will be on the third party and as with levy by service, the debtor may not receive notice in time to contest the levy.[24]

b. Notice to Debtor

It is possible that in its amendment to section 5234 the Legislature intended the 15-day period to run from service of the 5222(e) notice.

A similar problem concerning notice to the debtor arises. Since section 5232 permits service of the notice within a year prior to the levy, the debtor may receive no notice of the actual levy until more than 15 days after service of the 5222(e) notice. Since the Legislature presumably intended to assure the debtor approximately two weeks after a levy within which to contest the levy before property is distributed, section 5234 should be interpreted in whatever way is necessary to effectuate this purpose.

In reality few of these problems should arise. The most typical levy situation will be service of an execution upon a garnishee, typically a bank. In that case, the debtor is likely to learn of the execution before the 15-day period has run and therefore be able to contest it. To the extent that it is possible under these amendments that neither the bank nor the sheriff nor the judgment creditor will notify the debtor of the actual execution, the statute may not satisfy the *Deary* court. A creditor can, of course, avoid that fact situation by giving notice to the debtor immediately after the sheriff levies. The *Deary* court indicated that with respect to the constitutionality of sections 5239 and 5240 it was willing to review the actual operation of the statute rather than its terms. Assuming a court is willing to do the same with respect to the 1982 Amendments, the statute should pass constitutional muster if creditors and courts interpret it to assure that debtors receive notice of executions in time to contest their validity and assert exemptions.[25]

III. CONCLUSION

If litigants follow the spirit rather than the letter of the recent amendments to the CPLR, the beneficial effects are readily apparent. While most creditor actions do not involve exempt property, the harm that even an occasional improper restraint of funds can create for a low income debtor looms large in contrast to the slight burden the new provisions place on the creditor, particularly with the inclusion of a customized form in the statute. The New York Legislature's swift response to these concerns is worthy of praise.

Footnotes

[1] N.Y. Civ. Prac. Law sec. 5222 (McKinney 1978 and Supp. 1982-83).

[2] N.Y. Civ. Prac. Law sec. 5230 (McKinney 1978 and Supp. 1982-83).

[3] 395 U.S. 337 (1969).

[4] 4407 U.S. 67 (1972).

[5] 416 U.S. 600 (1974).

[6] The Louisiana statute required that the writ of sequestration be issued by a judge, that the creditor prove specific facts to support issuance of the writ, and that the creditor post bond to protect the debtor against injury resulting from an improper sequestration.

[7] 419 U.S. 601 (1975).

[8] *See, e.g.*, Catz & Robinson, *Due Process and Creditors Remedies: From Sniadach and* Fuentes to Mitchell, North Georgia *and Beyond*, 28 Rutgers L. Rev. 541, 564 (1975). *Cf. Sugar v. Curtis Circulation Co.*, 383 F. Supp. 643 (S.D.N.Y. 1974), *vacated and remanded on other grounds*, 425 U.S. 73 (1976).

[9] N.Y. Civ. Prac. Law secs. 6201-6226 (McKinney 1978 and Supp. 1982-83).

[10] *See, e.g.*, *Sharrock v. Dell Buick-Cadillac, Inc.*, 45 N.Y.2d 152, 379 N.E.2d 1169, 408 N.Y.S.2d 39 (1978).

[11] 11 N.Y. Lien Law sec. 181 (McKinney 1978 and Supp. 1982-83).

[12] 95 Misc. 2d 720, 410 N.Y.S.2d 950 (Sup. Ct. Broome Cty. 1978).

[13] *See Endicott-Johnson v. Encyclopedia Press*, 266 U.S. 285 (1924).

[14] David Siegel, Supplementary Practice Commentaries, N.Y. Civ. Prac. Law C5222:1 (McKinney Supp. 1982-83).

[15] 534 F. Supp. 1178 (S.D.N.Y. 1982).

[16] *See* Note 13, *supra*.

[17] Courts outside of New York have split on this issue. In *Brown v. Liberty Loan Corp. of Duval*, 539 F.2d 1355 (5th Cir. 1976), the court reversed a district court finding that a Florida garnishment statute was unconstitutional. It found that the freezing of a debtor's assets pending resolution of an exemption claim creates for the creditor a "secure debtor resource" at some but not an overriding disadvantage to the debtor. The court found the *Endicott-Johnson* rationale regarding notice to be still valid. However, in *Finberg v. Sullivan*, 634 F.2d 50 (3rd Cir. 1980), the court found a post-judgment garnishment procedure to violate both the due

process and supremacy clauses because it did not provide notice to the debtor regarding availability of exemptions or the method for asserting an exemption claim. In a lengthy dissent, Judge Aldisert found the notice requirement to constitute judicial legislation; queried whether at some future date a "laundry list" of exemptions would be required; and reviewed similar procedures in all 50 states.

[18] "(e) Content of notice. The notice required by subdivision (d) shall be in substantially the following form and may be included in the restraining notice: NOTICE TO JUDGMENT DEBTOR

Money or property belonging to you may have been taken or held in order to satisfy a judgment which has been entered against you. Read this carefully.

YOU MAY BE ABLE TO GET YOUR MONEY BACK

State and federal laws prevent certain money or property from being taken to satisfy judgments. Such money or property is said to be 'exempt.' The following is a partial list of money which may be exempt:

1. Supplemental security income (SSI);
2. Social Security;
3. Public Assistance (Welfare);
4. Alimony or child support;
5. Unemployment benefits;
6. Disability benefits;
7. Workers' compensation benefits;
8. Public or private pensions; and
9. Veterans benefits.

If you think that any of your money that has been taken or held is exempt, you must act promptly because the money may be applied to the judgment. If you claim that any of your money that has been taken or held is exempt, you may contact the person sending this notice. Also, YOU MAY CONSULT AN ATTORNEY, INCLUDING LEGAL AID IF YOU QUALIFY. The law (New York Civil Practice Law and Rules, article four and sections fifty-two hundred thirty-nine and fifty-two hundred forty) provides a procedure for determination of a claim to an exemption." N.Y. Civ. Prac. Law sec. 5222(e) (McKinney Supp. 1983).

[19] "Such notice shall be mailed to the defendant at his residence address; or in the event such mailing is returned as undeliverable by the post office, or if the residence address of the defendant is unknown, then to the defendant in care of the place of employment of the defendant if known, in a envelope bearing the legend 'personal and confidential' and not indicating on the outside thereof, by the return address or otherwise, that the communication is from an attorney or concerns a judgment; or if neither the residence address nor the place of employment of the defendant is known then to the defendant at any other known address." N.Y. Civ. Prac. Law sec. 5222(d) (McKinney Supp. 1983).

[20] *Siegel, supra*, note 11, at C5222:11. A creditor's attorney who has sent out many of the new notices has yet to have a debtor respond to one. However, if contacted, he stated that his procedure would consist of staying any execution process, investigating thoroughly any claim of exemption, and responding to the debtor. Conversation with Stanley Stern of Stern and Peskhin, New York, September 1, 1983.

[21] *See, e.g., Sugar v. Curtis Circulation Co.*, 383 F. Supp. 643 (S.D.N.Y. 1974), vacated and remanded on other grounds, 425 U.S. 73 (1976).

[22] *See, e.g., Walter v. Doe*, 93 Misc. 2d 286, 402 N.Y.S.2d 723 (1978).

[23] *Siegel, supra*, note 14, at C5222:11.

[24] *Siegel, supra*, note 14, at C5234:1.

[25] It should be noted that the *Deary* court also found that the procedures in question violated the Supremacy Clause of the Constitution to the extent that money exempt under federal law was involved. The court found that the possibility of a significant interruption in benefits ran counter to the intent of Congress to provide uninterrupted benefits. The amendments should also resolve this problem.

*The author is a Professor of Law at Brooklyn Law School and a Visiting Professor at Fordham University School of Law. The author thanks Mr. Andrew Schwartz, a third year student at Brooklyn Law School, for his invaluable assistance in the preparation of this chapter.

CHAPTER ELEVEN

EVALUATING COLLECTION PROSPECTS

Ronald Forster, Esq.

I. INTRODUCTION

After successfully obtaining judgment, attention must be focused on turning the judgment into cash as quickly and inexpensively as possible. In order to do this, it is necessary to obtain as much information about the judgment debtor and his/her assets as possible. The techniques are referrred to as "asset locating" and "skip tracing." If the whereabouts of the judgment debtor are known, then the total effort will be made toward locating those assets which can be subject to enforcement and satisfaction of the judgment. It is also very important to be familiar with what property is exempt from execution. Article 52 of the Civil Practice Law and Rules provides the mechanism for locating assets and enforcing a money judgment. It begins by identifying which property is subject to enforcement.[1] Assets are broken down into debts and property against which a money judgment can be enforced. The debt must be past due or certain to become due or upon demand of the judgment debtor such as a time deposit or checking or savings account at a bank. It matters not where the debt was incurred nor whether it was to or from a nonresident. A cause of action capable of being assigned or transferred is a debt whether it occurred within or without the state. Similarly, any property which could be assigned or transferred, vested or not, or consisting of a present or future right, can be the proper subject of the enforcement of a money judgment. The debt or property must not be exempt from application to the satisfaction of the judgment. Section 5205 covers personal property exemptions and sec. 5206 covers real property exemptions. Section 5222(e) mentions other exemptions under state and federal law.

After carefully considering all the exemptions, there still remains a multitude of examples of assets subject to enforcement and satisfaction of a judgment. However, there have been some interesting interpretations of section 5201. In *Glassman v. Hyder*,[2] the Court of Appeals held that future rental payments due to the judgment debtor were not a debt and not attachable since there was no certainty that they would become due. The Court considered future rents as contingent. However, the Court seemed to base its decision solely upon paragraph (a) of section 5201 dealing with debts and did not consider section (b) dealing with property. If future rents are not considered debts because there is no certainty that they will become due, why could they not be considered a property right which could be assigned or transferred? This seems to make more sense. Future rents certainly have value and therefore should be applicable to the satisfaction of a judgment as they become due. It has been pointed out that a judgment creditor can execute against the real property so it becomes moot as to whether or not you can execute against the rent.[3] The problem is that it may not be economically feasible to proceed against the property. The amount of the judgment would be controlling as to how to proceed. A real property execution can be costly and time consuming. The cost of advertising and sheriff's fees are substantial even though recoverable. If the judgment is relatively small, you would not choose this method. Also, many courts in New York are reluctant to sell real property to satisfy a judgment particularly if it also happens to be the judgment debtor's residence.

You must petition the court to permit such a sale where the value of the home exceeds ten thousand dollars above liens and encumbrances. Homes with a value under this amount are exempt from execution. The courts have been known to invoke protective orders against the sale where the debt is disproportionate to the value of the property and can also require that other remedies be exhausted first.[4]

Of course a receiver could be appointed under section 5228 who could collect the rents and apply them toward the judgment. Again it is time consuming and requires a lot of paper work. Certainly it would be preferable if the rents could be executed against like other property. In 1976, the Court of Appeals, in *Abkco Industries, Inc. v. Apple Films, Inc.*,[5] may have decided just that. This case involved a licensing agreement between a British company and a New York company to market in the United States a film involving the Beatles, a musical group. Under the agreement, a percentage of the profit was to be paid to the British firm. The court brushed over the contingent nature of the "debt" and treated the agreement as property capable of being assigned and subject to attachment. In reaching this conclusion, the court reviewed its decision in *Glassman v. Hyder, supra*. The real property in the *Glassman* case was located in New Mexico and since the situs of a leasehold of real estate is at the location of the real estate, the property was beyond the reach of New York courts and only the question of future rents as debts could be considered.

It would now appear possible that future rents could be reached as property under sec. 5201(b) so long as the situs of the real estate is within the jurisdiction of the New York courts. It is now clear that even if levy and execution cannot be maintained under sec. 5201(a) dealing with contingent debts, it can be maintained if the debt can be treated as property.

Property can be either real or personal. However, shares in a cooperative apartment, although not really real property, are treated as such for purposes of the homestead exemption pursuant to section 5206 of the CPLR. Unlike the condominium, which is treated as real property for all purposes,[6] one would execute on a co-op by levying upon the shares of stock. The homestead exemption of $10,000 above liens and encumbrances remains in effect for one year after payment to the judgment debtor. If the judgment debtor receives money as a result of a surplus after a mortgage foreclosure, there is no exemption. The surplus money becomes personalty and is subject to execution at any time thereafter.[7]

Irrespective of how property is classified, it must be found first in order to utilize any one of a number of judgment enforcement proceedings provided for under Article 52. In order to do this, you must use all of the available information at your disposal. The information you obtain should either lead to possible assets or the realization that the judgment debtor is judgment proof and that the claim is uncollectable for all practical purposes.

How much effort is put into collecting is really determined by the reward that can be gained. The larger the debt, the greater the effort that can be made and economically justified. Unfortunately the realities are that a majority of claims will go unpaid and a substantial number of judgments will not be satisfied. This is especially true when the claim or judgment is a retail as distinguished from a commercial claim. To a collection lawyer, a retail claim is against an individual, while a commercial claim is against a business. Retail claims generally consist of some type of consumer credit transaction. Commercial claims usually arise for nonpayment of goods or services used in connection with the business and are probably contested more than retail claims. A judgment against a commercial establishment that is still doing business should present no problems unless the assets are not subject to levy or are inconsequential as compared to the debt, such as a real estate office with just a few desks, chairs, filing cabinets and a typewriter which may be covered by a security agreement or lien. In those cases, efforts would turn toward examining the books and records of the debtor. The real problem is tracking down assets for individuals who are mobile, uncooperative and whose assets are not apparent. To do this one should always begin with the client's file.

II. CLIENT'S FILE

Nearly every creditor has made some effort to collect a past due account before turning it over to a collection agency or an attorney for suit. One should obtain any documentation that may be in the file. In many instances the client has personal knowledge of the debtor and knows where he/she banks or works. There may be a credit application which has information about assets. Even if the application is very old and might not have current information it is a good starting point. Credit applications usually have information about places of employment, banks, other income, home telephone numbers, social security numbers and names, addresses and telephone numbers of relatives. The social security number is very important as a means of identification, especially if the debtor has a common name or was a single women who is now married and using a different name. It is also useful for obtaining credit bureau reports, although not mandatory. Where the debtor is a "skip" (no longer at the address you have), contacting relatives can be useful in helping locate him/her.

III. PERSONAL CONTACT

Personal contact with the debtor should be attempted. Start with the white pages of the local directory. If there is no listing use the telephone number in your client's file. If you happen to make contact with the debtor, always start off by asking if there is any reason why the judgment has not been paid. If the debtor is willing to talk, you should be willing to listen. Assuming you do not learn that he/she is exempt from execution because of bankruptcy or receipt of public assistance, the conversation should be directed toward his/her income and employment. Any information you receive voluntarily will result in time and expense saved. Most debtors probably feel that they cannot afford to pay because their expenses for necessities leave nothing left over. "It is not that I don't want to pay, I just don't have the money right now," is a common reason given by debtors. Explore the possibilities of obtaining the resources with which to pay a judgment. There may be life insurance upon which money can be borrowed at relatively low rates of interest, or if employed, there may be a credit union from which to borrow. Sometimes debtors feel overwhelmed by the number of debts they have so they ignore all of them. A suggestion about a consolidation loan may be feasible. Some companies will extend credit to a person for the purpose of paying all other judgments and delinquencies. This is especially true where the salary and length of time on the job warrant consideration. If practical, the debtor will gain the advantage of borrowing to make one monthly payment and the creditor will be paid at once. This is certainly preferable to filing an income execution which requires follow up with the sheriff or marshal and periodic payments providing there are not other prior garnishees ahead of you.

IV. COLES DIRECTORY—REVERSE TELEPHONE BOOK

The more you know about a debtor, the greater the chance of collecting. One of the greatest tools for locating and obtaining information about a debtor is Coles Directory. Coles is a set of books broken down by borough in New York City and by county outside New York City. It is a street directory arranged by alphabetical street and address number, and a numerical directory arranged by telephone number. The listing under street will give you the name and telephone numbers of those persons living at that address. If there is no telephone or a non-published telephone, it will indicate that. The listing by telephone number will tell you to whom and at what address it is listed. This is important because you can now have the names and telephone numbers of your judgment debtor's neighbors. Neighbors can be a great source of information. This is especially true in a small community. Other valuable information supplied in Coles is a wealth code which designates the type of income area in which the debtor lives. People who live in high income areas will generally have more assets subject to execution. It also gives the year in which the listing first appeared, an indication of how stable the debtor is and how well known he/she might be. If he/she lived in a multiple dwelling for a long time, the landlord may be good source of information. Businesses and cross streets are also indicated in the directory. By merely running your finger down the list, you can determine if there are any banks or financial institutions in the area. People generally will bank where it is convenient, near their home or place of employment. Of course, if you know where the debtor is employed, you can also determine which banks are accessible. For new information not yet in the books, there is a private line service which will supply you with such information.

Another important aspect of this directory is that it can give you a pretty good indication as to whether the debtor may be a home owner. If the addresses are single listings, the chances are that they are private homes. Further investigation as to whether the house is owned by the judgment debtor would then be warranted. These books are updated and renewed each year.

V. CREDIT BUREAUS

There are a number of credit bureaus that collect and report the credit profile of individuals and businesses. Much valuable information can be gleaned from such reports. If your client reports to any of these agencies it could obtain a report for you or it may already have one in its files. For those doing volume collection work, arrangements can be made to tie directly into the credit bureau via teletype. The bureaus report positive and negative information. If the report is filled with negative information such as many unpaid judgments, it may be an indication that the chances of collection are slight or at least that a great effort will have to be made to discover assets. Sometimes hidden among the negative may be clues to collection. For example, there may be a number of credit card companies and banks reporting derogatory information about the payment history of the judgment debtor and one bank reporting positive. In this day and age the necessity of the checking account for the transaction of business is extremely important. It may very well be that a debtor does maintain an active checking account at that bank and a restraining notice served may capture for you the prize of collection.

Credit bureaus generally pick up the suits and judgments instituted and entered against debtors, and as far as practicable report those that are satisfied. In some courts there is a tremendous lag in recording the filing of a satisfaction piece. If a judgment has been recently satisfied and marked as such, a contact with the attorney may lead you to assets which will help in the collection of your judgment.

Also reported is current information pertaining to a place of employment. Debtors constantly apply for credit, and information listed on their application can be a source leading to collection.

Of course, one must be careful that the information reported applies to your debtor. There are many examples where there is a variance on the file such as a different social security number. Information should be checked carefully so as to avoid confusion and possible liability. Many fathers and sons have the same name and there is always confusion between Junior and Senior.

Bankruptcy is reported in many instances where you never received actual notice, or the credit profile may be so bad that you believe the debtor is a possible candidate for bankruptcy. Where bankruptcy is noted, the date of the filing of the petition should be checked to see if it encompasses the debt upon which the claim you are handling arises.

It is not unusual to receive a claim against one who has filed bankruptcy, especially one based on a credit card. The petition does not require that the account number be disclosed and even if it is, the notice mailed to the creditor does not refer to it. Accordingly, the creditor is left with a name and address from which to check their records. If the debtor has a common name or has moved recently and did not notify the creditor, it will be unable to identify the bankrupt. Any dunning or attempt to enforce collection will place you in violation of the automatic stay provision of the Bankruptcy Act and could subject you and your client to contempt of court.

Information against consumers can be reported by the credit bureau until obsolete. In the case of bankruptcies, you cannot report more than ten years from the date of adjudication; and for suits and judgments, not more than seven years from entry or until the governing statute of limitations has expired, whichever is *longer.*

Accounts placed for collection or charged off to profit and loss can be reported for seven years.

VI. LANDLORDS

When it comes to locating or verifying the address of a debtor, the landlord is a good place to start. The name and telephone number can be obtained from a variety of sources. As previously mentioned, if the Coles Directory is available to you, a call to a person living at that address will usually get you the information. A trip to the County Clerk's office for a look at the deed will provide you with the name of the landlord, which could lead to a telephone number. In New York City a company called Standard Abstract Corp. has provided a directory available for leasing containing the names, addresses and telephone numbers of the landlords arranged alphabetically by street address of apartment houses, hotels, tenements and rooming houses. Also broken down is an alphabetical listing of landlords containing the properties they own. This is available if you have a judgment debtor who is also a landlord.

Once you are able to make contact with the landlord, all available information should be obtained regarding the debtor. If they are uncooperative, this information can be subpoenaed, as will be discussed later.

Many times landlords will honor your requests for reports if you write to them. If the debtor is a skip, it is probable that he/she may have left owing the landlord money and thus the landlord would have a stake in trying to locate him/her. The volumes are supplemented periodically because of the frequency of change in ownership.

For single or two family residences, the County Clerk's office should be consulted to obtain information as to whether the judgment debtor owns real property. By obtaining the block and lot number, the deed, which is microfilmed, can be looked at. This will give you the current owner and you can also check previous deeds to see if your debtor ever owned the property. If he/she did, it is important to ascertain if the transfer was for a fair consideration and whether there is anything suspicious about the transfer such as a conveyance to a family member. Such conveyance may have been fraudulent as to creditors and subject to being overturned. Sometimes, for a reasonable fee, you can get someone to do title searches for you to establish current ownership.

VII. COUNTY CLERK

While at the County Clerk's office, a number of things can be checked. The defendant's book can be checked showing all judgments entered against a named individual. The book is arranged in alphabetical order and will list the judgment amount and whether it is satisfied.

The judgment roll book is then checked to determine if any of the judgments listed were entered against your particular debtor, which will be apparent if the addresses are the same. At this point your interest should be focused on recently satisfied judgments because, like the credit bureau reports, it can lead to assets if the attorney of record is contacted. This is not to say that other judgments, especially recent ones, should not be checked; only that the amount of judgments entered against someone with a common name could be voluminous and a lot of time may be spent to no avail. Of course, if only a few judgments have been entered, the attorneys of record should be contacted on all of them.

UCC filings of secured transactions can also be checked for individuals and businesses at the County Clerk's office. A list of property covered by the security agreement which may be available for levy if the debt has not been satisfied is listed. It will also indicate who the secured party is. Appropriate questions of the secured party may lead to additional assets subject to execution or information which can lead to additional assets. Also available for inspection are certificates of doing business and partnerships. This is especially important to establish if your debtor is the principal of a business. Where a judgment debtor is a partner, his/her interest is the partnership can be levied upon. Any other partner on behalf of the partnership is a proper garnishee in such matters.[8]

VIII. DEPARTMENT OF MOTOR VEHICLES

The Department of Motor Vehicles can provide you with information pertaining to a debtor's whereabouts and which can lead to assets. The DMV has a procedure whereby information pertaining to a licensed driver or owner can be obtained. What is particularly important is the date of birth. With the date of birth, information can be supplied readily. Of course, this information is not always available but it may be obtained from other sources such as past employers, if known.

There is a fee involved for each search, and for persons who do large volume searches a charge account can be set up. Currently there is a one hundred dollar set up fee and reports can be requested by telephone. Each request is two dollars. You can request either a license or registration search. Further information can be obtained from the New York State Department of Motor Vehicles. Individual forms can be obtained from any local office and can be done by mail together with payment in advance.

Also obtainable is the code of the insurance company which can be followed up for financial information. Of course the automobile itself is an asset capable of being levied upon and sold at public auction to satisfy a judgment. It is not exempt property unless it can be shown to bear a special relationship to his/her work and then exempt under CPLR sec. 5025(a)7 as a working tool.[9]

IX. PROCESS SERVER

Collection work requires that every lead be followed and every piece of information be digested. The process server, having been to the home address or business, is a source of valuable information. When affidavits of service are submitted to you, a code relating to type of area and which banks are nearby should be worked out with your process server. Other information could also be obtained. Since there is need to sometimes talk with neighbors or landlords (pertaining to nonmilitary service affidavits), questions about employment should be asked. Process servers are paid and should be required to provide us with any useful information which can be applied toward the satisfaction of a judgment, especially if it requires no real additional work.

X. NEW YORK CITY AGENCY

If your debtor happens to be a member of the diplomatic community, the City of New York has an agency which acts as a liason between diplomats and the business community. It is called the New York City Commission for the United Nations and Consular Corp., located at 809 United Nations Plaza, New York, New York 10017.

A letter addressed to the agency, together with a copy of your judgment asking them to intercede, is all that is necessary. They will write to the Ambassador of the appropriate mission and request assistance in seeing that just debts are satisfied. A copy of that letter will be sent to you.

XI. POST OFFICE

The post office can also be helpful in locating a debtor. A letter sent to the last known home address marked "address correction requested" will get you the forwarding address for a fee of twenty-five cents. The post office also has a procedure for obtaining a home address where the mailing address is a post office box number. If the post office box is used by a business, the public can obtain the mailing address without a fee. If it is a residence, only certain persons are entitled to obtain this information, such as persons authorized by law to serve legal process. (*See* Appendix A.) Also available is the name and address of the holder of a postage meter permit. For those people who send letters to you and use their employer's postage meter, the name and address where they are working can be obtained. All of these procedures can be requested from the Regional Director of the post office, which constitutes part of the Administrative Support Manual. Most local post offices have their own interpretations regarding post office regulations. The regional office should always be contacted for the proper interpretation in the form of a letter which can be sent along with your request to those post offices which are unfamiliar with the interpretation.

XII. UNIONS

Knowledge of the type of work the debtor does can determine the debtor's place of employment if he/she belongs to a union. Knowledge that the debtor is a carpenter or electrician means that it is likely he/she is a union member. Contact with the union can give you information about his/her current employment. It will also reveal if he/she is a paid up member, which would indicate that he/she still is employed in this line of work. Many union contracts provide for vacation money to accumulate and some of that can be reached by restraining notice and income execution. Other union benefits such as pensions could also be revealed. Whether pensions are subject to execution is cloudy.

A question to be decided is whether the federal government has, under the Federal Employment Retirement Income Security Act[10] (commonly known as ERISA, which governs pensions), pre-empted New York State Law on enforcement of money judgments and has prohibited execution thereon.

The First Department has held that such plans are entirely exempt under federal law. *Helmsley Spear Inc. v. Winter.*[11] The Second Department has held that although 90 percent of the income is exempt, there is no absolute pre-emption by virtue of ERISA's supersedure clause.[12] A 1981 federal case in the Ninth Circuit has held that garnishment of ERISA benefits for a spouse is not pre-empted by federal law. Also in *Plymouth Rock Fuel Corp. v. Bank of New York,*[13] the court held that assets belonging to a judgment debtor held by a custodian under a "Keough" profit sharing plan are subject to garnishment, levy or execution by general creditors.

XIII. SUBPOENAS

When you have no specific information regarding assets from which a judgment can be enforced, or it cannot be obtained voluntarily, then the disclosure devices of the CPLR should be utilized. Section 5223 allows disclosure "of all matters relevant to the satisfaction of the judgment." The devices used are subpoenas, which can be issued at any time prior to a judgment being satisfied or vacated.

The authority to examine is very broad and allows examination of the judgment debtor or of anyone who may be in possession of property belonging to the judgment debtor or persons who may have knowledge relevant to locating assets which are subject to enforcement under section 5201.

In the case of *Chemical Bank v. Sinoto,*[14] the court went so far as to force an attorney to reveal the address of his client, the judgment debtor. The court held that although there is an attorney-client relationship that could prevent the disclosure of confidential communication, the information "must be a confidential communication made to the attorney for the purpose of obtaining legal advice or services." There was no showing of that in this case.

It has also been held proper for a certified social worker to disclose names and addresses of persons constituting his/her account receivable.[15]

The subpoena must specify all of the parties to the action, contain the date and amount of the judgment as entered, the current balance due and the court in which it was entered. There must also be a statement that false swearing or failure to comply with the subpoena is punishable as a contempt of court.

There are three kinds of subpoenas. Any or all can be used. The first is the subpoena *ad testificandum*, requiring attendance for the taking of testimony upon oral or written questions. This provides a face to face confrontation with the person from whom you are seeking information and allows you to develop your line of questioning depending upon answers to previous questions.

The second is a subpoena *ducus tecum* requiring the production of books and records to be examined. When examining some witnesses such as the judgment debtor, you want both his/her testimony and books and records.

The third and perhaps the most useful for doing collection work is the information subpoena. The first two subpoenas are served in the same manner as a summons and are therefore governed by CPLR sec. 2303.

At least ten days notice is required for a deposition upon oral or written questions or an examination of books and records. The court can order a shorter notice, if it deems it warranted. The examination shall be held during regular business hours. If the party being examined is a party or officer, director, member or employee of a party, the examination must be noticed within the county where he/she resides, has an office for the regular transaction of business in person, or where the action is pending. For other witnesses, the place of examination depends on whether they are residents or not. If a resident, then in the county where they reside or are regularly employed or have an office for the regular transaction of business in person. If a nonresident, the examination shall be noticed to take place in the county where served, or regularly employed or where there is an office for the regular transaction of business in person.

If the person to be examined is a public corporation or officer, agent, or employee thereof, the examination is held in the court within the county where the action is pending. Parties may stipulate otherwise.

Depositions are usually taken before a notary public but cannot be taken before an attorney or employee of an attorney for a party or someone related by blood or affinity to a party.

There is no fee when a judgment debtor is subpoened. Others shall receive one day's attendance fee, currently two dollars, plus eight cents for each mile as travel expenses to the place where served and return.[16] If travel is wholly within a city, there is no mileage fee.

The examination is taken under oath. Since the main thrust of the examination is to discover assets or information leading to assets, it is better to write the questions and answers in longhand in order to save the expense of obtaining a stenographer. There are also a number of Blumberg forms that can be bought in any legal stationery store with questions for individual debtor, corporate debtor, third parties and financial institutions.

Any objections to the proceeding shall be noted, but the examination shall proceed subject to the right of the person to apply for a protective order. It is a good practice to notice examinations at the courthouse so in the event the witness or debtor refuses to answer a question, an application for a ruling can be made right there. Although the deposition shall be taken continuously and without unreasonable adjournment, the court can order it or the witness can agree. If the witness is the judgment debtor and does agree, it should be adjourned to a date to be agreed upon or a future date long enough to analyze and verify the answers already given. This is important since you cannot subpoena the judgment debtor or compel him/her to produce books and records within one year after the completion of a previous examination without leave of court,[17] which may not be granted freely without a strong showing of a compelling reason. It is interesting to note that no such restriction is placed upon a witness other than the judgment debtor. Thus protection is afforded to the person who owes money, but not to someone who may only have information. Of course, if they believe they are being harassed unnecessarily, they can apply to the court for a protective order.[18] The court can modify, deny or limit any enforcement procedure. It can also supervise the disclosure procedure itself or through a referee or attorney selected by the parties.[19] On the other hand, a restraining notice can only be served once upon the same person with respect to the same judgment without leave of court.[20] Thus you can examine a witness who may be in possession of property belonging to the judgment debtor more than once in a year, but can only serve a restraining notice once in a lifetime without leave of court.

After the deposition is taken, it is read to the witness and then signed by him/her, after making any changes in form or substance with a statement of the reason for the changes. The changes are entered at the end of the deposition.

The information subpoena is probably used more often by attorneys doing volume collection work than any other type of subpoena. It is more efficient, less costly and can be used to obtain certain information quickly. The information subpoena under the Civil Practice Act was intended to obtain information only from financial institutions regarding a judgment debtor's holding. There is no restriction under the CPLR and although it is still used to obtain information from financial institutions, it can be used to obtain information from any source relevant to the satisfaction of the judgment.

An information subpoena contains the same information as the other two and can also be served in the same manner as a summons. However, a big advantage is that it can be served by registered or certified mail, return receipt requested. Certified mail is less expensive than registered mail and less expensive than serving through a process server, considering the fees they get today. The subpoena is accompanied by an original and copy of a set of questions and a prepaid, self-addressed return envelope.

The answers must refer to the question to which it responds, and be made under oath. Answers must be returned with the original questions within seven days after receipt.

Except where the person subpoenaed is a debtor, a fee of fifty cents must accompany the subpoena in order to cover the cost of the notarial fee because the answers must be under oath. Where the judgment creditor is the state, municipality or an agency or office of either, the fee of course is waived.

When using subpoenas to discover assets it is wise to utilize the provisions of CPLR sec. 5222 relating to restraining notices. The restraining notice can be served simultaneously with the subpoena and in fact can be combined in one form. (*See* Appendix B.) This is particularly useful when serving banks or financial institutions. If you should discover assets by way of the subpoena, the restraining notice prohibits the transfer of any property which can allow you time to levy upon the asset and make it applicable toward the satisfaction of your judgment.

The restraining notice does nothing more than "freeze" the asset. It does not give priority to a judgment creditor, but allows him/her to select one of the other judgment enforcement proceedings to obtain priority, such as issuing a property execution to a sheriff or moving for a turnover order. In any case, time is of the essence and the subpoena and restraining notice should be combined whenever possible.

When examining the judgment debtor bear in mind that there is a high degree of probability that he/she will not be entirely candid, if there are assets. It stands to reason that if an examination is necessary, no real effort has been made to satisfy the judgment, and the judgment debtors are in no hurry to part with their money. If the judgment debtor is truly judgment proof, the examination will probably go smoother.

Think of the examination as an accountant preparing a balance sheet. In addition to discovering assets, check all liabilities, such as rent, family needs for food, clothing, transportation and telephone. A person's income must add up to at least what he/she needs to survive.

A person cannot tell you he/she pays rent of five hundred dollars a month and only has income from unemployment insurance of one hundred dollars a week. The answers must make enough sense that the debtor convinces you he/she can survive. More than likely, there are other sources of income such as from family or friends or bank accounts or odd jobs. Always ask for verification. Check the lease to see what the rent is, and check with the landlord to see if it has been paid. The landlord is a good source of information. Landlords generally take some credit information and will at least be able to give you a last known place of employment or a checking account if the rent is paid by check.

If the debtor no longer resides at the address given, the landlord can probably advise the date of departure. This could be important for skip tracing. One of the neighbors may have knowledge of the new address or even know the name of the moving company used. Those records can be subpoenaed to obtain the new address.

When examining the judgment debtor, always seek the production of tax returns pertaining at least to the three previous years. Requests to produce records going back beyond the time when the obligation was incurred would be unreasonable and could be met with a protective order. Recent returns are surely relevant, and can be subpoenaed from the accountant of the judgment debtor even if it was a joint return. In the case of *Siemens & Halske v. Gres*,[21] the judgment debtor was outside the jurisdiction of the court. The joint tax return was with the accountant within the jurisdiction and a subpoena *duces tecum* was served upon him. The court in citing *Leonard v. Wargon*[22] stated the public policy as "to put no obstacle in the path of one seeking to secure the enforcement of a judgment of a court of competent jurisdiction."

The tax returns can help you obtain information about current sources of income and can provide you with the basis for a line of questions regarding the disposal of assets. A transfer of assets may be fraudulent and subject to recovery by the judgment creditor. Questions pertaining to the concealment of assets or transferred assets in fraud of creditors are relevant to the satisfaction of the judgment. Under the Debtor and Creditor Law, if a conveyance is made or an obligation incurred which renders the judgment debtor insolvent, it is fraudulent if made without fair consideration. Actual intent to defraud need not be shown.[23] For example, if a judgment debtor transfers a house to a spouse for love and affection, it is fraudulent if it renders him/her insolvent and can be overturned.

Similarly, any conveyance made without fair consideration by a defendant during the pendency of an action which has been docketed is fraudulent as to the plaintiff without regard to actual intent if the judgment is not satisfied.[24] Accordingly, after the action has been commenced, any transfer of assets to a third party by the defendant can be reached by the judgment creditor. Conveyances by business persons which leave relatively small capital are fraudulent if made without fair consideration.[25]

If a person believes he/she is about to incur debts, conveyances are fraudulent if made without fair consideration.[26] This is of course more difficult to establish since it deals with intent. The line of questions will be geared to discover intent or at least lead to the inescapable conclusion that the conveyance was made with intent to defraud.

It is not necessary to move to set aside a fraudulent conveyance on a matured claim. Execution against the property conveyed can be maintained.[28] Such execution is of course subject to the rights of third parties to intercede.[29]

In many instances the judgment debtor will not appear for an examination even though properly served with a subpoena. This follows since most judgments are obtained on default also. In the field of collection work, it is an acceptable fact that the judgment debtors are not going to be very cooperative and help you to satisfy your judgment. Some will be cooperative, but most will not. The courts, from which a special proceeding can be commenced, are empowered to punish for contempt. Failure to obey a subpoena or false swearing to oral or written questions is punishable as a contempt of court. It is during such instances of noncompliance by judgment debtors that creditors must resort to contempt procedures in order to give substance to the provisions designed to aid in the enforcement of a judgment.

As previously mentioned, the information subpoena is the most useful and effective weapon in the entire discovery arsenal. This is so because of its basic simplicity. A set of questions is mailed and answers are received through the mail. Of course there are some problems. Since it must be signed for, the subpoena may be returned as unclaimed. It cannot be resent by ordinary mail.[30] Answers received may be incomplete or ambiguous.

The most common instances where an information subpoena is used is for verification of a place of employment or upon a banking institution. Most employers will answer a subpoena although it may not be within the seven days required. Some take a month or more and require a follow-up letter. The information asked for should pertain to current employment, salary, social security number, home address and telephone number. If not currently employed, you want to know the last day worked and whether they know where he/she is currently employed. Many past employers have records pertaining to new employment of the debtor.

Employers usually know a current home address since a W-2 form for income taxes would have been mailed for that portion of the year worked. Another very important question that must not be overlooked is whether there are any income executions currently against the salary or wages. There may be so many others as to make collection through income execution virtually impossible since there can only be one in operation at a time. In such a case, and if the amount of income warrants it, you might consider proceeding by way of an installment payment order.[31] An installment payment order can operate at the same time as an income execution.

Some places of employment will not answer the questions as outlined. Instead they may send you a response on their own letterhead stating that the judgment debtor is no longer employed. In other cases the answers may not be sworn to or even signed by the person who answered them. It is not easy to tell if this is done out of carelessness or as a cover-up. Usually a telephone call insisting upon compliance is enough or a follow-up letter enclosing a duplicate set of questions and answers with a reminder that failure to honor the subpoena is a contempt of court will suffice. Because there is no control as to who will receive a subpoena served upon a place of business by mail, it is not unlikely that the judgment debtor will wind up with it. In such a case it may go unanswered or the answers will be fabricated. This is why insistance upon the answers being notarized should be adhered to.

The post office requires subpoenas to be "so ordered" by a judge even though an attorney has the authority to issue same.

Banks rarely respond properly to an information subpoena. Usually they have their own form which is answered and returned. The emphasis is upon whether there are any active accounts belonging to the judgment debtor and the amounts in them that they have restrained. Also important is whether the bank, pursuant to Debtor and Creditor Law section 151, has any set-off against the account, which is a superior right.[32] In the case of *Industrial Commissioner v. South Shore Amusements, Inc.*,[33] the court held that:

> The appellant's right of set-off terminated with the levy. There is nothing in Section 151 which requires the nullification of such levy. While the section provides for right of set off notwithstanding the

fact that such right of set off shall not have been exercised by such debtor prior to the issuance of execution, it does not provide for such right after levy.

In some instances the bank may have information about current employment of the judgment debtor. You of course want to know whether there is a safe deposit box in which the judgment debtor has an interest. If the debtor will not open it voluntarily, the creditor will have to pay for a locksmith. Since the information subpoena is combined with a restraining notice, all assets up to twice the judgment amount are restrained. This is so even if the account is a joint account. There is a rebuttable presumption that all monies restrained in a joint account belong to the judgment debtor. In the case of *Denton v. Grumbach*,[34] the court stated that in a joint account there is a rebuttable presumption that the interest of the depositors are that of joint tenants. Joint tenants are said to be seized by the half and the whole. Therefore an attachment against the whole is proper.

Another problem is proper service upon a bank. Since banks generally have branches scattered all over, the question arises as to which bank constitutes proper service. In New York the law was well settled that proper service upon a bank consisted of serving the branch where the account was located.[35]

In *National Shipping and Trading Corp. v. Weeks Stevedoring Company*,[36] the court held that "each branch of a bank is a separate and distinct business entity." The court explained that unless each branch were treated separately, constant checking with other branches would have to be made before any check could be paid. This would be a detriment to normal banking procedures.

In 1980 along with the advancing technology in high speed computers came the case of *Digitrex Inc. v. Johnson*.[37] This was a federal case interpreting New York Law. This court reviewed the previous New York rule and, pursuaded by counsel for Manufacturers Hanover Bank, decided that service upon the main branch of a bank utilizing high speed computers with central indexing capabilities "promotes rather than endangers the orderly transaction of banking business."

The court then took judicial notice of the fact that most, if not all, New York City commercial banks have become largely computerized as described and rejected the previous rule:

> We do not believe that the New York courts would today perpetuate an obsolete interpretation of the attachment statute which would . . . not only render creditors remedies less effective but interfere with the orderly business of the very banking institution the interpretation was originally designed to protect. Believing that New York courts would today act in a sensible fashion, certainly the federal courts should not have to wait until some state court litigant brings a case to appellate attention before doing likewise.

It now appeared that New York had a new rule regarding service on a bank. Those that thought so were premature. In an excellent article in the *New York Law Journal* by Bradley E. Rock, Esq.,[38] the author points out that a broad interpretation of the *Digitrex* case would be unwise. In the *Digitrex* case the attack came from a judgment debtor whose account was restrained by service upon the main office. It is unlikely that a bank would be held liable for failing to honor a restraint if served at the main office instead of the branch where the account is located. The author points to the Uniform Commericial Code Section 4-106 which provides: "A branch or separate office of a bank is a separate bank for the purpose of . . . determining the place at or to which action may be taken or notices or orders shall be given under this Article and Article 3." Also added was another sentence: "The receipt of any notice or order by or the knowledge of one branch or separate office of a bank is not actual or constructive notice to or knowledge of any other branch or office of the same bank."

Not all banks have the capabilities discussed in the *Digitrex* case, and so in 1981, the court found in *Therm X Chemical & Oil Corp. v. Extebank*[39] that service upon the main branch was not sufficient to hold the bank liable for failing to restrain an account located at a branch without showing the branch received actual notice.

When dealing with a large bank equipped with sophisticated electronic equipment, service upon the main branch may get you the desired results faster, if you have no knowledge as to in which branch a debtor maintains an account, but you will not be able to hold the bank liable in the event they honor checks and withdrawals after service. Because service of information subpoenas and restraining notices are relatively inexpensive, it pays to take a chance on serving main offices of large banks in the hope that the judgment debtor has an account with the bank that can be discovered.

The combination of information subpoena and restraining notice can also be served upon a credit union. Many employers have set up credit unions for the benefit of their employees. Sometimes knowing the field of work a debtor is in can lead you to a credit union and assets. For example, if you suspect that a person works for the City of New York, but do not have specific knowledge as to the actual job, a restraint and subpoena directed toward the Municipal Credit Union may produce results. Not only might you restrain monies on deposit, but you can learn exactly where the debtor is employed and proceed to income execution.

Other important providers of information are unions, utilities such as the telephone company, and medical plans such as Blue Cross. The telephone company takes credit information when installing a telephone and if it is a relatively new installment, the information can be current. (*See* Appendix C.) Usually they have bank information as well as employment.

If there is a active Blue Cross policy and it happens to be a group plan paid for by an employer, this information can be obtained. It is necessary to have a social security number to obtain this information since the policy number is the same as the social security number. Sometimes an information subpoena is used to obtain the social security number from a previous employer and then Blue Cross can be checked.

It is not easy to discover assets and attention must be paid to every detail. You never know what piece of information will lead to discovery. Sometimes you will find yourself tracking leads like a detective lookin~

for clues. It is time consuming and can be expensive. How much effort is put into it must be weighed very carefully against the potential recovery. There is nothing more frustrating than spending time and effort in locating a debtor and assets and then discovering that the debtor has filed for bankruptcy. There are times that a debtor will threaten to file for bankruptcy and not do it until you have actually levied upon a bank account or instituted an income execution.

Most of the avenues outlined above are geared toward discovering a debtor's place of employment or bank account. It is through these two assets that most judgments are satisfied. Other assets can be discovered but are not as readily available and execution against them may be cumbersome and expensive. There will always be a need for attorneys to enforce collection of judgments. How successful you are is directly proportional to the effort you are willing to put in and the ability to interpret the information at your disposal. Locating the assets is only the first step. It is the enforcement devices which will lead to the satisfaction of the judgment.

Footnotes

[1] CPLR sec. 5201(a)(b).

[2] *Glassman v. Hyder*, 23 N.Y.2d 354, 296 N.Y.S.2d 783, 244 N.E.2d 259 (1968).

[3] Siegel, Practice Commentaries, McKinney's Consolidated Laws of New York, Book 7B, CPLR 5201:5 p. 53.

[4] *Gilchrist v. Commercial Credit Corp.*, 66 Misc. 2d 791, 322 N.Y.S.2d 200 (1971).

[5] 39 N.Y.2d 670, 385 N.Y.S.2d 511, 350 N.E.2d 899 (1976).

[6] RPL sec. 339-G.

[7] *First Federal Savings & Loan Association of Rochester v. Brown*, 78 A.D.2d 119, 434 N.Y.S.2d 306 (1980).

[8] CPLR sec. 5201(c).

[9] *Thorpe Elec. Supply, Inc. v. Deitz*, 104 Misc. 2d 994, 429 N.Y.S.2d 386 (1980).

[10] 29 U.S.C.A. sec. 1001 *et seq.*

[11] 74 A.D.2d 195, 426 N.Y.S.2d 778 (1980).

[12] *National Bank of North America v. International Brotherhood of Electrical Workers Local No. 3*, 93 Misc. 2d 590, 400 N.Y.S.2d 482 (1977), *aff'd*, 69 A.D.2d 679, 419 N.Y.S.2d 127, *appeal dismissed*, 48 N.Y.2d 752, 422 N.Y.S.2d 666, 397 N.E.2d 1333 (1979).

[13] 102 Misc. 2d 235, 425 N.Y.S.2d 908 (1979).

[14] N.Y.L.J. December 1, 1981, col. 3.

[15] *Scherz v. Scherz*, 110 Misc. 2d 137, 442 N.Y.S.2d 41 (1981).

[16] CPLR sec. 8002(a).

[17] CPLR sec. 5224(f).

[18] CPLR sec. 5240.

[19] CPLR sec. 3104(a)(b).

[20] CPLR sec. 5222(c).

[21] 37 A.D.2d 768, 324 N.Y.S.2d 639 (1971).

[22] 55 N.Y.S.2d 626 (1945).

[23] N.Y. Debtor and Creditor Law sec. 273.

[24] *Id.*, sec. 273-a.

[25] *Id.*, sec. 274.

[26] *Id.*, sec. 275.

[27] *Id.*, sec. 276.

[28] *Id.*, sec. 278(b).

[29] *Simon v. Bailey*, 172 Misc. 186, 14 N.Y.S.2d 822 (1939).

[30] *Carl v. Moyer*, 63 Misc. 2d 1052, 313 N.Y.S.2d 936 (1970).

[31] CLPR sec. 5226.

[32] *Aspen Industries, Inc. v. Marine Midland Bank*, 52 N.Y.2d 575, 439 N.Y.S.2d 316 (1981).

[33] *Industrial Commissioner v. South Shore Amusements Inc.*, 55 A.D.2d 141, 389 N.Y.S.2d 850 (1976).

[34] 2 A.D.2d 420, 157 N.Y.S.2d 91 (1956)

[35] *Bluebird Undergarment Corp. v. Gomez*, 139 Misc. 742, 249 N.Y.S. 319 (City Court, 1931); *Cronan v. Schilling*, 31 Misc.2d 759 100 N.Y.S.2d 474, *aff'd*, 282 A.D. 940, 126 N.Y.S.2d 192 (1950).

[36] 252 F. Supp. 275 (SDNY 1966).

[37] 491 F. Supp. 66 (SDNY 1980).

[38] Rock, "Proper Place to Serve Restraining Notice on Bank," N.Y.L.J., May 14, 1981, p. 1, cols. 2-3.

[39] 84 A.D.2d 787 (1981)

Appendix A

FORSTER & GARBUS
ATTORNEYS AT LAW
NASSAU PLAZA
ONE FULTON AVENUE
HEMPSTEAD, N. Y. 11550

RONALD FORSTER
MARK A. GARBUS

AREA CODE (516)
481-9800
AREA CODE (212)
895-5650

Date:

Postmaster

Re:
vs.
P.O. Box
Our File No.

Dear Sir/Madam:

This is to advise that we represent the above-referenced plaintiff.

Pursuant to Administrative Support Manual 352.44(e)(2), we are requesting the street address of the above box holder (defendant).

I certify that the information is required for me to effect service of legal process upon the box holder (defendant).

Our return envelope is provided for your reply.

Very truly yours,

FORSTER & GARBUS

By____________________________
RONALD FORSTER

Enc.

FG-5

Appendix B

County of **Court**

Index No.

INFORMATION SUBPOENA
WITH
RESTRAINING NOTICE
TO GARNISHEE

Plaintiff

against

Re: ____________________
Judgment Debtor

Address:

S.S. No.:
Account No.:

Defendant

The People of the State of New York

TO:
ADDRESS:

Garnishee: GREETING:

WHEREAS, *in action in the* *Court:*
County of *between*
plaintiff(s) and
defendant(s)
who are all the parties named in said action, a judgment was entered *19* *in favor of Judgment* *Creditor(s) and against Judgment Debtor(s) in the amount of $* *of which $* *together with interest thereon from* *19* *remains unpaid:*

NOW THEREFORE, WE COMMAND YOU, *that you answer in writing under oath, separately and fully, each question in the questionnaire accompanying this subpoena, and that you return the original questions and answers within seven (7) days after your receipt of this subpoena.*

FALSE SWEARING OR FAILURE TO COMPLY WITH THIS SUBPOENA IS PUNISHABLE AS A CONTEMPT OF COURT.

TAKE NOTICE THAT, *pursuant to Section 5222(b) of the Civil Practice Law and Rules, you are hereby FORBIDDEN TO MAKE OR SUFFER ANY TRANSFER OR OTHER DISPOSITION OF ANY PROPERTY IN WHICH JUDGMENT DEBTOR(S) HAS OR MAY HAVE ANY INTEREST, OR TO PAY OVER OR OTHERWISE DISPOSE OF ANY MONEYS DUE OR TO BECOME DUE TO JUDGMENT DEBTOR(S), except as therein provided.*

DISOBEDIENCE OF THIS RESTRAINING NOTICE IS PUNISHABLE AS A CONTEMPT OF COURT.

DATED:

NOTE:

Section 5222 (b) OF THE CIVIL PRACTICE LAW AND RULES.

Effect of restraint; prohibition of transfer; duration. A judgment debtor served with a restraining notice is forbidden to make or suffer any sale, assignment, transfer or interference with any property in which he has an interest, except upon direction of the sheriff or pursuant to an order of the court, until the judgment is satisfied or vacated. A restraining notice served upon a person other than the judgment debtor is effective only if, at the time of service, he owes a debt to the judgment debtor or he is in the possession or custody of property in which he knows or has reason to believe the judgment debtor has an interest, or if the judgment creditor has stated in the notice that a specified debt is owed by the person served to the judgment debtor or that the judgment debtor has an interest in specified property in the possession or custody of the person served. All property in which the judgment debtor is known or believed to have an interest then in and thereafter coming into the possession or custody of such a person, including any specified in the notice, and all debts of such a person, including any specified in the notice, then due and thereafter coming due to the judgment debtor, shall be subject to the notice. Such a person is forbidden to make or suffer any sale, assignment or transfer or, or any interference with, any such property, or pay over or otherwise dispose of any such debt, to any person other than the sheriff, except upon direction of the sheriff or pursuant to an order of the court, until the expiration of one year after the notice is served upon him, or until the judgment is satisfied or vacated, whichever event first occurs. A judgment creditor who has specified personal property or debt in a restraining notice shall be liable to the owner of the property or the person to whom the debt is owed, if other than the judgment debtor, for any damages sustained by reason of the restraint. If a garnishee served with a restraining notice withholds the payment of money belonging or owed to the judgment debtor in an amount equal to twice the amount due on the judgment, the restraining notice is not effective as to other property or money.

EMPLOYERS ANSWER NUMBERS 1,2,3,4,6,7,8,9,10,11,12,15 IN BACK OF THIS FORM

BANKS ANSWER ALL QUESTIONS

1-82

SEE REVERSE SIDE FOR QUESTIONS AND ANSWERS

QUESTIONS AND ANSWERS

STATE OF NEW YORK: COUNTY OF SS:

being duly sworn, deposes and says; that he is (officer; employer; landlord; tenant; relative) recipient of the within Information Subpoena, and original copy of questions thereon, and makes the following answers therto, from information and records of the recipient.

1. Q Is judgment debtor now employed by you? Q If not, when were they terminated?
   A .... A ....
   Capacity:
   Earnings:
   Social Security No.
   Badge No.

2. Q What is judgment debtor's full and correct name and social security number according to your records? (Note: social security number, if known, is listed on front). A ....

3. Q What is the correct name & address of your firm?
   A

4. Q What is judgment debtor(s) present home address and phone number?
   A

5. Q Are you holding any property of the judgment debtor(s), in which the judgment debtor(s) has an interest, in his own name, or with others, including but not limited to bank accounts, collateral, safe deposit box, debt, contract, lien, application, financial statement, security, or record of same, within one (1) year prior to the date hereof?
   A If yes, describe as indicated below:

exact title of a/c	amount held	date closed	value	collateral

6. Q Is judgment debtor(s) indebted to you? A...
   A If yes, describe as indicated below:

amount	date incurred	amount repaid	date repaid

7. Q Is judgment debtor receiving public assistance? A If so, give case #....................................

8. Q Are there any income executions, orliens against earnings presently in effect or awaiting placement?
   A If yes, give name(s) of judgment creditor(s); or lienor(s)-
   Name(s) of Marshal or Sheriff-
   Balance of each item:

9. Q Is judgment debtor(s) a stockholder or partner in your firm?
   A If yes, give details:

10. Q Do you maintain or contribute to a vacation fund, or severance fund for your employee including judgment debtor(s)?
    A If yes, give full details:

11. Q Is judgment debtor(s) a member of a union?
    A If yes, give name and address of union, union number, status of membership:

12. Q State the name and address of judgment debtor(s) present or last known employer.
    A

13. Q Are you the owner of premises located at--
    A

14. Q What is the monthly rental or carrying charges paid by judgment debtor(s)? State the amount of security you are holding
    A

15. Q Are you in any way related to judgment debtor(s) either by blood ties or through marriage?
    A If yes, state and

A A If yes, state said relationship:

Sworn to before me this
day of 198

____
(print name of signer below)

Appendix C

QUESTIONS AND ANSWERS

STATE OF NEW YORK: COUNTY OF ss

being duly sworn, deposes and says, that he is a security officer of the N.Y. Telephone Co., recipient of the within Information Subpoena, and original copy of questions thereon, and makes the following answers thereto, from information and records of the recipient.

SET FORTH FROM YOUR RECORDS & APPLICATION:

1. If an unlisted phone, the number is

2. Address & floor or Apt. # of telephone

3. Exact listing of telephone

4. Connect date of telephone

5. Billing dates & amounts, last two months

6. Date & amount of last payment

7. Credit service history

8. Reach numbers, names & locations

9. Additional listings

10. Customer's place of business

11. Customer's bank

Sworn to before me this
day of

CHAPTER TWELVE

PROCEDURES

Richard J. Miller, Esq.

I. OVERCOMING THE CONSTITUTIONAL CHALLENGE AS IT HAS SUCCEEDED

Now that we have given due consideration to the constitutional challenge brought to bear on CPLR Article 52, seemingly, the Bar has succeeded in allaying the objections raised. It is evident that the challenge at hand relates primarily to consumer cases. As a practical matter, sheriffs and other third parties in interest (such as bank employees, municipal authorities, insurance carriers, tenants, etc.) will decline to enforce a creditor's rights, absent proof of appropriate notification to the judgment debtor.

To this end, it is suggested that a special notice be forwarded to the judgment debtor immediately upon the entry of judgment, and, certainly, prior to invoking any enforcement measure. Exhibit 1 attached hereto will provide adequate notice, as that contemplated by the relatively recent legislative amendment to Article 52.

In addition to this special notice, it is advisable to forward proof of notification by a copy thereof plus an affidavit of service (as more fully described by Exhibit 2) to the sheriff or third party involved with the judgment debtor. This will obviate the need for any action on the sheriff's part, and will demonstrate that the judgment creditor has fully complied with the law as made and provided. Moreover, it is advisable to diary the file for a period of one year following service of the initial notification given, so that a subsequent notice may be given following the expiration of a year and prior to further enforcement measures if applicable (necessary).

It also should be noted, merely for the sake of procedure, that there is no method or statement of the mechanics by which the constitutional challenge is to be implemented or the exemption claimed. This being the case, it is anticipated that a debtor may well be slow to respond other than by a motion to vacate or set aside the judgment.

II. PROCEDURES TAKEN AGAINST THIRD PARTIES

A. Restraining Notice (with subpoena *duces tecum* and questionnaire)

1. Pursuant to CPLR sec. 5222, the judgment creditor's attorney may issue a restraining notice and serve it on the judgment debtor or a garnishee (one who owes the judgment debtor money or holds money or property in trust for the judgment debtor), as set forth in Exhibit 3. This notice acts to enjoin the transfer of any property belonging to or in which the debtor has an interest. Failure to heed the notice (effectively, an injunction) is punishable as contempt of court.

The purpose of the notice is to restrain the property in question until the opportunity can be gained to levy upon or seize it. The restraining notice is served either in the same manner as a summons or by registered or certified mail. It is effective against the judgment debtor until the judgment is satisfied or vacated; it is effective against a third party only if, at the time of service, the third party owes a debt to the judgment debtor or he/she is in the possession or custody of property in which the judgment debtor has an interest. Further, it is effective against a garnishee only until the expiration of one year after the notice is served upon him/her.

This measure ordinarily is employed with banks or tenants of a landlorddebtor. Leave of court is required to serve more than one restraining notice upon the same person with respect to the same judgment. It is followed by a property execution and notice to garnishee, if appropriate.

2. Kinds of subpoenas—pursuant to CPLR sec. 5224, three different and distinct types of subpoenas may be served with the restraining notice:

a. A subpoena requiring attendance for the taking of a deposition upon oral or written questions. *See* Exhibit 4;

b. A subpoena *duces tecum* requiring the production of books and papers for examination. *See* Exhibit 5;

c. An information subpoena accompanied by a copy and original of written questions and a prepaid addressed return envelope. *See* Exhibit 6.

To be noted is that virtually the most effective and practical combination of the foregoing is the restraining notice with subpoena *duces tecum* and questionnaire. Exhibit 7 attached hereto confirms the usefulness of this particular procedure and clarifies the mechanics of practice.

When using this procedure with respect to a bank, certain considerations must be kept in mind. Include a fifty-cent fee made payable to the bank; otherwise, the questionnaire will not be completed and returned as requested. Note that the general rule in New York is that the creditor must serve the branch where the account is or the bank will not be bound by the restraining notice, unless the bank is computerized. In the latter circumstance, the main office would be sufficient. *See Digitrix, Inc. v. Johnson*, 491 F. Supp. 66 (1980); *Therm-Chemical & Oil Corp. v. Extebank*, 84 A.D.2d 787 (1981).

B. Turnover Motions

1. Special proceedings for the payment or delivery of property of the judgment debtor—should a third party resist, refuse or fail to turn over property to the judgment creditor which is in the third party's possession or custody and in which the judgment debtor has an interest—may be brought by the judgment creditor as part of the action pending to require such person to comply. Exhibit 8 represents the preferable format; the papers are to be served on the judgment debtor, the garnishee and the sheriff, if involved, in the same manner as a summons or by registered or certified mail, return receipt requested.

To be noted here also is that CPLR sec. 5225(a), as compared with foregoing CPLR sec. 5225(b), applies to property in the possession of the judgment debtor, and that, pursuant to a special proceeding brought by the judgment creditor, the judgment debtor may be made subject to a delivery or payment order, directly.

2. Special proceedings for the payment of debts owed to the judgment debtor— Exhibit 9 depicts the procedure contemplated by CPLR sec. 5227. This proceeding is similar to CPLR sec. 5225, but is one commenced against any person who it is shown is, or will become, indebted to the judgment debtor.

Consider these special proceedings when seeking recovery of a bank account, rent and security deposits, insurance proceeds or accounts receivable. Again, they are not separate, independent lawsuits, but, rather, are to be brought within and as part of the action already reduced to judgment.

A word of caution: restraining notices may be served and turn over motions may be brought upon or against any person *except the employer* of a judgment debtor where the property sought to be restrained or seized consists of wages or salary due or to become due to the judgment debtor. *See* CPLR sec. 5222(a).

III. PROCEDURES TAKEN AGAINST THE JUDGMENT DEBTOR

A. Property Execution

1. Records search—prior to invoking section 5232 or section 5235 of the CPLR, it is advisable to conduct a search of the various records maintained in connection with personal and real property and fixtures. There is little advantage in levying upon and selling property if it is subject to a superior lien or interest. The following should be considered:

a. Mot. Veh. sec. 901 relative to 1973 or newer vehicles required to be registered (titled) with the Department of Motor Vehicles. *See* Exhibit 10.

b. UCC form 3 for older model vehicles, personal property and fixtures. *See* Exhibit 11.

c. Abstract (stubsearch) for update on title to real estate.

Of course, even if it is determined that there is a prior lien or superior interest, this does not necessarily mean that the property execution should be withdrawn. Inquire as to the balance, if any, on the obligation in question and then make the decision as to how to proceed.

2. Identify property—it is always helpful to the sheriff or marshal if specific property is identified in relation to the execution issued. An example of this is found in Exhibit 12 attached hereto.

3. Nature of property—some obvious examples of property subject to this type of execution are as follows:

a. Vehicles

b. Equipment and Inventory

c. Fixtures and Real Estate

d. Bank Accounts and Safe Deposit Boxes

e. Machinery

f. Accounts Receivable

g. Insurance Proceeds

h. Generally, Tangible and Intangible Personal Property

4. Time limitations—ordinarily a property execution must be returned by the sheriff or marshal within 60 days after it is issued. Nonetheless, it is recognized that the execution can be levied on personal property in two different ways. If the property is capable of delivery, the sheriff

levies upon it by taking it into his/her custody. This is a levy by seizure under CPLR sec. 5232(b); the execution then is governed by the 60-day provision period.

On the other hand, if the property is not capable of delivery, the sheriff is to serve a copy of the execution on the party in possession of the property (garnishee) in the same manner as a summons. *See* CPLR sec. 5232(a). In this instance, the garnishee has 90 days within which to transfer the property to the sheriff; if the transfer is not made within the 90-day period, the execution is to be returned.

Therefore, it is important either to enforce the execution or have it extended so that it may be enforced; otherwise, it will be returned "unsatisfied." The 60-day period may be extended by the judgment creditor's attorney once, as a matter of right. *See* CPLR sec. 5230(c).

A levy upon real property is governed by CPLR sec. 5235. A levy in this case involves neither a seizure nor the service of the execution on a third party. But such an execution also must be pursued with the sheriff or it, too, will be returned by the sheriff, "unsatisified."

5. Selling the property—for the purposes of sale, attention should be given to the detail set forth in the following sections of the CPLR:

a. CPLR sec. 5233—sale of personal property;

b. CPLR sec. 5234—distribution of proceeds of personal property, priorities;

c. CPLR sec. 5236—sale of real property.

As an incidental note, reference should be made to Exhibit 13 when proceeding against real estate. The proposed format ordinarily encourages the sheriff to take the execution seriously and follow through with the attorney acting on behalf of the creditor. Executions levied against real estate are cumbersome and involve significantly more work of the sheriff than other duties performed by that office.

6. Exempt property—not all property belonging to or claimed by a judgment creditor is subject to execution. Various items of personal property as well as certain realty are exempt. Before proceeding toward the satisfaction of a judgment by means of a property execution, care should be taken to review the following provisions of the CPLR:

a. CPLR sec. 5205—personal property exempt from application to the satisfaction of money judgments;

b. CPLR sec. 5206—real property exempt from application to the satisfaction of money judgments;

c. CPLR sec. 5207—enforcement involving the State;

d. CPLR sec. 5208—enforcement after death of judgment debtor, leave of court, extension of lien.

As a point of information, personal bankruptcy exemptions claimed by a debtor involved in an insolvency proceeding under the Bankruptcy Code now are restricted to those enumerated under Article 10-A of the Debtor and Creditor Law. *See* Exhibit 14.

B. Income Execution

1. Restraining notice—again, consider the proscription of CPLR sec. 5222 against restraining wages or salary due or to become due to the judgment debtor. In this regard, however, a close question often arises when the judgment creditor encounters money earned by a judgment debtor in irregular installment payments, through a tax shelter, periodic payments from a municipality or governmental agency or under a construction contract.

2. Form of income execution—pursuant to CPLR sec. 5231, a judgment creditor may issue an income execution, *see* Exhibit 15, to the sheriff of the county in which the judgment debtor resides (or, where he/she is a nonresident, the county in which he/she is employed), con-

taining a notice to the judgment debtor that he/she shall commence payment of the installments specified to the sheriff and that, upon his/her default, the execution will be served upon the person from whom he/she is receiving or will receive money.

3. The wage requirements—subdivision (b) of CPLR sec. 5231 has been pre-empted by Federal Law. The $85.01 criteria is no longer the hard and fast rule to be used in determining if a judgment debtor qualifies; the judgment creditor now must look to the Federal Wage Garnishment Law. *See* 15 U.S.C. sec. 1671, *et seq.* as more fully expressed in Exhibit 16 attached hereto. Federal Law now requires that the judgment debtor earn at least $100.51, take-home, which would thereby entitle the judgment creditor to:

a. 10% of the gross wage earned; or

b. 25% of the net wage earned; or

c. The amount earned over $100.50, whichever is the least.

(Note: Legislation presently is pending in the New York State Legislature to amend CPLR sec. 5231(b) to conform to the Federal provisions; it is anticipated that, following a series of amendments to the bills proposed, a law will be enacted which will track the Federal Wage Garnishment Law. At this time, the proposed (S.2622-B/A.2957-A) eliminates inconsistent references to net and gross wage. These bills tend not to alter the current New York standard of 10 percent; *Dreary* is being challenged as unconstitutional.)

4. The two stages—the income execution is issued to the sheriff for service on the judgment debtor (and his/her employer, upon a default in payment) in the same manner as a summons or by certified mail, return receipt requested:

a. On the debtor—within 20 days after an income execution is delivered to the sheriff, the sheriff shall serve a copy of it upon the judgment debtor.

b. On the employer—if a judgment debtor fails to pay installments pursuant to an income execution served upon him/her for a period of 20 days, or if the sheriff is unable to serve an income execution upon the judgment debtor within 20 days after the execution is delivered to the sheriff, the sheriff shall levy upon the money that the judgment debtor is receiving or will receive by serving a copy of the income execution upon the person from whom the judgment debtor is receiving or will receive money.

5. Miscellaneous considerations—when employing this particular enforcement device, it is advisable to refer to the following points in the nature of practice guides:

a. If there is a default in the first stage and the employer is in the same county (ordinarily the debtor's residence), the same sheriff will serve the employer; if the employer is in a different county, the first sheriff will (or should) return the execution unsatisifed, and the judgment creditor's attorney then will have to forward it to the sheriff of the employer's county.

b. If the judgment debtor is a nonresident, the execution may be delivered directly to the sheriff of the employer's county.

c. If the debtor resides either within or without the State of New York, and is employed outside of the State of New York, but the employer has a place of business within the State of New York, refer to Exhibit 17 attached hereto.

d. The United States Postal Service (and correspondingly, its employees) is not immune from commercial garnishment proceedings to enforce judgments in state courts. Garnishment proceedings are within the scope of the United States Postal Service's authorization to "sue and be sued." *See* 39 U.S.C. 401(1).

e. The majority opinion is that an employer is required to make simultaneous deductions from an employee-judgment debtor's wages pursuant to an income execution and concurrent Family Court payroll deduction support order. *See Costa v. Chevrolet-Tonawanda, Division of General Motors Corp.*, 53 Misc. 2d 252 (1963), *aff'd*, 24 A.D.2d 732 (1965); *Manufacturers and Traders Trust Company v. Forestville*, 57 Misc. 2d 973 (1968); *Lincoln Nat. Bank & Trust Co. v. Colgan*, 71 Misc. 2d 908 (1972); *Southampton Hospital Association v. Hampton Cablevision Corp.*, 64 Misc. 2d 998 (1970); section 49-b of the Personal Property Law (McKinney as interpreted by the Attorney General 22 Op. Att'y Gen. (1968)).

f. Where a judgment creditor has issued an income execution to a sheriff, which states that there remains unpaid on the judgment a specified sum with interest thereon from the date of judgment, the sheriff has the duty to compute and collect the additional interest due on the judgment from the date of the judgment. *See Beneficial Discount Co. of New York, Inc. v. Spike*, 91 Misc. 2d 733 (1977); CPLR sec. 2223.

g. If a sheriff returns an execution without collecting the interest due on the judgment, but has not filed a satisfaction piece with the County Clerk, a new income execution may be issued for service and filing to collect the balance due; if a sheriff returns an execution without collecting the interest due on the judgment, but has in fact satisfied the judgment of record by filing a satisfaction piece with the County Clerk, the judgment creditor may move to vacate the satisfaction of judgment and, thereafter, reissue the execution. *See* Exhibit 18.

h. Where an employer dismisses or lays off an employee to avoid compliance with an income execution, *see* CPLR sec. 5252.

C. Installment Payment Orders

1. Purpose—CPLR sec. 5226 permits a judgment creditor to apply to the Court for an order directing that the judgment debtor make specified installment payments to the judgment creditor, where it is shown that the judgment debtor is receiving or will receive money from any source. *See* Exhibit 19. This device is used primarily where:

a. The judgment debtor ostensibly is rendering services without adequate compensation;

b. The judgment debtor appears to be concealing income;

c. The judgment debtor is self-employed;

d. The judgement debtor has succeeded in avoiding an income execution by reason of his/her position with the employer (as the general manager);

e. The judgment debtor can afford more than the terms of an income execution will provide.

2. Preliminary disclosure—before applying to the court for an installment payment order, it is advisable to examine the judgment debtor in order to obtain the necessary details to sustain the application:

a. Special information subpoena. *See* Exhibit 20 attached hereto;

b. Personal examination by deposition. *See* Exhibit 4 attached hereto.

Both subpoenas noted above and the installment payment order ultimately awarded are enforceable by the appropriate contempt proceedings. *See* CPLR sec. 5210 and CPLR sec. 5251.

3. Service—as indicated above, the application is brought by motion, captioned in the original action; the motion papers are served on the judgment debtor in the same manner as a summons or by registered or certified mail.

IV. PRIORITY AND MODIFICATION OF EXECUTIONS

A. The Property Execution

1. Priority among execution creditor—CPLR sec. 5234(b) provides in pertinent part, that:

a. Where two or more executions or orders of attachment are issued against the same judgment debtor and delivered to the same enforcement officer, they should be satisifed out of proceeds of personal property or debt levied upon by the officer in the order in which they were delivered;

b. Where two or more executions or orders of attachment are issued against the same judgment debtor and delivered to different enforcement officers, and personal property or debt is levied upon within the jurisdiction of all of the officers, the proceeds shall be first applied in satisfaction of the execution or order of attachment delivered to the officer who levied, and thereafter should be applied in satisfaction of the executions or orders of attachment delivered to those of the other officers who, before the proceeds are distributed, make a demand upon the officer who levied, in the order of such demands;

c. An execution or order of attachment returned by an officer before a levy or delivered to him/her after the proceeds of the levy have been distributed shall not be satisifed out of the proceeds.

(Note: for the statement of priority of other judgment creditors, *see* CPLR sec. 5234(c).)

2. Proceeding to determine adverse claims—often, a judgment creditor seeking to recover under a property execution will be competing with other creditors of the judgment debtor. These other creditors may have liens or claims based upon other types of instruments or court-ordered documents. CPLR sec. 5239 allows for a special proceeding to be commenced to arrive at a determination of the priority of the claims of the respective parties in interest. *See* Exhibit 21.

3. Modification of the property execution—CPLR sec. 5240 allows for the modification of a property execution or the grant of a protective order:

a. The Court may at any time, on its own initiative or the motion of any interested person, make an order denying, limiting, conditioning, regulating, extending or modifying the use of this enforcement measure;

b. Further, sec. 3104 of the CPLR is applicable to procedures found under Article 52 of the CPLR.

B. The Income Execution

1. Priority—CPLR sec. 5231(a) provides that:

a. Two or more income executions issued against the same judgment debtor, specifying the same person from whom the money is received and delivered to the same or different enforcement officers, should be satisifed out of that money in the order in which the executions are delivered to an officer authorized to levy in the county in which the debtor resides or, where the judgment debtor is a nonresident, the county in which he/she is employed.

b. The priority of an income execution delivered to a sheriff within 20 days after its return by each previous sheriff shall be determined by the time of delivery to the first sheriff.

2. Modification—CPLR sec. 5231(g) permits either the judgment creditor or the judgment debtor to move for an order modifying an income execution. *See* Exhibits 21 and 22 attached hereto.

EXHIBIT 1

Plaintiff,

Date of Judgment:

-against-

Amount of Judgment:

Defendant.

$

TO:

Judgment has been entered against you in this case as shown above.

This office is now considering what steps it will take to enforce payment of the amount due. Such steps may include issuing an execution to take your property or income or serving a restraint against a third party, such as a bank, holding any of your property.

You should know that under the laws of this state and of the United States, certain of your property may be exempt. Common exemptions include payments from the Social Security Administration, unemployment insurance, a percentage of your wages, certain kinds of insurance, certain household goods, and certain real estate. This is not an exact nor complete list. You may be entitled to certain other exemptions.

As we are anxious not to take anything from you that is exempt, we urge you to call this office as soon as possible to discuss your exemptions and ability to pay the judgment.

Of course, you are free to consult with your own lawyer if you wish. If you have no lawyer, you may seek help from your nearest Legal Aid Society, if you qualify, or from the Lawyers Referral Service of your County.

Dated:

Attorney for Judgment Creditor

Richard J. Miller & Associates, P.C.
14 Corporate Woods Blvd.
Albany, New York 12211
Phone: (518) 465-7591

EXHIBIT 2

STATE OF NEW YORK
SUPREME COURT ALBANY COUNTY

NEW YORK STATE HIGHER EDUCATION
SERVICES CORPORATION,

Plaintiff,

-against- AFFIDAVIT OF SERVICE

Defendant.

STATE OF)
COUNTY OF) ss.:

being duly sworn, deposes and says:______________________

I am over the age of 18 years, I am not a party to this action, and I am authorized by the laws of the place of service to serve legal process; I served the summons and complaint on the defendant above named in the following manner:

1. [ ] *PERSONAL (also complete 6 below)*
   By delivering to and leaving with said defendant personally a true copy thereof at

   ____
   (ADDRESS, CITY AND STATE)
   on __________, 19 ____ at ________________ M. O'clock.
   (DATE OF SERVICE) (TIME OF SERVICE)

2. [ ] *SUITABLE AGE PERSON (also complete 4 and 6 below)*
   By delivering a copy of the summons and complaint to a person of suitable age and discretion, to wit: ________________
   (PERSON WITH WHOM LEFT)
   at ____
   (ADDRESS, CITY AND STATE)
   on ___________, 19 ____ at ________________ M. O'clock.
   (DATE OF SERVICE) (TIME OF SERVICE)

   that being said defendant's [ ] dwelling place, [ ] usual place of abode, [ ] actual place of business.

3. [ ] *AFFIXING TO DOOR (also complete 4 and 5 below)*
   By affixing a true copy thereof to the door of said premises, the same being the defendant's [ ] dwelling place, [ ] usual place of abode, [ ] actual place of business, there being no person of suitable age and discretion to be found.

4. [ ] *MAILING (use with 2 or 3 above)*
   Deponent completed service by depositing a copy of the summons and complaint in a postpaid envelope, properly addressed to the defendant, in an official depository of the United States Post Office on ____________________________, 19____.
   (DATE OF MAILING)

5. [ ] *PREVIOUS ATTEMPTS (Use with 3 above)*
   Deponent had previously attempted to serve the above named defendant

   on ________, 19__ at ____M. O'clock; Results ________
   on ________, 19__ at ____M. O'clock; Results ________
   on ________, 19__ at ____M. O'clock; Results ________

6. [ ] *DESCRIPTION (Use with 1 or 2 above)*
A description of the defendant or other person served on behalf of the defendant is as follows:

Approximate age ________ Approximate weight ________
Approximate height ______ Sex __ Color of skin ________
Color of hair ________________ Other ______________
____

7. [ ] *NOT FOUND IN COUNTY*
I Certify that I received the annexed civil process, and that after due search, careful inquiry and diligent attempts at the dwelling place, usual place of abode and/or actual place of business, I have been unable to make personal delivery of said process in the County of ___________, on the following person named therein, to wit:
NAME OF DEFENDANT: ___________________________
ADDRESS ATTEMPTED:____________________________
REASON:_____________________________________

That at the time of service of process, I made investigation and I ascertained the defendant is not on active duty in the military service of the United States.

by ________________________________

(PRINT NAME BELOW SIGNATURE)

Sworn to before me this
__________ day of ____________, 19____.

____

(NOTARY PUBLIC) (COMMISSIONER OF DEEDS)

NOTE: IF THIS AFFIDAVIT WAS EXECUTED OUTSIDE THE STATE OF NEW YORK, A CERTIFICATE OF THE NOTARY'S AUTHORITY MUST BE ATTACHED.

EXHIBIT 3

Plaintiff,	INDEX NO.
-against-	SUBPONEA DUCES TECUM AND RESTRAINING NOTICE
Defendant(s).	

TO:

You are hereby required to appear before a person authorized by the laws of this state to administer oaths at on , 19 , at M. and at any recessed or adjourned date and place for the purpose of taking your deposition under oath on all matters concerning defendant's income, property, and means and ability to pay or otherwise satisfy the judgment herein duly rendered, entered and perfected in favor of the plaintiff above named and against the defendant(s) above named for the sum of $ on , 19 , in the Court, County of , a transcript of which judgment was filed in the County Clerk's Office on 19 ; and on which there still remains unpaid and due the sum of $ with interest from , 19 .

You are REQUIRED to produce for examination at such time and place all books, papers, writings, records and memoranda in your possession or control which have or may contain information relative to the purpose of the examination.

FAILURE to appear at the time and place mentioned is punishable as a contempt of court.

TAKE NOTICE of Section 5222(b) of the Civil Practice Law and Rules set forth in full on the reverse side hereof.

DISOBEDIENCE OF THIS RESTRAINING NOTICE IS PUNISHABLE AS A CONTEMPT OF COURT.

Dated: Albany, New York

Richard J. Miller & Associates, P.C.
Attorney for Plaintiff
14 Corporate Woods Blvd.
Albany, New York 12211
Phone: 518-465-7591

You will be relieved of the provisions of this document if, before the return date, you pay the plaintiff's attorney, at its office, the sum of $ with interest from , 19 .

YOUR ATTENTION IS DIRECTED TO THE RESTRAINING NOTICE PROVISIONS ON THE REVERSE SIDE.

IMPORTANT

NOTE THAT YOU ARE *PROHIBITED* AND *RESTRAINED* FROM TRANSFERRING ANY PROPERTY OF THE DEFENDANT OR PAYING ANY MONEY OR OTHER ITEM OF VALUE TO HIM. READ THE FOLLOWING PROVISION OF LAW FOR DETAILS.

CIVIL PRACTICE LAW AND RULES

Section 5222(b): Effect of restraint; prohibition of transfer; duration. A judgment debtor served with a restraining notice is forbidden to make or suffer any sale, assignment, transfer or interference with any property in which he has an interest, except upon direction of the Sheriff or pursuant to an order of the court, until the judgment is satisfied or vacated. A restraining notice served upon a person other that the judgment debtor is effective only if, at the time of service, he owes a debt to the judgment debtor or he is in the possession or custody of property in which he knows or has reason to believe the judgment debtor has an interest, or if judgment creditor has stated in the notice that a specified debt is owed by the person served to the judgment debtor or that the judgment debtor has an interest in specified property in the possession or custody of the person served. All property in which the judgment debtor is known or believed to have an interest then in and thereafter coming into the possession or custody of such a person, including any specified in the notice, and all debts of such a person, including any specified in the notice, then due and thereafter coming due to the judgment debtor, shall be subject to the notice. Such a person is forbidden to make or suffer any sale, assignment, or transfer of or any interference with, any such property, or pay over or otherwise dispose of any debt, to any person other than the Sheriff, except upon direction of the Sheriff or pursuant to an order of the court, until the expiration of one year after the notice is served upon him, or until the judgment is satisfied or vacated, which ever event first occurs. A judgment creditor who was specified personal property or debt in a restraining notice shall be liable to the owner of the property or the person to whom the debt is owed, if other than the judgment debtor, for any damages sustained by reason of the restraint. If a garnishee served with a restraining notice withholds the payment of money belonging or owed to the judgment debtor in an amount equal to twice the amount due on the judgment, the restraining notice is not effective as to other property or money.

EXHIBIT 4

,

Plaintiff,

-against- SUBPOENA

,

Defendant.

To the above-named judgment debtor,

WHEREAS, a certain judgment in the sum of $ has been recovered by , the judgment creditor against , the judgment debtor, in the Court of County on the day of , 19 , said judgment having been docketed in the Office of the Clerk of , on the day of , 19 ;

NOW, therefore, we command you to appear and attend before at , to be examined under oath concerning the property, income, or other means of , judgment debtor, for satisfying such judgment, and failure to attend and false swearing at such examination, shall be punishable as a contempt of court.

WITNESS, Honorable , one of the Justices of our said Court at the day of , 19 .

LYNN, LYNN & MILLER, P.C.
Attorney for Judgment Creditor
99 Washington Avenue
Albany, New York 12210
Phone: (518) 465-7591

EXHIBIT 5

INDEX NO.

Plaintiff,

-against-

SUBPOENA DUCES TECUM AND RESTRAINING NOTICE

Defendant(s).

TO:

You are hereby required to appear before a person authorized by the laws of this state to administer oaths at
on , 19 , at M. and at any recessed or adjourned date and place for the purpose of taking your deposition under oath on all matters concerning defendant's income, property, and means and ability to pay or otherwise satisfy the judgment herein duly rendered, entered and perfected in favor of the plaintiff above named and against the defendant(s) above named for the sum of $ on , 19 , in the Court, County of , a transcript of which was filed in the County Clerk's Office on , 19 ; and on which there still remains unpaid and due the sum of $ with interest from , 19 .

You are REQUIRED to produce for examination at such time and place all books, papers, writings, records and memoranda in your possession or control which have or may contain information relative to the purpose of the examination.

FAILURE to appear at the time and place mentioned is punishable as a contempt of court.

TAKE NOTICE of Section 5222(b) of the Civil Practice Law and Rules set forth in full on the reverse side hereof.

DISOBEDIENCE OF THIS RESTRAINING NOTICE IS PUNISHABLE AS A CONTEMPT OF COURT.

Richard J. Miller & Associates, P.C
Dated: Albany, New York Attorney for Plaintiff
, 19 14 Corporate Woods Blvd.
Albany, New York 12211
Phone: 518-465-7591

You will be relieved of the provisions of this document if, before the return date, you pay the plaintiff's attorney, at its office, the sum of $ with interest from

YOUR ATTENTION IS DIRECTED TO THE RESTRAINING NOTICE PROVISIONS ON THE REVERSE SIDE.

IMPORTANT

NOTE THAT YOU ARE *PROHIBITED* AND *RESTRAINED* FROM TRANSFERRING ANY PROPERTY OF THE DEFENDANT OR PAYING ANY MONEY OR OTHER ITEM OF VALUE TO HIM. READ THE FOLLOWING PROVISION OF LAW FOR DETAILS.

CIVIL PRACTICE LAW AND RULES

Section 5222(b): Effect of restraint; prohibition of transfer; duration. A judgment debtor served with a restraining notice is forbidden to make or suffer any sale, assignment, transfer or interference with any property in which he has an interest, except upon direction of the Sheriff or pursuant to an order of the court, until the judgment is satisfied or vacated. A restraining notice served upon a person other that the judgment debtor is effective only if, at the time of service, he owes a debt to the judgment debtor or he is in the possession or custody of property in which he knows or has reason to believe the judgment debtor has an interest, or if judgment creditor has stated in the notice that a specified debt is owed by the person served to the judgment debtor or that the judgment debtor has an interest in specified property in the possession or custody of the person served. All property in which the judgment debtor is known or believed to have an interest then in and thereafter coming into the possession or custody of such a person, including any specified in the notice, and all debts of such a person, including any specified in the notice, then due and thereafter coming due to the judgment debtor, shall be subject to the notice. Such a person is forbidden to make or suffer any sale, assignment, or transfer of or any interference with, any such property, or pay over or otherwise dispose of any debt, to any person other than the Sheriff, except upon direction of the Sheriff or pursuant to an order of the court, until the expiration of one year after the notice is served upon him, or until the judgment is satisfied or vacated, which ever event first occurs. A judgment creditor who was specified personal property or debt in a restraining notice shall be liable to the owner of the property or the person to whom the debt is owed, if other than the judgment debtor, for any damages sustained by reason of the restraint. If a garnishee served with a restraining notice withholds the payment of money belonging or owed to the judgment debtor in an amount equal to twice the amount due on the judgment, the restraining notice is not effective as to other property or money.

EXHIBIT 6

File #

INDEX NO.

Plaintiff(s),

-against-

INFORMATION SUBPOENA

Defendant(s).

TO:

WHEREAS a certain judgment in the sum of $ has been recovered by the plaintiff(s), against , defendant(s), in Court, County on , 19 , a transcript of which was filed in the County Clerk's Office on , 19 , and there is still due and owing on said judgment the sum of $ with interest from , 19 ;

NOW, THEREFORE, in the name of THE PEOPLE OF THE STATE OF NEW YORK you are hereby REQUIRED to answer in writing upon oath the attached written questions, of which a copy thereof is also attached, relevant to the satisfaction of the said judgment. Each question is to be answered separately and in full, and each answer is to refer to the question to which it responds, and is to be returned to the undersigned, together with the original of the questions, within seven days after receipt.

FALSE SWEARING OR FAILURE TO COMPLY WITH THIS SUBPOENA IS PUNISHABLE AS A CONTEMPT OF COURT.

Dated: Albany, New York

, 19

____

As an Officer of the Court
Richard J. Miller & Associates, P.C.*
Attorney for Plaintiff
14 Corporate Woods Boulevard
Albany, New York 12211
Phone: (518) 465-7591

*Formerly the Law Offices of Lynn, Lynn & Miller, P.C.

EXHIBIT 7

RE:

VS: FILE #:

PLEASE ANSWER QUESTIONS ON *BOTH* SIDES

1. Q. Give the name and address of your present employer.
   A.

2. Q. What is your position with the employer?
   A.

3. Q. What is your gross wage (before deductions)? How often are you paid this amount (weekly, every other week, etc.)?
   A.

4. Q. Do you own an automobile?
   A.

5. Q. If so, state the year, make, model, color and current license plate number.
   A.

6. Q. Do you own any real estate?
   A.

7. Q. If so, give location, stating the county, street and number of said real estate; also from whom purchased and the approximate date of purchase.
   A.

8. Q. What is your Social Security number?
   A

9. Q. What is your present address?
   A.

10. Q. What is your present home telephone number?
    A.

11. Q. What is your present business telephone number?
    A.

12. Q. Give the name(s) and address(es) of the bank or banks in which you have an account.
    A.

13. Q. If you are not presently employed, outline your prospects for employment, including the type of work you are seeking, and when you expect to find it.

    A.

14. Q. Do you have any other assets or income, such as property, debts due you, insurance settlements, etc., which could be used to pay the judgment in whole or in part? If so, give complete details.

    A.

15. Q. If you cannot pay the entire judgment at this time, our client will accept reasonable monthly installment payments, as a matter of courtesy and forbearance. Please indicate how much you will send us per month, and on what date we can expect your first payment. (Payments should be as substantial as possible, as interest is continuing to accrue.)
    A.

____

(Please sign)

PLEASE NOTE: If you wish to telephone our office to make arrangements for reasonable monthly installment payments, you may call us COLLECT at: (518) 465-7591, 465-5235

LYNN & LYNN, P.C.

EXHIBIT 8

INDEX #:

Plaintiff,

NOTICE TO GARNISHEE

-against-

Defendant,

TO:

ADDRESS:

WHEREAS it appears that you are indebted to the judgment debtor above named or in possession or custody of property in which the judgment debtor has an interest, including, without limitation, the following specified debt and property:

NOW, THEREFORE, YOU ARE REQUIRED forthwith to transfer and deliver to the Sheriff all personal property in which the judgment debtor is known or believed to have an interest now in or hereafter coming into your possession or custody including but not limited to any property specified in this notice; and to pay to the sheriff, upon maturity, all debts now due or hereafter coming due from you to the judgment debtor, including but not limited to any debts specified in this notice; and to execute any documents necessary to effect such transfer, delivery or payment;

AND TAKE NOTICE that until such transfer, delivery or payment is made or until the expiration of ninety days after the service of this execution upon you or such further time as is provided by any order of the court served upon you, you are forbidden to make or suffer any sale, assignment or transfer of, or any interference with, any such property, or pay over or otherwise dispose of any such property or debt, to any person other than the Sheriff, except upon direction of the Sheriff or pursuant to an order of the court;

AND TAKE FURTHER NOTICE that at the expiration, or of such further time as after a levy is made by service of the execution, or of such further time as the court has provided, this levy shall be void except as to property or debts which have been transferred, delivered or paid to the Sheriff or as to which a proceeding under § 5225 or § 5227 of the Civil Practice Law and Rules has been brought.

This notice to garnishee is to be attached to and is made a part of the execution herein dated , 19 .

WITNESS, HON. Justice of the Supreme Court, County Judge, at the Court House, , New York, ______________ , 19 .

s/____________________________________

Richard J. Miller & Associates, P.C.
Attorney for Judgment Creditor
14 Corporate Woods Blvd.
Albany, New York 12211
Phone: (518) 465-7591

EXHIBIT 9

,

Plaintiff,

-against-

NOTICE OF MOTION

,

Defendant.

PLEASE TAKE NOTICE that upon annexed affidavit of , sworn to the day of , 19 , upon the restraining notice heretofore served upon , on the day of , 19 , pursuant to CPLR 5222, upon the deposition of , taken pursuant to CPLR 5223, on the day of , 19 , and upon all of the proceedings heretofore had in the above entitled action, the undersigned will move the Supreme Court of County, at a Special Term thereof to be held at the Court House in the City of , New York, on the day of 19 , at o'clock in the noon of that day, or as soon thereafter as counsel may be heard, for an order requiring , judgment debtor to pay over to , judgment creditor, the sum of $ in his possession, in satisfaction of a judgment entered in the above entitled action, in the Court of County, New York on the day of , 19 [or deliver to , Sheriff of County, New York, the following described personal property in his possession, or so much as is sufficient to satisfy the judgment entered in the above entitled action in the Court of County, New York] [or assign and deliver to , Sheriff of the County of , New York].

____

LYNN, LYNN & MILLER, P.C.
Attorney for Judgment Creditor
99 Washington Avenue
Albany, New York 12210
Phone: (518) 465-7591

TO: [Judgment Debtor]

,

Plaintiff,

-against-

,

Defendant.

AFFIDAVIT IN SUPPORT OF MOTION FOR PAYMENT OR DELIVERY OF PROPERTY OF JUDGMENT DEBTOR

STATE OF NEW YORK)
COUNTY OF) ss.:

, being duly sworn, deposes and says:

1. I am of , the plaintiff in the above-entitled action, a corporation.

2. [State nature and status of action]

3. A restraining notice was served upon the judgment debtor herein on the day of , 19 , pursuant to CPLR 5222, as will more fully appear from the copy thereof, together with due proof of service thereof, hereto attached.

4. , the judgment debtor herein, disclosed by deposition taken pursuant to CPLR 5223 on the day of , 19 , a copy of which is hereto attached, that he was in possession of the sum of $, which sum is sufficient to satisfy the judgment obtained by , judgment creditor herein against the said , in the above entitled action on the day of , 19 , which judgment is filed in the Clerk's Office of County, New York.

WHEREFORE, deponent prays that an order be made herein, requiring , judgment debtor, to pay over to deponent so much of said funds in his possession as are sufficient to satisfy the said judgment.

____

Sworn to before me
this day of , 198 .

____

NOTARY PUBLIC

Exhibit 10

MV-901 (9/80)

STATE OF NEW YORK — DEPARTMENT OF MOTOR VEHICLES

NOTICE OF RECORDED LIEN

FIRST LENDER BANK
1 LIEN ST
LIEN CITY NY 12345

Vehicle I.D. Number	Year	Make
12A3456B78C9DEFG	1978	AMAKE

1

Weight	Fuel	Cyl.	Body Type	Color
4000	GAS	4	SEDN	BL

Owner: If you have moved and have not yet notified this Department of your new address, cross out the address shown and print your new address in its place.

OWNER

MOTORIST,MIKE,M
20 SWAN ST
ALBANY NY 12228

FORMER OWNER

MOTORIST,FORMER,F
3 FORMER ST
OLD CITY NY 11223

The following information applies only to the lienholder shown in the box above.

☐ Our security interest in the vehicle described in this notice has been satisfied.

☐ We have assumed ownership of this vehicle. We are transferring ownership to:

____

☐ We have assigned our security interest in this vehicle to:

Name ______ Date of Assignment ______

No. and Street ______

City ______ State ______ ZIP ______

Authorized Signature ______ Date ______

ADDITIONAL LIENHOLDERS

SECOND LENDER BANK
AND TRUST CO.
2 LENDER ST
LIENVILLE NY 11111

THIRD LENDER BANK
3 LIEN AVE
LENDERVILLE NY 33333

VOID

If you are the owner named on this notice, mail this notice with your Certificate of Title to:

DEPARTMENT OF MOTOR VEHICLES, TITLE BUREAU,
THE GOVERNOR NELSON A. ROCKEFELLER EMPIRE STATE PLAZA
ALBANY, NEW YORK 12228
A NEW TITLE WILL BE MAILED TO YOU AT NO CHARGE.

00040 103078

Exhibit 11

Uniform Commercial Code — FINANCING STATEMENT CHANGE — Form UCC-3

JULIUS BLUMBERG, INC. N. Y. C. 10013

IMPORTANT — Read instructions on back before filling out form.

This STATEMENT is presented to a filing officer for filing pursuant to the Uniform Commercial Code.	No. of additional Sheets Presented:	3. ☐ The Debtor is a transmitting utility.
1. Debtor(s) (Last Name First) and Address(es):	2. Secured Party(ies) Name(s) and Address(es):	4. For Filing Officer: Date, Time, No. Filing Office

5. This statement refers to original Financing Statement No. ________ filed (date) ________ with ________

6. ☐ A. Continuation — The original Financing Statement bearing the above file number is still effective.

☐ B. Termination — The Secured Party of record no longer claims a security interest under the Financing Statement bearing the above file number.

☐ C. Release — From the Collateral described in the Financing Statement bearing the above file number, the Secured Party of record releases the following:

☐ D. Assignment — The Secured Party of record has assigned the Secured Party's rights in the property described below under the Financing Statement bearing the above file number to the Assignee whose name and address are shown below:

☐ E. Amendment — The Financing Statement bearing the above file number is amended as set forth below: (Signature of Debtor and Secured Party is Required)

☐ This statement is to be indexed in the Real Estate Records Section Block Lot

By ________ Signature(s) of Debtor(s) (only on amendment)

By ________ Signature(s) of Secured Party(ies)

EXHIBIT 11

(1) Filing Officer Copy-Numerical

(5/82) STANDARD FORM - FORM UCC-3 — Approved by the Secretary of State of New York, Pennsylvania & Texas

Exhibit 12

Law Offices
LYNN & LYNN, P.C.
Twin Towers, Capitol Hill
99 Washington Avenue
Albany, New York 12210
(518) 465-7591

[Date]

[Albany County Sheriff]
[Albany County Court House]
[Albany, New York 12207]

Re: [New York State Higher Education Services Corporation]
Vs: [Robert Jones]
Our File: #[123456]

Dear Sheriff:

Please make one demand for payment upon the debtor. If payment is not forthcoming at the time of your demand, please levy upon the debtor's real property.

Do not return the execution; if payment is not made as a result of the demand and your levy, notify this office and we will furnish a complete description of the property and a list of all lienors, judgment creditors and others who may have an interest in debtor's realty.

We intend to proceed with the sale of the property, and when notified, will furnish the necessary advance for the expenses of advertising, etc.

Very truly yours,

[Morton M. Z. Lynn]

[ML/dh]

[Enc.]

[COVER LETTER SENDING PROPERTY EXECUTION TO THE SHERIFF TO EXECUTE ON REAL PROPERTY]

[469]

[cc to Whomever]

EXHIBIT 13

File #

INDEX NO.

Plaintiff(s),

-against-

PROPERTY EXECUTION

Defendant(s).

THE PEOPLE OF THE STATE OF NEW YORK: TO THE SHERIFF OF ANY COUNTY

Judgment having being entered in the above entitled action on 19 , in Court, County of , in favor of the plaintiff(s) and against the defendant(s) in the sum of $, a transcript of which was entered in the County Clerk's Office , 19 and there still being due and unpaid thereon $, with interest from , 19 ;

NOW, THEREFORE, WE COMMAND YOU to satisfy the said judgment out of the real and personal property of the defendant(s) against whom the judgment was taken and the debts due to him; AND TO RETURN this execution to the Clerk of the Court within 60 days after issuance unless a levy has been made pursuant to 5232(b) CPLR or within extensions of that time made in writing by the attorney for the judgment creditor.

Dated: Albany, New York

, 19

____

As an Officer of the Court
RICHARD J. MILLER & ASSOCIATES,
P.C.*
Attorney for Plaintiff(s)
14 Corporate Woods Boulevard
Albany, New York 12211
Phone: (518) 465- 7591

Address of Judgment Debtor:

Location of Property:

SHERIFF IS TO COLLECT $, PLUS INTEREST FROM 19 , PLUS HIS FEES.

*Formerly the Law Offices of Lynn, Lynn & Miller, P.C.

Exhibit 14

UNITED STATES BANKRUPTCY COURT
NORTHERN DISTRICT OF NEW YORK
OFFICE OF THE CLERK
311 U.S COURTHOUSE
UTICA, N.Y. 13501

RUBY W. HARRIS
CLERK
(315) 793-8101

DIVISIONAL OFFICE
3RD FLOOR - U.S. COURTHOUSE
ALBANY, N.Y. 12201

August 19, 1982

TO: Attorneys -- Previously filed petitions in Northern District of New York under 11 U.S.C.

IN RE: EXEMPT PROPERTY - NEW YORK STATE DEBTOR AND CREDITOR LAW

Effective SEPTEMBER 1, 1982 the New York State Debtor and Creditor Law has been amended by ARTICLE 10-A to provide for claiming exemptions in bankruptcy. Section 284 provides for the "Exclusivity of exemptions" and removes the option of debtors claiming exemptions under the federal or state statute.

After 9/1/82 debtors filing petitions in New York State are not permitted to claim exemptions under the federal statute (11 U.S.C. §522).

Enclosed is a sample form for itemizing exemptions under ARTICLE 10-A. This form should be included as a supplement to Schedule B-4 for all petitions filed on and after SEPTEMBER 1, 1982, in New York State.

We hope this form will assist you and avoid the necessity of objections to exemptions claimed improperly under 11 U.S.C. §522 after 9/1/82.

RUBY W. HARRIS
Clerk

UNITED STATES BANKRUPTCY COURT
NORTHERN DISTRICT OF NEW YORK

IN RE

DEBTOR(S)

CASE NO.____________________

NEW YORK STATE-PROPERTY CLAIMED AS EXEMPT - SCHEDULE B-4

Following property is claimed exempt pursuant to ARTICLE 10-A of the NEW YORK DEBTOR AND CREDITOR LAW effective September 1, 1982, and supplements Schedule B-4:

REAL PROPERTY - §282(CPLR 5206) Location and Brief Description	Market Value	Mortgage or Lien Lienholder	CLAIMED EXEMPT
	$________	$________	$________
	Lienholder:________		

MOTOR VEHICLE - §282(1) Year, Make, Model	Market Value	Amt.of Lien Lienholder	CLAIMED EXEMPT
	$________	$________	$________
	Lienholder:________		
	$________	$________	$________
	Lienholder:________		

PERSONAL PROPERTY - §283(1) (Household, Personal, Annuity Contracts)	Market Value	Aggregate Amount CLAIMED EXEMPT
ITEMIZE:		
TOTAL	$________	$________

(See Reverse Side)

507 NDNY (9/82)

CASH EXEMPTION - §283(2)	Claimed Exempt
Cash	$__________
Bonds	$__________
Checking/Savings Accounts	$_______
Income Tax Refunds	$__________
Other:	$__________

RIGHT TO RECEIVE BENEFITS AND/OR PROPERTY §282(2)&(3):

Brief Description:

Dated:____________________ Debtor(s)____________________

____

STATE OF NEW YORK
EXECUTIVE CHAMBER
HUGH L. CAREY, GOVERNOR

Stephen J. Morello, Press Secretary
518-474-8418
212-977-2716

FOR RELEASE:
IMMEDIATE, TUESDAY
JULY 20, 1982

STATE OF NEW YORK
EXECUTIVE CHAMBER
ALBANY 12224

July 20, 1982

MEMORANDUM filed with Assembly Bill Number 11207-A, entitled:

#36
(Chapter 540)

"AN ACT to amend the debtor and creditor law, in relation to providing exemptions for debtors in federal bankruptcy proceedings"

A P P R O V E D

The bill amends the Debtor and Creditor Law by adding a new Article 10-A to provide personal bankruptcy exemptions for debtors domiciled in the State who file in a federal bankruptcy proceeding on or after September 1, 1982.

At present, the personal bankruptcy exemptions are those established by the federal Bankruptcy Reform Act of 1978. The Act does, however, authorize each state to adopt its own set of bankruptcy exemptions.

The basic thrust of the bill is to replace the federal bankruptcy exemptions with the personal property and homestead exemptions applicable to actions for the satisfaction of money judgments under sections 5205 and 5206 of the Civil Practice Law and Rules (CPLR).

The exemptions under the bill differ from those under the federal bankrupty law in several respects. The value of the personal residence exemption is increased from $7,500 to $10,000, and the value of the bankruptcy exemption for a motor vehicle from $1200 to $2400. A $5,000 ceiling is imposed on the aggregate amount of other personal property a debtor may exempt under the bill, while the federal bankruptcy law does not impose a ceiling. Although the federal law makes the $7,500 exemption available both to homeowners and to those who are not homeowners, the bill limits a non-homeowner's exemption to $2,500, and counts that amount toward the $5,000 ceiling imposed on the aggregate personal property exemption.

The bill reflects the Legislature's judgment that the present federal bankruptcy exemptions allow debtors to retain too great a portion of their assets, that the level of federal exemptions has contributed to the sharp rise in personal bankruptcy filings which have occurred since the federal law took effect, and that the bill will enable the debtor in bankruptcy to keep sufficient property to permit a fresh start following a filing in bankruptcy.

Concern has been expressed with respect to the reduced amount of the property the bill will permit a debtor to keep, and over those property interests which are protected by the bill and those which are not. The enactment of the bill will not foreclose consideration of those issues which are of legitimate concern. I am confident, based on the widespread interest shown in the bill, that enactment will not discourage continued study of bankruptcy problems, including the effects of the bill on debtors, to assure that the bill does, in fact, enable debtors to make a fresh start after bankruptcy on a basis which is fair and reasonable.

Approval of the bill is recommended by the Business Council of New York State, Inc., the New York State Council of Retail Merchants, Inc., the New York Chamber of Commerce and Industry, the New York State Bankers Association and the National Federation of Independent Business.

The bill is approved.

EXHIBIT 15

File #

INDEX NO.

Plaintiff(s),

-against-

INCOME EXECUTION

Defendant(s).

THE PEOPLE OF THE STATE OF NEW YORK: TO THE SHERIFF OF ANY COUNTY

Judgment having been entered on , 19 , in Court, County of , in favor of the plaintiff(s) and against the defendant(s) in the sum of $, a transcript of which was entered in the County Clerk's Office 19 , and there being unpaid thereon $ with interest from , 19 ; and whereas the defendant, , is receiving or will receive from , the garnishee, disposable installment income of at least $100.50 per week; the SHERIFF within 20 days is to serve a copy of this execution upon the said DEFENDANT who is REQUIRED to pay to the Sheriff 10% of all income received hereafter from the garnishee until the judgment and sheriff's fees are paid, and on his default hereunder, this execution is to be served on the garnishee. If he is unable to serve the said defendant within 20 days, or if the defendant so served fails to pay pursuant hereto for a period of 20 days, the sheriff is to levy upon the money the defendant will receive by serving a copy of this execution upon the garnishee within the sheriff's county. the GARNISHEE (EMPLOYER) is DIRECTED to withhold and pay over to the sheriff installments equal to 10% of the GROSS of any money due to the defendant at the time of, or after, service of this instrument upon him until the judgment together with interest thereon and the sheriff's fees are fully paid. If this execution remains unpaid in whole or in part because he is unable to find the garnishee within his county, the sheriff is to return this execution to the attorney for the plaintiff(s), endorsed to indicate the extent to which paid installments have satisfied the judgment, and the attorney may deliver this execution to the sheriff of any county in which the garnishee may be found, AND THE SHERIFF OF SUCH COUNTY is to levy upon the money that the defendant will receive from the garnishee, by serving a copy hereof on the garnishee within such sheriff's county, AND THE GARNISHEE IS DIRECTED to withhold and pay over to the sheriff of such county installments in the same amounts and for the same period as hereinabove provided. The SHERIFF is to account for and pay over to the attorney for the plaintiff(s) all money collected, less his fees, and when fully paid, to return this execution with his proceedings hereon to the Clerk of the Court where the judgment is entered.

Dated: Albany, New York
, 19

____

Address of Defendant:

As an Officer of the Court
RICHARD J. MILLER & ASSOCIATES,
P.C.
Attorney for Plaintiff(s)
14 Corporate Woods Boulevard

Address of Employer (Garnishee):

Albany, New York 12211
Phone: (518) 465-7591

*Formerly the Law Offices of Lynn, Lynn & Miller, P.C.

Exhibit 16

THE FEDERAL WAGE GARNISHMENT LAW[1]

(Title III of the Consumer Credit Protection Act)

(15 U.S.C. 1671, et seq.)

AN ACT

To safeguard the consumer in connection with the utilization of credit by requiring full disclosure of the terms and conditions of finance charges in credit transactions or in offers to extend credit; by restricting the garnishment of wages; and by creating the National Commission on Consumer Finance to study and make recommendations on the need for further regulation of the consumer finance industry; and for other purposes.

Be it enacted by the Senate and House of Representatives of the United States of America in Congress assembled,

§ 1. Short title of entire Act

This Act may be cited as the Consumer Credit Protection Act.

(This reprints only that portion of the Consumer Credit Protection Act contained in Title III—Restriction on Garnishment.)

TITLE III—RESTRICTION ON GARNISHMENT

Sec.

301. Findings and purpose.
302. Definitions.
303. Restriction on garnishment.
304. Restriction on discharge from employment by reason of garnishment.
305. Exemption for State-regulated garnishments.
306. Enforcement by Secretary of Labor.
307. Effect on State laws.

§ 301. Findings and purpose

(a) The Congress finds:

(1) The unrestricted garnishment of compensation due for personal services encourages the making of predatory extensions of credit. Such extensions of credit divert money into excessive credit payments and thereby hinder the production and flow of goods in interstate commerce.

(2) The application of garnishment as a creditors' remedy frequently results in loss of employment by the debtor, and the resulting disruption of employment, production, and consumption constitutes a substantial burden on interstate commerce.

(3) The great disparities among the laws of the several States relating to garnishment have, in effect, destroyed the uniformity of the bankruptcy laws and frustrated the purposes thereof in many areas of the country.

(b) On the basis of the findings in subsection (a) of this section, the Congress determines that the provisions of this title are necessary and proper for the purpose of carrying into

---

[1] Revised text showing new or amended language as follows:

Typeface Used	Public Law	Date Enacted	Effective Date	Statute Citation
Century	90–321	5/29/68	7/1/70	82 Stat. 162
Italics	95–30	5/23/77	6/1/77	91 Stat. 161

U.S. DEPARTMENT OF LABOR
Employment Standards Administration
Wage and Hour Division

WH Publication 1280 (Rev. 8/77)

execution the powers of the Congress to regulate commerce and to establish uniform bankruptcy laws.

§ 302. Definitions

For the purposes of this title:

(a) The term "earnings" means compensation paid or payable for personal services, whether denominated as wages, salary, commission, bonus, or otherwise, and includes periodic payments pursuant to a pension or retirement program.

(b) The term "disposable earnings" means that part of the earnings of any individual remaining after the deduction from those earnings of any amounts required by law to be withheld.

(c) The term "garnishment" means any legal or equitable procedure through which the earnings of any individual are required to be withheld for payment of any debt.

§ 303. Restriction on garnishment

(a) Except as provided in subsection (b) and in section 305, the maximum part of the aggregate disposable earnings of an individual for any workweek which is subjected to garnishment may not exceed

(1) 25 per centum of his disposable earnings for that week, or

(2) the amount by which his disposable earnings for that week exceed thirty times the Federal minimum hourly wage prescribed by section 6(a)(1) of the Fair Labor Standards Act of 1938 in effect at the time the earnings are payable,

whichever is less. In the case of earnings for any pay period other than a week, the Secretary of Labor shall by regulation prescribe a multiple of the Federal minimum hourly wage equivalent in effect to that set forth in paragraph (2).

(b)(1) The restrictions of subsection (a) do not apply in the case of

(A) any order for the support of any person issued by a court of competent jurisdiction or in accordance with an administrative procedure, which is established by State law, which affords substantial due process, and which is subject to judicial review.

(B) any order of any court of bankruptcy under chapter XIII of the Bankruptcy Act.

(C) any debt due for any State or Federal tax.

(2) The maximum part of the aggregate disposable earnings of an individual for any workweek which is subject to garnishment to enforce any order for the support of any person shall not exceed—

(A) where such individual is supporting his spouse or dependent child (other than a spouse or child with respect to whose support such order is used), 50 per centum of such individual's disposable earnings for that week; and

(B) where such individual is not supporting such a spouse or dependent child described in clause (A), 60 per centum of such individual's disposable earnings for that week;

except that, with respect to the disposable earnings of any individual for any workweek, the 50 per centum specified in clause (A) shall be deemed to be 55 per centum and the 60 per centum specified in clause (B) shall be deemed to be 65 per centum, if and to the extent that such earnings are subject to garnishment to enforce a support order with respect to a period which is prior to the twelve-week period which ends with the beginning of such workweek.

(c) No court of the United States *or any State*, and no State (or officer or agency thereof), may make, execute, or enforce any order or process in violation of this section.

§ 304. Restriction on discharge from employment by reason of garnishment.

(a) No employer may discharge any employee by reason of the fact that his earnings have been subjected to garnishment for any one indebtedness.

(b) Whoever willfully violates subsection (a) of this section shall be fined not more than $1,000, or imprisoned not more than one year, or both.

§ 305. Exemption for State-regulated garnishments

The Secretary of Labor may by regulation exempt from the provisions of section 303(a) *and (b)(2)* garnishments issued under the laws of any State if he determines that the laws of that State provide restrictions on garnishment which are substantially similar to those provided in section 303(a) *and (b)(2)*.

§ 306. Enforcement by Secretary of Labor

The Secretary of Labor, acting through the Wage and Hour Division of the Department of Labor, shall enforce the provisions of this title.

§ 307. Effect on State Laws

This title does not annul, alter, or affect, or exempt any person from complying with, the laws of any State

(1) prohibiting garnishments or providing for more limited garnishments than are allowed under this title, or

(2) prohibiting the discharge of any employee by reason of the fact that his earnings have been subjected to garnishment for more than one indebtedness.

EXHIBIT 17

,

Judgment Creditor,

-against- ORDER

,

Judgment Debtor.

Upon reading and filing the affirmation of , dated , 19 , and the original income execution herein, and it appearing to the satisfaction of the Court that service of the income execution herein, upon the judgment debtor, is impractical under CPLR 308, paragraphs 1, 2, 3 or 4;

NOW on motion of Lynn & Lynn, P.C., the attorney for the judgment creditor herein, for an order directing the manner of service of the income execution herein pursuant to paragraph 5 of CPLR 305; it is hereby

ORDERED that the income execution in the above entitled action be served on the judgment debtor, , by the [Sheriff] of , or his deputy, (a) by delivering copies to [her] personally, or (b) by mailing a copy thereof by certified mail return receipt requested to the debtor at , and, in addition thereto, by mailing a copy thereof by regular mail to the debtor at , and a copy thereof to the debtor in care of , and it is further

ORDERED that service of the income execution herein on the judgment debtor by the Sheriff in the manner above set forth shall be and is notice to the judgment debtor of the proceedings to be taken with respect to the income execution; and it is further

ORDERED that the judgment debtor pay the amount of the judgment directly to the judgment creditor's attorney, Lynn & Lynn, P.C., 99 Washington Avenue, Albany, New York 12210, in installments of 10% of [her] gross wages as required by the income execution commencing within twenty days of service thereof upon [her]; and it is further

ORDERED that on failure of the judgment debtor to pay as aforesaid, the plaintiff may file the income execution with any Sheriff in the State of New York for service on the employer in like manner as an execution issued against a resident of this State who has failed to make voluntary payments to the Sheriff in his county of residence.

Dated: Albany, New York

, 19

____

(JUSTICE OF THE SUPREME COURT)

INDEX NO.

,

Judgment Creditor,

-against-

AFFIRMATION

,

Judgment Debtor.

, under penalties of perjury, affirms and says:

1. I am a attorney at law and of counsel to the attorney for the plaintiff herein.

2. On , 19 , a judgment was entered in Court, County against the above named judgment debtor in the sum of $. The judgment is unsatisfied, the balance due being $ with interest from , 19.

3. Pursuant to such judgment, we conducted an investigation which revealed that the judgment debtor is employed by , at a salary of $.

4. The records of the judgment creditor and its attorney, Lynn & Lynn, P.C., indicate that the judgment debtor is not working within the State of New York and that he now resides at , but that the employer, , is doing business in this State and subject to the jurisdiction of this court.

5. It is not possible for a New York State Sheriff to serve the income execution upon as required by CPLR 5231(c).

6. In accordance with the decision of the court in *Oysterman's Bank and Trust Company v. Bernard Manning*, 59 Misc. 2d 144, we may

not dispense with service upon the judgment debtor where he is not within the state, but must make application for an order authorizing service of the income execution on the judgment debtor by a sheriff in the county of the state where the judgment debtor is residing.

7. We therefore pray for the annexed order and that notice of this application to the defendant be dispensed with.

Dated: Albany, New York

, 19

____

LYNN & LYNN, P.C.
Attorney for Judgment Creditor
99 Washington Avenue
Albany, New York 12210
Phone: (518) 465-7591

EXHIBIT 18

SUPREME COURT ALBANY COUNTY

NEW YORK STATE HIGHER EDUCATION SERVICES CORPORATION,

Plaintiff,

-against-

THOMAS MICHAEL ROWLAND,

Defendant.

ORDER VACATING SATISFACTION OF JUDGMENT

PRESENT: HON. ROGER J. MINER, Justice.

The plaintiff above named duly moved this Court at a Special Term of the Court held at the Court House, Albany, New York on November 9, 1978 for an order vacating the satisfaction of judgment filed herein;

NOW, on reading and filing the notice of motion and affirmation of Richard J. Miller, dated October 3, 1979, respectively, with proof of due sevice thereof, and after hearing Lynn & Lynn, P.C. (Richard J. Miller, of counsel), attorney for plaintiff, in support of said motion, and no one having appeared in opposition thereto, and due deliberation having been had, now on motion of Lynn & Lynn, P.C., attorney for the plaintiff; it is

ORDERED that the said motion be, and the same hereby is granted; and it is further

ORDERED that the satisfaction of judgment filed by the Sheriff of Ulster County with the Albany County Clerk be, and the same hereby is vacated; and it is further

ORDERED that the Albany County Clerk and the Ulster County Clerk be, and they hereby are directed to mark their records accordingly; and it is further

ORDERED that the plaintiff herein be, and it hereby is authorized and permitted to proceed with the collection of the balance due of the judgment remaining on record by means of whatever enforcement measures may be available to it.

Dated: Hudson, New York
November , 1978

____

JUSTICE OF THE SUPREME COURT

SUPREME COURT ALBANY COUNTY

NEW YORK STATE HIGHER EDUCATION SERVICES CORPORATION,

Plaintiff,

-against-

THOMAS MICHAEL ROWLAND,

Defendant.

NOTICE OF MOTION TO VACATE SATISFACTION OF JUDGMENT

SIR:

PLEASE TAKE NOTICE that upon the annexed affirmation of Richard J. Miller, dated October 3, 1978, the summons and complaint, affidavit of service, default judgment, income execution and satisfaction of said judgment filed with the Albany County Clerk on or about September 18, 1978, and all prior proceedings hereinbefore had, the undersigned will move this Court at a Special Term (Part I) thereof to be held at the Court House, Albany, New York on November 9, 1978 at 9:30 A.M., or as soon thereafter as counsel can be heard, for an order vacating the satisfaction of judgment filed herein, together with such other and further relief as to the Court may seem just and proper.

PLEASE TAKE FURTHER NOTICE that answering affidavits, if any, are required to be served five (5) days prior to the return date of this motion.

Dated: Albany, New York
October 3, 1978

Yours, etc.

LYNN & LYNN, P.C.
Attorney for Plaintiff
99 Washington Avenue
Albany, New York 12210
Phone: (518) 465-7591

TO: THOMAS MICHAEL ROWLAND
Defendant
P.O. Box 125
Mount Marion, New York 12456

ULSTER COUNTY SHERIFF
County Office Building
Kingston, New York 12401

SUPREME COURT ALBANY COUNTY

NEW YORK STATE HIGHER EDUCATION SERVICES CORPORATION,
Plaintiff,

-against-

THOMAS MICHAEL ROWLAND,
Defendant.

AFFIRMATION IN SUPPORT OF MOTION TO VACATE SATISFACTION OF JUDGMENT

RICHARD J. MILLER, under penalties of perjury, affirms and says:

1. I am an attorney at law and of counsel with Lynn & Lynn, P.C., the attorney of record for the plaintiff herein. I am familiar with the facts set forth in this affirmation from my own knowledge or from the information contained in our file.

2. On January 8, 1973, copies of the summons and complaint herein with reference to the above were duly served on the defendant named. The defendant did not and has not served an answer to the plaintiff's complaint, and be thereby allowed the matter to be put into default.

3. On February 27, 1973, the Albany County Clerk entered a judgment by default in the total sum of $3,004.52 on its records. A transcript of said judgment was duly filed with the Ulster County Clerk on March 1, 1973.

4. Pursuant thereto and on or about March 26, 1973, an income execution was issued and delivered to the Ulster County Sheriff's Offices. By reason thereof, payments totalling $3,400.87 were made by the Ulster County Sheriff to the plaintiff herein. The last payment in the amount of $1,479.02 was received by this office on behalf of the

plaintiff on September 26, 1978. At the time, we were advised that the Sheriff of Ulster County had filed a satisfaction of judgment with the Albany County Clerk.

5. To be noted is that there is a balance of $528.37 as of September 28, 1978 still due and owing on the judgment. Further, interest continues to accrue on the judgment at the rate of $.09 per diem. Apparently, the Ulster County Sheriff failed and neglected to take into account and compute the interest due on the judgment as required by law.

6. Under the circumstances, it is respectfully submitted that the judgment herein should not have been satisfied and that the plaintiff is entitled to the balance thereof in the nature of interest which has accrued and will continue to accrue. Plaintiff therefore requests that the satisfaction of judgment filed by the Ulster County Sheriff be vacated, and that the plaintiff be permitted to pursue the enforcement of said judgment by re-issuing the income execution herein.

WHEREFORE, the judgment having been satisfied in the Albany County Clerk's Offices, I pray for an order vacating the satisfaction of judgment and directing the Albany County Clerk to expunge the satisfaction from his records.

Dated: Albany, New York
October 3, 1978

s/Richard J. Miller

LYNN & LYNN, P.C.
Attorney for Plaintiff
99 Washington Avenue
Albany, New York 12210
Phone: (518) 465-7591

EXHIBIT 19

	INDEX NO. 4076-69
, Plaintiff,	
-against-	NOTICE OF MOTION TO SET INSTALLMENT PAYMENTS
, Defendant.	

SIR:

PLEASE TAKE NOTICE that on the pleadings herein and the annexed affirmation of Richard J. Miller, dated March 15, 1974, and on the judgment herein, dated July 8, 1969, and upon all the papers and proceedings hereinbefore had herein, the undersigned will move this Court at a Special Term of the Court held at the Court House, Albany, New York on April 5, 1974 at 9:30 A.M. or as soon thereafter as counsel can be heard for an order pursuant to CPLR § 5226 directing the above named judgment debtor to pay monthly installments of $75.00 each to the above named judgment creditor until the judgment entered herein, plus interest and costs and expenses of this motion, have been paid, and for such other and further relief as to the court may seem just and proper; and further

PLEASE TAKE NOTICE that answering affidavits, if any, are required to be served five (5) days prior to the return date of this motion.

Dated: Albany,New York
March 15, 1974

Yours, etc.,

LYNN & LYNN, P.C.
Attorney for Plaintiff
11 North Pearl Street
Albany, New York 12207
Phone: (518) 465-7591

TO:

Defendant
Buffalo, New York

SUPREME COURT ALBANY COUNTY

,	INDEX NO. 4076-69
Plaintiff,	
-against-	AFFIRMATION IN SUPPORT OF MOTION TO SET INSTALLMENT PAYMENTS
,	
Defendant.	

Richard J. Miller, under penalties of perjury, affirms and says:

1. I am an attorney duly admitted to practice in this State and of counsel with Lynn & Lynn, P.C., the attorney for the plaintiff herein. I am familiar with the facts set forth in this affirmation from my own knowledge or from the information contained in our file.

2. On July 8, 1969, judgment was entered in Supreme Court, Albany County in favor of the plaintiff herein against the above named judgment debtor in the sum of $1,467.35, including costs.

3. A number of payments on account have been made by the judgment debtor in satisfaction of the judgment on record, thereby leaving a balance due and owing in the sum of $581.59 with interest thereon from November 15, 1971. A copy of the judgment creditor's ledger card is attached hereto and marked Exhibit "A".

4. On May 4, 1973, this office caused an information subpoena to be issued against the defendant. The defendant answered the questionnaire annexed thereto stating that he was a self-employed attorney earning approximately $250.00 per week. A copy of the answers annexed to the information subpeona are attached hereto and marked Exhibit "B".

5. The judgment creditor herein then obtained a current Assets and Income Report dated February 26, 1974 which verified the answers as

set forth above indicating the judgment debtor to be a self-employed earning approximately $15,000.00 to $20,000.00 per year. A copy of the report is attached hereto and marked Exhibit "C".

6. It will be noted that by reason of the information found in the Current Assets and Income Report, it was discovered that the defendant resides with his mother at her home. In addition, it is suggested that the judgment debtor has no financial difficulties and apparently has the ability to make payments in satisfaction of the judgment herein.

7. It would appear that the judgment debtor is living well and that all of his reasonable needs are taken care of without difficulty and with little personal expense. Because of the nature of the judgment debtor's income, an income execution is not practicable. The judgment debtor has refused to make any effort to satisfy the balance due on his obligation, and the only recourse available to the judgment creditor is an order setting installment payments.

WHEREFORE I respectfully pray for an order directing to make regular monthly installment payments of $75.00 each to the judgment creditor, together with such other and further relief as may seem proper.

Dated: Albany, New York
March 15, 1974

____

Richard J. Miller
LYNN & LYNN, P.C.
Attorney for Plaintiff
11 North Pearl Street
Albany, New York 12207
Phone: (518) 465-7591

,	INDEX NO.
Plaintiff,	
-against-	ORDER SETTING INSTALLMENT PAYMENTS
,	
Defendant.	

PRESENT: HON. , Justice of the Supreme Court

The plaintiff above named having duly moved this Court at a Special Term of the Court held at the Court House, Albany, New York on April 5, 1974, the notice of motion dated March 15, 1974, under 1526 CPLR for an order directing the above named judgment debtor to pay monthly installments of $75.00 each to the above named judgment creditor;

Now, on reading and filing the complaint therein, the affirmation of Richard J. Miller dated March 15, 1974, with proof of due service thereof, and after hearing Lynn & Lynn, P.C., attorney for plaintiff, in support of said motion, and no one appearing in opposition thereto, and due deliberation having been had, now on motion of Lynn & Lynn, P.C., attorney for plaintiff; it is

ORDERED that the said motion be, and the same hereby is granted, and it is further

ORDERED that the judgment debtor herein be and he hereby is, directed to pay the judgment creditor's attorney, Lynn & Lynn P.C. at their offices located at 11 North Pearl Street, Albany, New York, the sum of $75.00 per month, the first payment in such amount to be made on the first day of May, 1974 and such payments thereafter to be made on the first day of each succeding month, or the next business day thereafter, until the balance due on the judgment herein in the sum of $581.59, with interest accruing thereon, is satisfied.

Dated: Troy, New York
April , 1974

____

JUSTICE OF THE SUPREME COURT

EXHIBIT 20

File #

INDEX #

Plaintiff,

-against-

INFORMATION SUBPOENA

Defendant.

TO:

WHEREAS a certain judgment in the sum of $ has been recovered by the plaintiff(s), against , defendant(s), in Court, County on , 19 , a transcript of which was filed in the County Clerk's Office on 19 , and there is still due and owing on said judgment the sum of $ with interest from , 19 ;

Now therefore in the name of THE PEOPLE OF THE STATE OF NEW YORK you are hereby REQUIRED to answer in writing upon oath the attached written qùestions, of which a copy thereof is also attached, relevant to the satisfaction of the said judgment. Each question is to be answered separately and in full, and each answer is to refer to the question to which it responds, and is to be returned to the undersigned, together with the original of the questions, within seven days after receipt.

FALSE SWEARING OR FAILURE TO COMPLY WITH THIS SUBPOENA IS PUNISHABLE AS A CONTEMPT OF COURT.

Dated: Albany, New York

, 19

____

As an Officer of the Court
LYNN, LYNN & MILLER, P.C.
Attorney for Plaintiff
99 Washington Avenue
Albany, New York 12210
Phone: (518) 465-7591

1. Q. Give the name and address of your present employer.

   A.

2. Q. What is your position with the employer?

   A.

3. Q. What is your gross wage and in what installments (weekly, bi-weekly, etc.) are you paid?

   A.

4. Q. Give the name and address of any additional employer for whom you may work part-time, regularly or irregularly.

   A.

5. Q. If applicable, state the total gross wages earned from such part-time employment over the last six months, including tips or gratuities as shown on payroll tax returns.

   A.

6. Q. Do you have any other source of income whatsoever?

   A.

7. Q. If so, state the exact source and amounts of such income, estimating the total gross receipts for the last six months.

   A.

8. Q. If married, give the name of your spouse.

   A.

9. Q. Does your spouse have any income whatsoever? If so, state complete details, including source, amounts, and in what installments (weekly, bi-weekly, etc.) it is received.

   A.

10. Q. Are there any other persons contributing to the support and maintenance of yourself or your family?

    A.

11. Q. If so, please state their name(s), address(es), the source of their income and in what installments (weekly, bi-weekly, etc.), they are paid.

    A.

12. Q. What are the amounts of you and your spouse's net "take-home" wages for the applicable pay periods specified above?

    A.

13. Q. List all items ordinarily deducted from your gross wage for each pay period, estimating the ordinary and usual amount of each deduction so itemized.

A.

14. Q. State your net taxable income for the 1974 taxable year as entered on your federal tax return.

A.

15. Q. Do you own an automobile, boat, trailer, snowmobile or any other type of motor vehicle?

A.

16. Q. If so, please state the year, make, model, color and current license plate number of each vehicle.

A.

17. Q. Do you own any real estate or have any interest in any real property?

A.

18. Q. If so, please give the location, stating the county, street and number of said real estate; also from whom purchased, and the approximate date of purchase.

A.

19. Q. If so, please state the name or names of the titleholders of record for each parcel of property.

A.

20. Q. If so, please state any indebtedness outstanding thereon.

A.

21. Q. Do you rent or own your home?

A.

22. Q. If you rent, to whom do you pay rent and how much do you pay per month?

A.

23. Q. If your landlord is a relative, state the relationship to him.

A.

24. Q. Give the name(s) and address(es) of the bank or banks in which you have an account or with which you prefer to do business.

A.

25. Q. State the amount or amounts presently contained in each of the accounts referred to hereinabove.

A.

26. Q. Do you have any personal property which is listed as security for an outstanding indebtedness (i.e., car, boat, etc.)?

A.

27. Q. If so, describe that property below indicating the total amount of in debtedness outstanding, to whom owed, and the amount per month being paid to discharge said indebtedness.

A.

28. Q. Are there any judgments of record which have been entered against you? If so, itemize below showing creditor, amount of judgment and when obtained.

A.

29. Q. How many individual exemptions will be claimed on your 1975 taxreturn?

A.

30. Q. State the full name and relationship to you of each person so claimed.

A.

30-a. Q. If you have any children, state the name, age, and school currently attended for each child.

A.

31. Q. How much money do you contribute directly to each child's educational expenses and tuition per year? Itemize per child below.

A.

32. Q. Estimate and itemize the average weekly expenditures for the family unit of the following: food, transportation, utilities and any other necessary family expenses.

A.

33. Q. Do you own any insurance policies?

A.

34. Q. If so, state the face value of each policy and estimate the current cash surrender value of each.

A.

35. Q. List below all your current accounts payable, stating to whom incurred, for what purpose, the estimated current balance outstanding.

A.

36. Q. What is your present address?

A.

37. Q. What is your present home telephone number?

A.

38. Q. Is there any person who could help you satisfy this obligation?

A.

39. Q. Please state your social security number.

A.

40. Q. Indicate below the maximum amount of a monthly installment payment which you believe you can afford.

A.

41. Q. List further any extraordinary expenses not heretofore listed above indicating amounts ordinarily paid, in what installments (weekly, bi-weekly, etc.) paid and the current balance outstanding.

A.

EXHIBIT 21

SUPREME COURT WARREN COUNTY

,

Petitioner,

-against-

,

Respondents.

NOTICE OF PETITION IN SPECIAL PROCEEDINGS TO DETERMINE ADVERSE CLAIMS

SIRS:

PLEASE TAKE NOTICE that upon the annexed petition of , verified on November 7, 1975, and on all prior proceedings hereinbefore had, the undersigned will move this Court at a Special Term of the Court held at the Court House, Schenectady, New York, on December 9, 1975 at 9:30 a.m., or as soon thereafter as counsel can be heard, for a judgment pursuant to 5239 CPLR, determining the rights of the petitioner in certain property held by the Warren County Sheriff on behalf of , and restrained by a property execution levied against said property with notice to garnishee, dated August 20, 1975, served in favor of , as plaintiff and pursuant to a judgment taken against , as defendant, together with such other and further relief as to the Court may seem just and proper; and further

PETITIONER designates Warren County as the place of trial, on the ground that the property is restrained in said County; and further

PLEASE TAKE NOTICE that answering affidavits, if any, are required to be served five (5) days prior to the return date of this motion.

Dated: Albany, New York
November 25, 1975

Yours, etc.,

LYNN & LYNN, P.C.
Attorney for Petitioner
99 Washington Avenue
Albany, New York
Phone: (518) 465-7591

TO:

SUPREME COURT WARREN COUNTY

,

Petitioner,

-against-

,

Respondents.

PETITION IN SPECIAL PROCEEDINGS TO DETERMINE ADVERSE CLAIMS

TO: The Supreme Court of the State of New York.

The petition of , by its Assistant Secretary, , respectfully shows:

1. is a Delaware corporation, duly authorized to transact business in the State of New York. The petitioner's offices and principal place of business are located at

2. This proceeding is brought pursuant to § 5239 of the CPLR in order to determine the propriety of certain adverse claims which involve certain personal property now in the possession of and subject to the control of the Warren County Sheriff.

3. I am the Assistant Secretary of , the petitioner herein. I make this petition on behalf of for the purpose of obtaining a judgment to determine the rights of the petitioner in cer-

tain property held by the Warren County Sheriff at this time. The statements hereinafter contained are on information and belief, the source of my information and the grounds of my belief being books and records in my possession and maintained by the petitioner during the regular course of business.

4. On or about January 12, 1975, , one of the respondents above named, entered into a security agreement with of Glens Falls, New York in the nature of a retail installment contract, pledging the chattel in question as security for the said purchasers' outstanding obligation as represented by the said parties' agreement, a copy of which is attached hereto and marked Exhibit "A."

5. For good and valuable consideration, the said conditional sale contract was duly assigned to and is now the property of the petitioner herein.

6. Subsequent to the execution of the said security instrument, the said respondent, , defaulted under the terms thereof, not having maintained the requisite payments as required by the terms of the contract.

7. By reason of the foregoing, the petitioner is the owner and entitled to the immediate possession of One (1) 1974 Tree Farmer Skidder, Model C 5 D, Serial Number 5311-356, Six (6) New C.C. Chockers and Two (2) Used C.C. Chains for 18.4 X 26 Tires, all having an estimated total market value of $15,000.00.

8. In order to properly protect its security interest in the subject property held by respondent , the petitioner herein caused a duly executed financing statement to be filed with the Warren County Clerk, as well as with the Secretary of State of the State of New York on or about January 20, 1975. A copy of the financing statement is attached hereto and marked Exhibit "B."

9. Upon information and belief, it is petitioner's understanding that respondent , filed a voluntary petition in bankruptcy on August 7, 1975 with the United States District Court for

the Northern District of New York. Apparently, the first meeting of creditors was held at the United States Court Room No. 2, United States Post Office and Court House, Albany, New York on September 4, 1975, and, at that time, was appointed Trustee of bankrupt estate. Upon consultation with counsel, I have learned that the said Trustee abandoned the personal property subject to the security instrument aforesaid to the bankrupt, inasmuch as the outstanding obligation which remained due and owing from respondent , to the petitioner herein far exceeded the value of the subject property. A copy of notice of first meeting of creditors is attached hereto and marked Exhibit "C."

10. Following the first meeting of creditors and the abandonment made by the Trustee, petitioner learned that a certain execution was issued against the property described in petitioner's security instrument, with notice to garnishee, on behalf of respondent , as a judgment creditor of respondent . Pursuant to the said property execution, the Warren County Sheriff, a named respondent herein, was directed to and did in fact take possession of petitioner's security, and, upon information and belief, said respondent is now in possession of that property which forms the basis for this motion. A copy of the execution with notice to garnishee is attached hereto and marked Exhibit "D."

11. By reason of the security instrument described above, petitioner acquired a purchase money security interest in the equipment as more fully described therein. There is presently due from respondent , to the petitioner on said security instrument the sum of $24,918.11. Petitioner has appraised the property covered by said security instrument, and it appears that the value of said property is no greater than the balance due to petitioner as indicated above.

12. For lack of payment, respondent is presently in default, and, as a result thereof, petitioner is entitled to the immediate possession of the aforesaid property or to be paid the sum of the unpaid balance due to it. Upon information and belief, said property is now in the possession of the Warren County Sheriff, a respondent named herein, and it has not been applied to the satisfaction of any judgment.

WHEREFORE, on behalf of the petitioner herein, I demand that a judgment pursuant to 5239 CPLR be entered herein determining that the property described in this petition is the property of , and that the said petitioner is entitled to its possession, setting aside any restraining notices or levies which may have been made upon said property and directing the respondent, the Warren County Sheriff, to deliver said property to the petitioner, and for such other and further relief as to the Court may seem proper.

Dated: Milwaukee, Wisconsin
November 7, 1975

By ______________________

STATE OF WISCONSIN)
COUNTY OF MILWAUKEE) ss.:

, being duly sworn, deposes and says: deponent is the Assistant Secretary of , a Delaware corporation, the petitioner in the within action; deponent has read the foregoing petition and knows the content thereof; and the same is true to the deponent's own knowledge, except as to the matters therein stated to be alleged upon information and belief, and as to those matters deponent believes it to be true. This verification is made by deponent because is a corporation and deponent is an officer thereof.

____

NOTARY PUBLIC

SUPREME COURT WARREN COUNTY

INDEX NO.

Petitioner,

-against- ORDER

Respondents.

PRESENT: HON. , Justice.

The petitioner above named, having duly moved this Court at a Special Term of the Court held at the Court House, Schenectady, New York on January 13, 1976, under CPLR 5239 for an order determining the rights of the petitioner in certain property held by the Warren County Sheriff and restrained by a property execution levied against said property with notice to garnishee served in favor of respondent ;

Now, on reading and filing the petition of , verified November 7, 1975, the notice of petition, dated November 25, 1975, with proof of due service thereof, the affidavit of attorney of the law firm of , attorneys for , the affidavit of respondent , verified December 1, 1975, submitted in support of petitioner's motion, and respondent having consented to the relief sought herein, and after hearing Lynn & Lynn, P.C., (Richard J. Miller, of counsel), attorney for petitioner, in support of said motion, and no one appearing in opposition thereto, and due deliberation having been had, now on motion of Lynn & Lynn, P.C., attorney for petitioner; it is

ORDERED that the said motion be, and the same hereby is granted, and it is further

ORDERED that , the petitioner herein, be, and it hereby is, determined to be the owner of the property described in the annexed petition, and it is further

ORDERED that the said petitioner be, and it hereby is, entitled to the possession of the said property, setting aside any restraining notices or levies which may have been made upon said property, and directing the respondent, The Warren County Sheriff, to deliver said property to said petitioner.

Dated: Schenectady, New York
January 13, 1976

____

JUSTICE OF THE SUPREME COURT

CHAPTER THIRTEEN

EFFECT OF BANKRUPTCY ACT

Michael J. Kaplan, Esq.

I. INTRODUCTION

The filing of a Chapter 7, 11, or 13 petition by or against a judgment debtor pursuant to 11 U.S.C. secs. 101 *et seq.* presents several immediate challenges to collection counsel.

As discussed later, unless you are collecting alimony or support arrearages you must immediately discontinue collection activities, and perhaps undo some of what has been done between the time of the filing of the petition and the time you hear of it.

Then you must reevaluate your client's claim in light of numerous factors arising out of the consequences of each of the several bankruptcy Chapters relative to the various types of judgment debts owed by the different types of debtors eligible to file under the bankruptcy law. In so doing, you may find that bankruptcy does not necessarily "dead end" the collection process.

Lastly, you must plan and execute in the Bankruptcy Court the strategy that emerges from the above analysis, or in some instances refer the matter to expert bankruptcy counsel.

This chapter will enlighten you on the impact of the bankruptcy on enforcement of a judgment, introduce you to the principle considerations governing evaluation of the prospects for recovery on the debt through the bankruptcy process or thereafter, and outline common bankruptcy practice techniques in sufficient degree to permit you to determine whether to study further toward handling the matter yourself, or to refer it to bankruptcy counsel.

II. THE BANKRUPTCY STAY; ITS EFFECT AND DURATION

Under 11 U.S.C. sec. 362, nearly all collection activity must cease at the moment the bankruptcy petition is filed, whether it is filed under Chapter 7, 11, or 13 of the Bankruptcy Code. If you continue collection activities after learning of the filing you place both your client and yourself in danger of being found in contempt, and actual and punitive damages may be awarded.

Because of this stay, and because of 11 U.S.C. sec. 549, any activity even innocently undertaken after the moment of filing is at least voidable, if not void. Therefore, you might be well-advised to comply with a debtor's request to undo such activity. For example, upon request your client should return money collected from post-petition wages pursuant to a wage execution unless the nature of the underlying debt is one dealt with by the exemptions in 11 U.S.C. sec. 362(b) which permits, for example, the collection of alimony, maintenance, or support to continue in certain instances.

11 U.S.C. sec. 108(c) provides a tolling of limitation periods, claims-assertion periods, and the like, so that the section 362 stay will not cause your client a loss of time-related rights.

As to "passive" collection activities such as pending or ongoing sheriff's executions or wage orders you should advise the sheriff or employer to cease, at least until you have had a chance to study the exceptions to the stay set forth in section 362(b) and (by incorporation through section 362(b)(3)) those set forth at 11 U.S.C. secs. 546(b) and 547(e)(2)(A).

If the debtor has filed under Chapter 7 or 11, voluntary wage assignments need not cease if the debtor does not want them to, since post-petition wages are not "property of the [bankruptcy] estate" under those Chapters, 11 U.S.C. sec. 541(a)(6), and the debtor's decision to pay one or more debts out of post-petition earnings in these Chapters does not prejudice the rights of other creditors. 11 U.S.C. sec. 524(f). But under Chapter 13, post-petition wages belong to the bankruptcy estate, 11 U.S.C. sec. 1306, and are likely to be found not to be subject to the debtor's pre-petition voluntary wage assignment.

With few exceptions, then, the automatic stay of section 362 maintains the status quo as it existed at the time of the filing of the bankruptcy petition.

The duration of the automatic stay is set forth in 11 U.S.C. sec. 362(c)-(f). While that section contemplates points in time at which the automatic stay dissolves itself, or may be terminated by order of the court, another stay (in fact a permanent injunction) is provided at 11 U.S.C. sec. 524 which specifies the effect of a discharge in bankruptcy. Most notably, that section specifies that a discharge in bankruptcy voids any judgment at any time obtained insofar as the judgment is a determination of the personal liability of the debtor with respect to any discharged debt, and it provides that the discharge is an injunction against the commencement or continuation of an action, the employment of process, or an act of any sort, to collect, recover, or offset any discharged debt as a personal liability of the debtor. The statute specifies that these effects cannot be waived by the debtor although the debtor may, as indicated above, choose to voluntarily repay any debt. Additionally, as discussed elsewhere in this chapter, the debtor may choose to "reaffirm," and thereby become legally obligated to repay debts of the debtor's choice.

The questions of what debts are discharged or not discharged in the bankruptcy case, of reaffirmed debts, and of the fact that judgment liens are not discharged in a bankruptcy proceeding, are discussed later in this chapter.

III. ASSESSING THE CHANCES OF RECOVERY IN THE CASE

A. Judgment Liens vs. Non-Lien Claims

As discussed later in this chapter, liens are subject to many forms of attack in a bankruptcy case. But liens which are not attacked or which survive these attacks are not discharged in bankruptcy. Moreover, they are subject to numerous protections, some of which are discussed in this chapter. Perhaps most importantly, once the value of a lien has been established and allowed as a secured claim pursuant to 11 U.S.C. sec. 506 (*see* the Procedural Guide at Part VI of this Chapter), the lienor is entitled to the retention of the lien, the surrender of the property securing the lien, or the value of the lien, regardless of whether the bankruptcy is a Chapter 7, 11, or 13 proceeding. *See, e.g.*, 11 U.S.C. secs. 725, 1129(b)(2)(A), 1325(a)(5). To the extent the lien fails to survive these attacks, or is determined pursuant to 11 U.S.C. sec. 506 to have no value supporting it, then the judgment lienor stands in no better stead than any unsecured creditor.

Judgment lienors whose liens have been set aside as discussed elsewhere in this chapter, as well as judgment lienors to the extent that their lien has been found to be without value, stand in the same stead as judgment creditors who have no lien. And that is the same stead stood in by unsecured lenders and unsecured providers of goods or services.

Most notable among the liens potentially held by a judgment creditor in the State of New York is the lien provided by CPLR sec. 5203 on real property, provided that the judgment is entered in the office of the clerk of the county in which such real property is located.

B. Dischargeability

Whether or not a judgment is secured by a lien, judgments are discharged in bankruptcy—which is to say that enforcement of the debt as a personal liability of the debtor is forever barred—unless the obligation underlying the judgment falls into a category of "non-dischargeable debts." 11 U.S.C. sec. 523(a) sets forth the categories of such debts.

The fact that an obligation has been reduced to judgment does not preclude inquiry by the bankruptcy court into the true nature of the underlying obligation for purposes of applying 11 U.S.C. sec. 523. Therefore, even if you see a provision of section 523 which appears to clearly speak to the type of judgment you are seeking to enforce, it may be necessary for you to examine the case law under section 523. For example, debts for alimony, maintenance, or support are non-dischargeable debts, but only if they are truly "in the nature of" alimony, maintenance or support, and the bankruptcy court is not bound by the labels used by the state court in its judgment or decree—a state court decree specifying that a particular obligation is "support" may be viewed by a bankruptcy court as instead being in the nature of a dischargeable property settlement.

Bearing this example in mind, it can be stated that the other non-dischargeable debts which may be proved, as discussed in part IV-B of this chapter include certain categories of: taxes; debts incurred through use of a materially false financial statement upon which the creditor relied; debts which the debtor failed to duly list or schedule in his/her bankruptcy case (so long as the creditor had no actual notice or knowledge of the case); debts resulting from willfull or malicious injury; debts resulting from fraud, embezzlement, or larceny; debts resulting from injuries caused by driving while intoxicated; debts incurred by the purchase, on credit, of luxury goods or services on the eve of bankruptcy; and debts which had not been discharged in an earlier bankruptcy proceeding involving the same debtor. The qualifications and limitations regarding each of these categories of nondischargeable debt require careful scrutiny.

It is imperative to note that under 11 U.S.C. sec. 1328, all of the above categories of non-dischargeable debts are applicable only if a Chapter 13 debtor fails to complete his/her Chapter 13 plan—if the debtor completes the Chapter 13 plan it is only debts for alimony, maintenance, or support that are non-dischargeable regardless of the fact that the plan itself may have only provided for the payment of debts in part, rather than in whole.

For purposes of a Chapter 7 bankruptcy case, attention is called to 11 U.S.C. sec. 727 which sets forth a number of grounds on which a debtor can be denied a discharge, which grounds, if alleged and proven, will result in the debtor emerging from the bankruptcy case with all obligations still intact. Simplified, these grounds are: failure of the debtor to obey a lawful order of the court; having obtained a prior bankruptcy discharge, under certain circumstances, within the past six years; and various forms of concealment or other fraudulent or criminal conduct in connection with the case or with a related bankruptcy case.

The procedures governing objections to discharge and objections to the dischargeability of particular debts require prompt and diligent action by the attorney for the creditor as discussed later in this chapter.

C. Vulnerability Of Judgment Liens and Underlying Judgments

Unlike such liens as duly-perfected purchase-money security interests, judgment liens are subject to many forms of attack in a bankruptcy case. Among the more commonly used are the following.

If the debtor is an individual or a husband and wife filing jointly, judgment liens on real property that are subject to the homestead exemption provided by CPLR sec. 5206 may be set aside on motion by the debtor to the extent that the lien impairs the debtor's exemption. 11 USC sec. 522(f)(1). Therefore, if by setting aside all judgment liens on the homestead, the debtor can thereby free up equity in the property that would be exempt under CPLR sec. 5206, the debtor may set aside all judgment liens. On the other hand, if the equity thus freed up would be in excess of the permissible exemption amount, the debtor cannot set aside the portion of one or more prior judgment liens that are supported by the excess value over the exempt amount.

Any judgment lien taken after 90 days before the filing of the bankruptcy petition (one year before the filing of the petition if the creditor taking a lien is one having inside knowledge of the debtor's financial condition) can be set aside completely as a "preferential transfer" under 11 U.S.C. sec. 547 and this is without regard to the type of debtor or the nature of the property involved. This must be accomplished by a proceeding commenced by summons and complaint, Bankruptcy Rule 7001, and is subject to a two-year statute of limitations measured usually from the date of the filing of the petition. 11 U.S.C. sec. 546. (*See* the Procedural Guide at Part VI of this Chapter for hints in defending such an action.)

Pre-bankruptcy seizures of property may be vulnerable to the same type of attack as above, and to attack under 11 U.S.C. sec. 554 under which the representative of the estate is vested with the powers of a hypothetical judgment lien creditor who has had execution returned unsatisfied.

Under 11 U.S.C. sec. 506(d), as to which case law is still developing, it is possible that a judgment lien can be declared void to the extent that the encumbered property does not have sufficient value to support the lien. Thus, for example, it is possible that $4,000 of a $5,000 judgment lien could be set aside if there is only $1,000 of otherwise-unencumbered value in the property to which the lien has attached. In a similar vein, under some circumstances in a case under Chapter 7 of the Bankruptcy Code, the debtor may "redeem" the property from any type of lien by paying only the value supporting the lien. 11 U.S.C. sec. 722.

To the extent that any of the above attacks are successful, the judgment lienor is relegated to a status of holding only an unsecured claim, and the lien itself will be preserved for the benefit of the estate, 11 U.S.C. sec. 551, or of the debtor, 11 U.S.C. sec. 522(g), to prevent junior liens from moving up in status.

As to state court judgments themselves, the doctrine of res judicata generally applies—the bankruptcy court does not sit as a court of appellate jurisdiction regarding state trial court decisions. However, where a state court judgment must be interpreted in light of provisions of the Bankruptcy Code, the bankruptcy court may look behind the judgment. This is most commonly encountered in the context of disputes regarding the dischargeability of the debt in bankruptcy, as discussed elsewhere in this chapter. Suffice it to say for the moment that a state court judgment to the effect that a debt was incurred through fraud does not preclude inquiry by the bankruptcy court into whether the debtor engaged in the type of fraud which, under 11 U.S.C. sec. 523, would result in the passing of the debt through bankruptcy unaffected.

D. Liquidation Cases vs. Rehabilitation Cases

Putting aside the fact that a case may convert from one chapter of the Bankruptcy Code to another, a case under Chapter 7 of the Bankruptcy Code is always a liquidation case, a case under Chapter 13 of the Bankruptcy Code is almost always a rehabilitation case, a case under Chapter 11 of the Bankruptcy Code can be either.

Assessing the chances of recovery in the case is sometimes made easier by virtue of these facts. For example, if the case is a Chapter 7 case or a Chapter 11 case in which the debtor intends to undertake an orderly liquidation, it can often be determined whether the liquidation value of the debtor's assets will be sufficient to generate monies for the payment of the types of claims represented by that of your client. If, at liquidation values, there is no equity above the total value of senior liens, there will be no recovery for your client.

On the other hand, if rehabilitation is contemplated, and is feasible, many considerations come into play in determining the likelihood of recovery for your client. For example, a Chapter 11 or 13 plan must propose to pay section 507 priority claims in full; hence, if your client holds a claim entitled to priority under 11 U.S.C. sec. 507 (such as a claim for certain types of unpaid wages earned within certain time frames) the prospects for full recovery are as good as the debtor's prospects for being able to meet the obligations set forth in the proposed rehabilitation plan.

By way of another example, although a debtor in a Chapter 11 case need not promise to pay general unsecured creditors any more than those creditors would receive in a Chapter 7 liquidation of the debtor, it is very common for a Chapter 11 debtor to propose full and immediate payment to all creditors holding claims below a certain relatively small dollar amount or who are willing to reduce their claims to that amount.

And by way of yet another example, it is required in Chapter 13 cases that the debtor propose to commit all projected net disposable income to the payment of creditors during the life of the Chapter 13 plan. Hence, the prospects of recovery depend not on the value of the debtor's assets, but on the size of the debtor's income relative to his/her expenditures and to the amounts needed to satisfy the claims of senior classes of debt.

In sum, then, assessing the chances of recovery in the case can sometimes be accomplished by knowing the chapter under which the debtor is proceeding in conjunction with the debtor's expressed intentions, but at other times you must adopt a wait-and-see attitude. In the latter case, however, counsel should not overlook the possibility of participating in the negotiation and formulation of a rehabilitation plan, and the need to assure that proposed plans treat your client in full accord with applicable law, as discussed elsewhere in this chapter. (As to filing objections to confirmation of plans, *see* the Procedural Guide at Part VI of this Chapter.)

E. Debtor's Assets and Exemptions; "Priority of Claims"

As suggested in the previous section, it can be useful, in assessing the chances of recovery in the case, to examine the extent to which the debtor's assets, if sold at liquidation prices, would be sufficient to satisfy the claims of creditors. This analysis must be accomplished in light of 11 U.S.C. sec. 726, which specifies the fashion in which assets of the assets are to be distributed to creditors. By virtue of 11 U.S.C. secs. 1129 and 1325, the amounts which creditors would receive under section 726 are the minimum amounts that a debtor in a Chapter 11 or 13 case may propose to pay each creditor under the Chapter 11 or Chapter 13 plan.

By examining the debtor's schedules of assets and making additional inquiries of the debtor at the meetings of creditors, it is possible to estimate the liquidation values of the assets, the value of superior liens on those assets, and the debtor's available real property and personal property exemptions, if any. (Exemptions for debtors who are individuals are exclusively set forth at Article 10A of the New York Debtor and Creditor Law.) What remains is available for other creditors.

An example best demonstrates the analysis. The debtor is a corporation in Chapter 7. Your judgment lien has no value because the real property of the corporation is overencumbered by prior mortgages or judgment liens. Hence, your client will be treated as a general unsecured creditor. Examination discloses that the debtor's inventory and equipment is unencumbered and can reasonably be expected to bring $50,000 at the trustee's auction. To determine whether any portion of that $50,000 will be made available in payment of the claim of your client, it is necessary to consult section 726. Doing so, you find that all claims of a kind specified in 11 U.S.C. sec. 507 must be paid in full, and in the sequence specified in section 507, before monies can be distributed under section 726 to holders of "general" as opposed to "priority" unsecured claims.

You check section 507 to determine if the claim underlying the judgment you are collecting is a priority claim, such as a claim by a consumer for a deposit placed with the debtor for goods or services which the debtor never delivered. If the claim is such a priority claim, then you would know that if higher priority claims do not deplete the $50,000 in assets, your client will be next in line along with other creditors holding the same type of claim, and thereby stand a good chance of at least partial, and possibly full, recovery. On the other hand, if an examination of the schedules discloses an unpaid tax liability in excess of $50,000, you know that the unencumbered assets of the estate are not sufficient to reach your client's claim.

Presume, however, that your client does not hold a priority claim, and that $25,000 will be available for distribution after payment of all priority claims. An examination of the total dollar amount of timely filed claims against the estate by other general unsecured creditors permits you to project what the likely prorated distribution to your client will be.

One should never overlook the possibility that there may exist assets, even substantial assets, not disclosed in the debtor's schedules. Therefore, one should never refrain from timely filing a proof of claim, even if it appears from the papers that there will be no distribution to creditors. It is not uncommon for a trustee to determine that grounds exist for the recovery of a fraudulent transfer of sufficient amount to satisfy the claims of timely filed creditors in full. Moreover, it is also not uncommon for a small amount of assets to go exclusively to a small number of creditors because other creditors have refrained from filing proofs of claims; although section 726 permits late-filed claims to receive a distribution, it requires that they receive nothing until filed claims have been paid in full.

The type of examination discussed above is useful toward providing a client with the type of information needed to make the business decisions confronting a creditor in the early days of the bankruptcy case and later, particularly with regard to whether it is cost-effective for you to become actively involved in the bankruptcy case.

F. Pre-Bankruptcy Collections as "Preferential Transfers"

The word "transfer" is defined at 11 U.S.C. sec. 101 very broadly, to include any method of disposing of an interest in property, whether voluntary or involuntary, direct or indirect. And it is provided at 11 U.S.C. sec. 547 that certain types of transfers are "preferential" and may be set aside in bankruptcy by the trustee or debtor in possession, or even by the debtor if the subject property is exempt (pursuant to 11 U.S.C. sec. 522).

Generally speaking, a preferential transfer is a transfer of property of the debtor within the 90 days preceding bankruptcy, for application on a prior unsecured debt, while the debtor is insolvent (and the statute creates a presumption of insolvency), the result of which transfer is to enable the transferee to obtain a higher degree of repayment of its debt than the transferee would have obtained had the transfer not been made and were the transferee to receive only its appropriate distribution under a Chapter 7 bankruptcy.

Thus, for example, the taking of a judgment lien within 90 days before bankruptcy is usually a voidable preferential transfer, as discussed elsewhere in this chapter. However, the Second Circuit Court of Appeals, in the case of *In re Riddervold*, 7 Bankr. 921 (Bankr. 2d Cir. 1981) has ruled that where a wage execution was entered more than 90 days before the filing of the petition, the wage deductions received by the judgment creditor during the 90-day period before bankruptcy are not preferential transfers because, the court ruled, under New York law the "transfer" at issue is completely consumated upon the entry of the wage execution.

Presumably, the result would be different if the wage execution is entered during the 90 days preceding bankruptcy.

11 U.S.C. sec. 547 sets forth a list of transfers or transactions that are immune from attack as preferential transfers even though they would otherwise meet all the criteria for avoidance. Most notable in the context of collections is an immunity provided by the July 10, 1984, amendments for preferential transfers amounting to less than $600. The twelve possible defenses to a preference attack are set forth in the Procedural Guide at Part VI of this Chapter.

G. Is There a Co-Debtor?

With at least two exceptions, the filing of a petition under any chapter of the Bankruptcy Code by one obligor affords no protection whatsoever to a co-obligor. The first exception is statutory and is contained in 11 U.S.C. sec. 1301. That provision protects a Chapter 13 debtor by providing an automatic stay of collection activities directed against the debtor's co-obligors, provided that the consideration for the obligation flowed to the debtor rather than to the co-obligor. Although the details of local practice may differ, the statute generally provides that collection activities may begin or be resumed against the co-obligor twenty days after the creditor has filed a request for relief from the stay, unless the debtor, co-obligor, or another party with standing has requested a hearing. The creditor is entitled to relief to proceed against the co-debtor only to the extent that the Chapter 13 debtor is proposing, in his, her or their Chapter 13 plan, to provide less than full recovery to the creditor.

The second exception is found in a few cases in which the court determined that a Chapter 11 debtor's efforts to reorganize would be thwarted were a creditor not to be temporarily stayed from seeking to recover against a coobligor who was an affiliate of the debtor, such as a debtor-corporation's principal officer. As a practical matter, a corporate principal who is liable for some of the corporate debtor's debt will seek to maximize the corporation's contribution toward satisfaction of those debts, to the extent that this does not violate law.

Apart from these exceptions, and subject, of course, to the caveat that the method of proceeding against a co-debtor should never in fact be tantamount to harassment of the debtor who is in bankruptcy, the filing of a bankruptcy petition in no way curtails efforts to recover against a non-bankrupt co-obligor.

It should lastly be noted that if recovery from the co-debtor requires the commencement or continuation of an action or other proceedings against the debtor, even just in name only, it will be necessary to obtain relief from the section 362 stay to that extent, in accordance with the procedures discussed later in this chapter.

H. Miscellaneous Considerations

Bankruptcy cases can be unpredictable, despite popular belief to the contrary. It is simply not true that all bankruptcy cases constitute disaster for creditors. It is a common occurrence in Chapter 7 bankruptcy cases, for example, that meager assets have been discovered, but so few creditors have filed claims against those assets, even after repeated notice, that a "surplus" results for return to the debtor. Similarly, it is not uncommon for a bankruptcy trustee, a committee of creditors, or others, to uncover frauds or concealments which when pursued result in sizeable distributions to creditors, not to mention possible criminal prosecution of the wrongdoers.

Moreover, outside the scope of this chapter are a multitude of provisions of the Bankruptcy Code that provide rights or remedies to creditors uniquely situated, or which offer substantial rewards to the clients of diligent and innovative counsel.

As but one example, at least one instance comes to mind in which an attorney for a judgment creditor had knowledge that a Chapter 13 debtor, who was proposing a small payout to unsecured creditors, was in the process of attempting to sell his home for substantially more money than the value scheduled by the debtor in his bankruptcy papers. By bringing this properly to the attention of the court, this attorney not only brought about an amendment to the debtor's Chapter 13 plan that provided a 100 percent payout to all creditors, but prompted a criminal investigation of both the debtor and his attorney relating to the circumstances surrounding the undervaluation.

You are therefore encouraged to learn as much as you can about bankruptcy law and about the "bankrupt" party from whom you are attempting to collect.

IV. SELECTED REMEDIES

A. Relief from Stay: Adequate Protection of Judicial Lien

It is rare for a creditor to establish grounds to be relieved from the automatic stay in order to commence an action on a dischargeable debt or to continue a pending state court action regarding such a debt unless there is a non-bankrupt co-obligor or insurer and the creditor is seeking relief from the stay only because of state practice requirements to the effect that the debtor be named as a party defendant. In such latter instances, relief from the stay can generally be obtained by an order based on stipulations that the creditor will not seek to enforce any judgment obtained against the debtor.

It is much more common for a bankruptcy court to grant relief from the automatic stay to permit a judgment creditor to realize upon a duly perfected, non-avoidable judgment lien. Indeed, upon suitable motion by such a creditor, the bankruptcy court has no choice but to grant relief from the stay unless the existence of certain conditions is established, as follows.

Relief from the stay is governed by 11 U.S.C. sec. 362(d). The procedure is a motion procedure governed by Bankruptcy Rules 4001, 9014 and 9006. The following discussion presumes that there is value supporting the lien, for if there is not, then for many purposes in bankruptcy a judgment lien creditor stands in no better stead than an unsecured creditor.

Let us presume a simple hypothetical situation. You wish to foreclose a judgment lien on otherwise unencumbered and nonexempt real property owned by a Chapter 11 debtor. The judgment is for $50,000 and the real property is worth $20,000.

All you need do, subject to local practice, is file and serve your motion and notice of motion requesting relief from the stay to permit foreclosure, alleging that the debtor has no equity in the property and that your client has not been offered adequate protection of your client's interest in the property. 11 U.S.C. sec. 362 and the applicable rules of Bankruptcy Procedure require a prompt hearing and determination of such a motion. And after hearing, the court "shall" grant relief from the stay unless the debtor in this hypothetical situation can establish both of two things—that the property is necessary to an effective Chapter 11 rehabilitation, and that the debtor can and will provide "adequate protection" insuring that the creditor will suffer no loss from the continuation of the stay. (If the debtor has equity in property, the equity can sometimes be used as, or obviate the need for, "adequate protection." In reality, much stay litigation revolves around the value of the property, for if the debtor can establish that there is equity in the property the debtor has established much toward obtaining a continuation of the stay.)

If the property in our example is unrelated or otherwise nonessential to the debtor's rehabilitation plans, the debtor will fail in satisfying the first criterion.

As to the second criterion, the debtor must offer some effective means of the type recognized in 11 U.S.C. sec. 361 (which contains the definition of "adequate protection") for assuring no diminution in the value of your client's lien and for compensating your client for the loss of the use of the money your client would obtain were foreclosure to be permitted. Moreover, the debtor must demonstrate the wherewithal to execute this proposal. In the hypothetical situation, the debtor might propose to make periodic payments of "interest" on the $20,000 value pending the development of a reorganization plan that would retire the debt.

What a bankruptcy court will approve as "adequate protection" is largely for case-by-case determination. But if the court does find you to be adequately protected by the debtor's proposals, it is imperative (if you wish to avoid relitigating the same issues at a future time) that you ask the court for an order under which the stay is automatically limited in your favor should the debtor default in its promises.

Of course, if you are successful in obtaining relief from the stay you will be free to resort or return to New York State collection law practices.

It is often advantageous, when the holder of a judgment does not have any burning desire to foreclose the judgment, to forego seeking relief from the stay, but limit the motion instead to a motion for the court to determine "adequate protection." Such a motion demonstrates a willingness to let the debtor continue in possession of the property, but seeks to protect the client from any losses that may result from the debtor's continued use. A debtor may even propose beginning periodic payments to retire at least the secured portion of the judgment debt over the course of the bankruptcy case and after.

An examination of sections 361 and 362 of the Bankruptcy Code in light of this greatly-simplified example will enlighten you as to the many innovative ways in which you may beneficially represent the holder of a valuable judgment lien.

The procedures discussed above are summarized in outline form in the Procedural Guide found at Part VI of this Chapter.

B. Dischargeability Litigation

While non-dischargeable categories of tax debts, unscheduled debts, debts for alimony, maintenance or support, non-compensatory fine, penalty, or forfeiture claims, student loan debts, drunk driving liabilities, and certain debts related to an earlier bankruptcy proceeding, are non-dischargeable in Chapter 7 cases and some Chapter 11 cases without the need for the creditor to take any procedural steps in the bankruptcy case, 11 U.S.C. sec. 523(c) provides that debts, even judgment debts, resulting from the use of a false financial statement, fraud, defalcation, embezzlement, larceny, or willful or malicious injury are discharged unless the creditor holding such debt obtains in a timely fashion a judgment of non-dischargeability from the bankruptcy court.

All creditors are notified of the time within which complaints objecting to the dischargeability of such debts must be filed and served, and generally the time set is 60 days after the date of the first meeting of creditors.

Under Bankruptcy Rule 7001(6), seeking a determination of non-dischargeability requires the filing of a complaint (and the payment of a $60 filing fee) and adherence to the rules contained in Part VII of the Rules of Bankruptcy Procedure. These rules approximate the Federal Rules of Civil Procedure. Hence, dischargeability litigation can be costly. It is important to additionally note that 11 U.S.C. sec. 523(d) provides that such litigation, when based upon the alleged use of a false financial statement, can result in a judgment in favor of the debtor for costs and attorneys' fees, if the court finds that the position of the creditor was not substantially justified.

As noted in Part III-B of this chapter, the bankruptcy court may look behind the State Court judgment to determine the true nature of a judgment debt.

If the debt that is the subject of the dischargeability litigation was not previously reduced to judgment, and if the bankruptcy court determines that the debt is non-dischargeable, then the bankruptcy court may grant a money judgment, thereby eliminating the need to later litigate the debt in State Court. 28 U.S.C. secs. 1961 *et seq.* and Bankruptcy Rule 9021 should be consulted for the effect of a judgment, and Bankruptcy Rule 7069 for execution thereon.

Debts that are non-dischargeable even without litigation in the bankruptcy court may be sued upon or executed upon in State Court as if the bankruptcy had not occurred, once the creditor is free of the restraints of the bankruptcy stay. The debtor might raise, in State Court, defenses going to the construction of the section 523 definitions of non-dischargeable debts, and the State Court is perfectly competent to address these issues. However, if either party should choose to return to the Bankruptcy Court to determine those issues (indeed, the debtor may choose to reopen his/her bankruptcy case to bring a contempt motion against the creditor for violation of the injunctive effects of the debtor's discharge), it is generally agreed that the jurisdiction of the bankruptcy court to determine matters relating to the dischargeability of particular debts is paramount and supersedes that of the State Court.

Very significantly, a creditor who holds a non-dischargeable debt may be in an extremely good position to recover upon that debt in light of the discharge of the debtor as to other debts. For this reason, it is usually much preferrable for a creditor to establish the non-dischargeability of the particular debt held by that creditor than it would be for the creditor to seek to block the discharge of the debtor as to all debts as is provided in 11 U.S.C. sec. 727 and 11 U.S.C. sec. 1141(d)(3).

Litigation to block the discharge of all debts is generally subject to the same time restraints, and is prosecuted in the same manner, as litigation to determine the dischargeability of those particular types of debts that the law provides will be discharged unless the bankruptcy court is timely asked to address them.

Dischargeability litigation procedure is outlined in the Procedural Guide found at Part VI of this Chapter.

C. Reaffirmation

Although a debtor may choose to voluntarily repay any debt, 11 U.S.C. sec. 524(f), it is only by a procedurally-sufficient "reaffirmation agreement" that a debtor becomes legally obligated to repay a discharged debt.

The procedures governing reaffirmation agreements are set forth at 11 U.S.C. sec. 524(c),(d). Any such agreement should be negotiated only through the attorney for the debtor, if the debtor has one. If the debtor has no attorney, you should be careful not to make overtures toward the debtor that might be construed as a violation of the bankruptcy stay.

Since a debtor usually reaffirms only on secured debts (in order to retain the collateral), reaffirmation in the collections context are generally likely only as to non-dischargeable debts and debts owed nongovernmental persons with whom the debtor would like to do business in the future, such as the family doctor. As to prohibitions against some forms of discrimination against debtors, *see* 11 U.S.C. secs. 366, 525.

Under 11 U.S.C. sec. 524(c),(d), reaffirmation agreements need not be approved by the court if the debtor is not represented by an attorney. But if the debtor is not represented by an attorney, the debtor (not the creditor) must move the court to approve the agreement as not imposing an undue hardship on the debtor or on a dependent of the debtor, and as being in the best interest of the debtor, except where the debt is a consumer debt secured by real property.

All reaffirmation agreements must be entered into by the debtor before the debtor has been granted a discharge. In other words, those efforts to obtain a reaffirmation agreement from the debtor that are undertaken after the debtor has been granted a discharge may be a violation of the injunctive effects of the discharge of the debtor, may result in contempt of the injunctive order of the court, and will taint any agreement thus obtained. In most consumer cases under Chapter 7, the debtor's discharge will be entered by the court—and is thereby "granted" by the court within the purview of the above restriction— upon the expiration of the time set for the filing of complaints objecting to the debtor's discharge. This is before, sometimes long before, the date set for the debtor's "discharge hearing." Therefore, you should be focusing on the last day for the filing of complaints objecting to discharge, not the date of the debtor's discharge hearing, as your deadline for having a reaffirmation agreement "in the can."

The procedure discussed above, and other steps regarding reaffirmations, are outlined in the Procedural Guide at Part VI of this Chapter.

D. Participation in Chapter 11 and 13 Rehabilitation Plans

If properly prodded, a Chapter 11 or 13 debtor must propose under a rehabilitation plan to pay at least the amount that each creditor would have received had the debtor sought relief, and been liquidated, under Chapter 7 of the Bankruptcy Code. 11 U.S.C. sec. 1129(a)(7), sec. 1325(a)(4). This is known as the "Chapter 7 test." Thus, all of the rules discussed elsewhere in this chapter regarding the debtor's assets and exemptions, claims filed against the estate and the priority thereof, assets rendered unencumbered by the setting aside of liens, and so forth, come into play in setting the minimum amount that debtors seeking rehabilitation must propose to pay to creditors. How much in excess of this threshold amount creditors are able to obtain from the debtor is purely a matter of negotiations that must obviously be tempered by reality.

Although only the debtor may propose a rehabilitation plan in Chapter 13, it is required by 11 U.S.C. sec. 1325(b) that if the holder of an unsecured claim objects to confirmation of the plan, then the court must find that all of the debtor's "projected disposal income" is being promised to creditors under the plan for at least the initial three-year period. This requirement, when properly asserted, can result in a substantially higher payment to creditors then would be required under the Chapter 7 test. Moreover, any creditor may raise, in opposition to the confirmation of a Chapter 13 plan, the standards for confirmation set forth in 11 U.S.C. sec. 1325, the most notable of which might be the fact that a plan must be proposed in "good faith," which is generally thought to mean that the plan must be fundamentally fair.

In Chapter 11, any creditor may file a plan of reorganization once there has lapsed the period of time (statutorily a 120-day minimum) for the debtor's exclusive right to do so. 11 U.S.C. sec. 1121. The possibility, then, that someone else may propose a confirmable plan of reorganization combines with several other factors to give creditors of a potentially profitable debtor significant bargaining leverage. Among these additional factors are: the potential for ousting the present management of the debtor in favor of a court appointed trustee, 11 U.S.C. sec. 1104; the potential for conversion or dismissal of the Chapter 11 case,

11 U.S.C. sec. 1112; and the fact that the shareholders of the debtor may not retain any equity in the debtor under a plan of reorganization unless creditor classes have either agreed to let them retain equity or are being proposed to be paid in full under the plan. 11 U.S.C. sec. 1129(b)(2)(ii), which requires, pursuant to 11 U.S.C. sec. 1129(b)(1), a suitable objection to confirmation.

Therefore, familiarity with the financial standards mandated by Chapters 11 or 13, or available under those Chapters upon suitable process initiated by a creditor, can result in significant benefits.

Presuming that a favorable (under the circumstances) plan has been obtained and confirmed by the court, the failure of the debtor to abide by the terms of the plan gives rise to remedies on behalf of creditors. For example, under 11 U.S.C. sec. 1112 a creditor of a Chapter 11 debtor who has defaulted in performance of a confirmed Chapter 11 plan may move to convert the case to Chapter 7 or to dismiss the case. And under 11 U.S.C. sec. 1329 an unsecured creditor may move to amend a confirmed Chapter 13 plan.

It can be seen from the above that a significant creditor of a Chapter 11 debtor ought not to pass up the opportunity to participate in the formulation of a Chapter 11 plan (such as through participation on a committee of creditors), and a creditor of a Chapter 13 debtor should not fail to monitor the debtor's pre-confirmation proposals as well as his/her post-confirmation performance. Under either Chapter, active involvement on behalf of the creditor, such as through well-founded objections to confirmation of a plan, may be invaluable.

The procedure for such objections is outlined in the Procedural Guide at Part VI of this Chapter.

V. SOME POST-BANKRUPTCY REMEDIES, WHEN AVAILABLE

A. In General

Except for the instances in which a discharged debtor has reaffirmed on discharged debts, as discussed in part IV-C above, the possibility of postbankruptcy remedies that do not constitute contempt of the injunction of the court resulting from a bankruptcy discharge are, in general, limited to: actions against property that is subject to a lien that has survived bankruptcy; execution on debts that have survived bankruptcy; and isolated instances in which "recoupment" is thought permissible. These are discussed in the following sections.

11 U.S.C. sec. 524 describes the effect of a discharge in bankruptcy in very broad terms, and you are advised against attempting to collect a debt after bankruptcy unless you fall within the ranks of those entitled thereto.

The possibility that your client was not notified of the bankruptcy, and had no actual knowledge or notice thereof should not be overlooked: this eventuality is specifically dealt with at 11 U.S.C. sec. 523(a)(3) and can result in the debt being non-dischargeable. However, the records of the court may show that your client did receive a notice of the bankruptcy under a name that your client would not have recognized. For example, if your client had retained a record of the account under the debtor's business style, and in fact the business and the bankruptcy were those of a sole proprietor, the question of whether your client truly received "notice" of the bankruptcy is subject to litigation. Therefore, it is not unwise to do a bankruptcy search on a defendant before you commence or continue collection efforts against an individual even where bankruptcy has not been mentioned by your client: as to a debtor who has remained local, and who would likely have filed bankruptcy in one locality nearby, the name search performed by the Bankruptcy Clerk costs only two dollars, and may save a contempt citation and other litigation.

B. Where Lien is Still Good, but Judgment Itself was Discharged

For purposes of the old axiom that where there is no obligation there is no lien, it may be said that a discharge in bankruptcy does not extinguish an obligation—it merely bars the remedy. Therefore, a lien which has survived bankruptcy remains valid even if the underlying obligation (and therefore the debtor's personal liability) was discharged.

Once the automatic stay has been terminated, in accordance with the provisions of 11 U.S.C. sec. 362, the lienor may proceed against the property that is subject to the lien.

While the debtor may, one year after discharge in bankruptcy, utilize N.Y. Debtor and Creditor Law sec. 150 in order that the judgment will be marked discharged in the records of the County Clerk, this has no effect on judgment liens which attached prior to bankruptcy; rather, it will protect the debtor's future creditability and his/her after-acquired property.

You are cautioned, however, that some bankruptcy courts might permit a debtor to reopen a case in order to set aside avoidable judgment liens that were overlooked during the pendency of the case.

C. Non-Dischargeable Debts

As is discussed in part IV-B above, non-discharged debts may be sued upon by the creditor once free of the bankruptcy stay; if reduced to judgment prior to bankruptcy, execution may resume.

See the discussion above, with regard to dischargeability litigation, for an assessment of the potential for further litigation arising out of the fact of the intervening bankruptcy discharge.

D. Other Post-Bankruptcy Remedies

11 U.S.C. sec. 524 makes it clear that even without a reaffirmation agreement, a debtor may choose to voluntarily repay a discharged debt in whole or in part. This, coupled with the fact discussed above that

it is only employment discrimination against a former bankrupt that is prohibited with regard to the private sector, gives rise to the possibility that a discharged bankrupt who wishes to continue, even on a cash-on-delivery basis, to obtain the goods or services of your client might not be able to do so without voluntarily repaying the discharged debt. It is imperative, however, that the creditor make no overtures to the debtor in this regard that might be viewed as an "act" to collect the discharged debt or to harass the debtor. That would be viewed as being a violation of the injunctive effect of discharge, and therefore a contempt of court.

Some cases have recognized that "recoupment" is not the same as "collection" of a discharged debt. These instances are limited, but deserve your study: *see In Re Main*, 32 Bankr. 452 (Bankr. W.D.N.Y. 1983); *Waldschmidt v. CBS, Inc.*, 14 Bankr. 309 (Bankr. M.D. Tenn. 1981); *In Re Yonkers Hamilton Sanitarium Inc.*, 22 Bankr. 427 (Bankr. S.D.N.Y. 1982); *but compare Lee v. Schweiker*, 739 F.2d 870, 11 Collier Bankr. Cas. 2d (MB) 834 (1984).

VI. PROCEDURAL GUIDE AND SAMPLE FORMS

The following outlines the basic procedural steps for undertaking some of the actions and strategies discussed in this chapter. Also included are sample forms provided by Richard J. Miller, Esq., Editor in Chief of this volume, for which contribution the writer is grateful.

A. Filing Proofs of Claims

1. Unsecured Creditors: Timely filing of a proof of claim on behalf of an unsecured creditor assures the creditor of a *pro-rata* share of whatever assets are available for distribution in the case. (*See* Exhibit 1.)

2. Secured Creditors: Filing a timely proof of claim on behalf of a secured creditor not only serves to assure that the trustee or debtor in possession is aware of your lien claim and its extent, but also preserves the creditor's opportunity to later assert, in an amendment to the claim,

any unsecured deficiency that is discovered after, for example, you have obtained a lifting of the stay to permit sale of the collateral. (*See* Exhibit 2.)

3. Caution: Filing of a proof of claim might be construed to be a consent to the jurisdiction of the bankruptcy court to adjudicate counterclaims which the debtor might have against the creditor. *See* 28 U.S.C. sec. 157(b)(2)(C).

B. Motions to lift the section 362 Automatic Stay

1. Grounds for Relief Under Sections 362(d), (e), (f):

a. For "cause, including the lack of adequate protection" of the value of a lien; or

b. Fact that the debtor has no equity in the property, and, additionally, the property is not necessary to an effective reorganization. (*See* Exhibit 3.)

2. Procedure:

a. Ask clerk's office whether such motions must be served with notice of motion specifying a return date for oral argument, and for any other local requirements.

b. Serve and file motion/notice of motion with supporting affidavit and exhibits; serve on debtor, debtor's counsel, trustee, trustee's counsel, and consider serving other lienors.

c. Determine whether hearing will be preliminary or final, and if preliminary whether to bring witnesses (on issue of value, etc.).

d. If there is default, or if motion is granted after trial, obtain order.

e. If motion is denied on condition that debtor observe court-mandated or agreed conditions for providing "adequate protection," seek order automatically lifting stay should debtor subsequently default.

C. Defending Action Against Creditor to Recover Preferential Transfer (*See* Exhibit 4)

1. Limitations: Two-year limitations period (measured from date of appointment of trustee, or from date of filing of Chapter 11 in which there is no trustee) is found in section 546.

2. Standing: Unless debtor is debtor in possession, debtor cannot bring preference action on own behalf unless preference involved exempt property. *See* sections 522(g),(h).

3. If you lose, or otherwise return property to estate, file proof of claim within thirty days under rule 3002(c)(3) so that *pro-rata* share will come back to creditor.

4. Twelve Defenses under section 547; and mitigation under section 550.

a. Was the transfer to or for the benefit of a creditor?

b. Was it on account of an antecedent debt?

c. Was the debtor insolvent at the time of the transfer? (Note that debtor is presumed insolvent during 90 days before bankruptcy petition.)

d. Was the transfer "made" within 90 days before bankruptcy (one year if transferee is "insider")? (Note that "made" is defined at section 547(e).)

e. Did transfer enable creditor to receive more than if transfer had not been made and creditor was to receive distributive share in a Chapter 7 case?

f. Was transfer intended to be and in fact a contemporaneous exchange for new value?

g. Was a transfer an ordinary payment of an ordinary debt?

h. Was the transfer a transfer of a security interest to secure the debt that enabled the debtor to purchase the collateral?

i. Did the creditor give new value to the debtor after the transfer?

j. Is the challenged transfer merely normal replacement of inventory or receivables subject to a floating lien?

k. Is the challenged transfer the fixing of a non-avoidable statutory lien? (Note that a judgment lien is not a statutory lien, under section 101's definitions.)

l. Is the debtor a consumer, and the amount of the challenged transfer less that $600?

m. Under section 550, is the transferee a good faith transferee entitled to a lien on the property transfereed?

D. Motions to Dismiss *(See* Exhibit 5)

1. Potential Grounds:

a. In Chapter 7: unreasonable delay in such matters as appearance at meeting of creditors, filing of required statements, schedules, lists, notices and in cooperating with trustee in marshalling assets of estate. *See* section 707.

b. In Chapter 11: continuing losses and absence of likelihood of rehabilitation; inability to effectuate a plan; unreasonable delay that is prejudicial to creditors; default in the provisions of a confirmed plan. *See* section 1112.

c. In Chapter 13: unreasonable delay; failure to timely file a plan; denial of confirmation of a plan and of a motion for additional time to file a confirmable plan; default in the terms of a confirmed plan. *See* section 1307.

d. In all Chapters, the interests of all parties, including the debtor, would be better served thereby. *See* section 305.

2. Procedure: see part B-2 above, except that it is unlikely that there would be a preliminary hearing. Even on motions to dismiss, the court might grant only a conditional order; for example, the court might condition an order dismissing on the debtor's failure to cure the irregularity that is complained of within a time set by the court.

3. Cautionary Note as to Notice and Hearing: The Rules (Rule 2002) require 20 days' notice to parties-in-interest of a hearing on a motion to dismiss. Consult with the clerk regarding who is to provide this notice. The court may require the moving party to provide it, and in a large case the cost might be substantial.

4. Special note regarding the 1984 Amendment's new requirement that a consumer debtor file, under section 521(2), a statement of intention with regard to collateral securing consumer debts: in the context of collection of money judgments, it is possible that if the judgment is on a consumer debt, and if the judgment lien is not avoidable as a preferential transfer under section 547 or as an impairment of an available exemption under section 522, this new requirement might apply to the debtor's intentions with regard to property encumbered by a judgment lien, in which case the debtor's failure to specify whether he intends to redeem, surrender, or negotiate a payment agreement with regard to the liened property might constitute grounds for dismissal.

E. Reaffirmation Agreements

1. Where the Debtor is Represented by an Attorney: The 1984 Amendments dispense with the need for court approval, but make sure that the agreement contains the rescission statement specified in section 524(c)(2), and that the agreement and a declaration by the debtor's attorney are filed with the court in accordance with section 524(c)(3). CAUTION: Subsection (c)(1) requires that the reaffirmation agreement be made before the granting of a discharge; in a routine

Chapter 7 case the discharge is usually granted 60 days after the first meeting of creditors, and therefore occurs well before the debtor's discharge hearing.

2. Where the Debtor is Not Represented by an Attorney:

a. Court approval required except as to consumer debts secured by real property.

b. File agreement, motion, notice of motion. (*See* Exhibit 6, except that the court might require the debtor to appear and take the stand to permit the court to find, as required by section 524(c)(6), that the agreement is in the best interest of the debtor and will not impose undue hardship.)

c. Obtain order approving.

F. Redemptions

1. Chapter 7 debtor may use section 722 to redeem certain types of property from liens.

2. *See* Exhibit 6, although applicability of section 722 to collection of money judgments is problematic, in light of fact that debtor cannot redeem real property under section 722.

G. Motions to Abandon

1. Under section 554(b) judgment lien creditor may move to obtain order abandoning property that is of inconsequential value to estate.

2. Procedure clears title as to interest of trustee.

3. Procedure: *see* part B-2 above, except that preliminary hearing is unlikely. (*See* Exhibit 8).

4. Obtain order:

a. Should contain legal description of property.

b. Important that order contain language like last paragraph of Exhibit 8's order, to avoid construction that would require further consummating document from Trustee.

H. Complaints Objecting to Discharge or to Dischargeability of Particular Debts

1. Determine whether facts support section 523 objection to dischargeability of particular debt or objection to discharge into under section 727:

a. Criminal provisions of 18 U.S.C. sec. 152 can bar settlement of section 727 complaints.

b. Rule 7041 can complicate withdrawal or other dismissal of section 727 complaints.

c. Creditor who holds the only debt that is nondischargeable has better chance of recovery than if all debts survive bankruptcy.

2. Complaints (*See* Exhibit 9):

a. File complaint and pay $60 fee for Adversary Proceeding. *See* Rules 7001 *et seq.*

b. Obtain summons from court.

c. Serve summons and complaint and file affidavit of service.

d. Preliminary hearing or pretrial is likely; determine whether witnesses need be present.

e. After trial, obtain order:

(1) If a section 727 objection to discharge, obtain order denying discharge.

(2) If a section 523 dischargeability complaint, obtain order declaring debt to be nondischargeable (and granting money judgment if in doubt about viability of judgment previously obtained in nonbankruptcy court).

I. Objections to Confirmation of Plans

1. Determine grounds for objection:

a. In Chapter 11, *see* section 1129.

b. In Chapter 13, *see* section 1325.

2. File objection. (*See* Exhibit 10.)

3. Attend scheduled confirmation hearing prepared to prove stated grounds.

J. Determining Value of Lien, and Therefore of Allowable Secured Claim, under section 506:

1. File secured claim, as above.

2. File and serve motion to allow it; use motion format discussed above.

3. Obtain order. (*See* Exhibit 11.)

4. This assists in establishing rights of creditor to such relief as "adequate protection" of lien, treatment as secured creditor in plan, etc.

5. Caution: Under section 506(a), valuation of lien for one purpose is not necessarily binding for another purpose.

K. Settling a Claim or Counterclaim by the Estate Against a Creditor (*See* Exhibit 12)

1. Negotiate proposed situation in settlement of trustee's or debtor in possession's motion or complaint.

2. Rule 2002 requires notice to creditors of estate's intent to settle or compromise, unless court orders otherwise.

3. After authority of trustee or debtor in possesison to settle has been established by requisite notice, and by hearing if necessary, submit stipulation and order approving.

L. Provisional Relief for Lienors Whose Collateral is in Danger (*See* Exhibit 13)

1. Seek relief from the automatic stay as discussed above.

2. Either as a part of that motion, or by separate motion filed after or at the same time, seek either a show-cause order or, pursuant to Rule 9006, an order shortening time for the return of your motion for provisional relief.

3. Consider use of Rule 4001(c) providing for *ex parte* relief from the automatic stay in unusual circumstances.

M. Representing the Creditor's Committee in Chapter 11 (*See* Exhibit 14)

1. In a change brought about by the 1984 amendments, the attorney for a creditor is no longer precluded from serving as attorney for the creditor's committee. *See* section 327(c).

2. When representing the committee, the attorney is compensable from the estate, rather than the client. *See* section 330.

3. It is essential that the attorney receive court approval *before* rendering any service for which compensation will be sought from the estate.

Exhibit 1 or 2

T 1031—Proof of Claim: Bankruptcy: Official Form No. 19 Power of Attorney: 8-83

UNITED STATES BANKRUPTCY COURT FOR THE DISTRICT OF

CASE NO.

In re

Debtor

PROOF OF CLAIM

Type or print all necessary parts. Incomplete or illegible claims may result in disallowance.

1. **If claimant is an individual claiming for himself** The undersigned, who is the claimant herein, resides at *

If claimant is a partnership claiming through a member The undersigned who resides at *

is a member of a partnership, composed of the undersigned and †

and doing business at *

and is authorized to make this proof of claim on behalf of the partnership.

If claimant is a corporation claiming through an authorized officer The undersigned, who resides at *

is the of , a corporation organized under the laws of

and doing business at *

and is authorized to make this proof of claim on behalf of the corporation.

If claim is made by agent The undersigned, who resides at *

is the agent of

of * and is authorized to make this proof of claim on behalf of the claimant.

2. The debtor was, at the time of the filing of the petition initiating this case, and still is indebted [*or* liable] to the claimant, in the sum of $

3. The consideration for this debt [*or* ground of liability] is as follows:

If filed in a chapter 7 or 13 case. This claim consists of $ in principal amount and $ in additional charges [*or* no additional charges]. **Itemize all charges in addition to principal amount of debt, state basis for inclusion and computation, and set forth any other consideration relevant to the legality of the charge.**

$5,000 or imprisonment for not more than five years or both—Title 18, U.S.C., Sec. 152.

PENALTY FOR PRESENTING FRAUDULENT CLAIMS.—Fine of not more than

4. [*If the claim is founded on writing*] The writing on which this claim is founded (or a duplicate thereof) is attached hereto [*or* cannot be attached for the reason set forth in the statement attached hereto].

5. [*If appropriate*] This claim is founded on an open account, which became [*or* will become] due on
as shown by the itemized statement attached hereto. Unless it is attached hereto or its absence is explained in an attached statement, no note or other negotiable instrument has been received for the account or any part of it.

6. No judgment has been rendered on the claim except

7. The amount of all payments on this claim has been credited and deducted for the purpose of making this proof of claim.

8. This claim is not subject to any setoff or counter-claim except

9. No security interest is held for this claim except

[*If security interest in property of the debtor is claimed*] The undersigned claims the security interest under the writing referred to in paragraph 4 hereof [*or* under a separate writing which (or a duplicate of which) is attached hereto, *or* under a separate writing which cannot be attached hereto for the reason set forth in the statement attached hereto]. Evidence of perfection of such security interest is also attached hereto.

10. This claim is a general unsecured claim, except to the extent that the security interest, if any, described in paragraph 9 is sufficient to satisfy the claim. [*If priority is claimed, state the amount and basis thereof.*]

11. This claim is filed as ☐ an Unsecured ☐ a Priority ☐ a Secured claim. $..............................
Total amount claimed

Claim Number
(For Office Use Only)

Dated: Signed:

....
Type or Print Name Signed

* State mailing address. † Name and mailing address of each partner.

No.........................

United States Bankruptcy Court

....DISTRICT OF

....

In Bankruptcy

IN THE MATTER OF

....

Debtor

Proof of Claim and Power of Attorney

AMOUNT OF CLAIM $......................

....

(NAME)

....

(ADDRESS)

....

JULIUS BLUMBERG, INC., NEW YORK CITY 10013

CORPORATION: by who says that he is the of the corporation named above and is authorized to execute this power of attorney in its behalf.

....

....

official character

* State post-office address.

POWER OF ATTORNEY

To

of *

The undersigned claimant hereby authorizes you, or any one of you, as attorney in fact for the undersigned and with full power of substitution, to vote on any question that may be lawfully submitted to creditors of the debtor in the above-entitled case; [if appropriate] to vote for a trustee of the estate of the debtor and for a committee of creditors; to receive dividends; and in general to perform any act not constituting the practice of law for the undersigned in all matters arising in this case.

Dated: Signed:..

[*If appropriate*] By..As..

Address:...

ACKNOWLEDGMENT

STATE OF COUNTY OF ss.:

INDIVIDUAL-PARTNERSHIP-CORPORATION: Acknowledged before me on

PARTNERSHIP: by who says that he is a member of the partnership named above and is authorized to execute this power of attorney in its behalf.

EXHIBIT 3

UNITED STATES BANKRUPTCY COURT
NORTHERN DISTRICT OF NEW YORK

In re:	IN BANKRUPTCY NO. ____________
______________,	
Debtor.	NOTICE OF MOTION TO VACATE STAY

PLEASE TAKE NOTICE that upon the annexed application of ______, by its attorney, RICHARD J. MILLER & ASSOCIATES, P.C., the undersigned will move this Court at United States Bankruptcy Court, U.S. Post Office and Court House, Albany, New York on , 1983 at ______ o'clock in the ____________noon, or as soon thereafter as counsel can be heard, for an order modifying the stay granted pursuant to 11 U.S.C., Section 362 to permit the applicant herein to obtain possession of the motor vehicle described in the annexed application pursuant to its duly perfected security interest, and for such other and further relief as may seem just and proper.

PLEASE TAKE FURTHER NOTICE that unless an answer to the application is served and filed, together with proof of service at least one (1) day before the return date herein, the relief demanded in the application will be deemed consented to by the respective parties in interest.

Dated: Albany, New York

Yours, etc.

RICHARD J. MILLER &
ASSOCIATES, P.C.
Attorney for Applicant
One Commerce Plaza, P. O. Box 2
Albany, New York 12260
Phone: (518) 465-7591

TO: ______________________
Attorney for Debtor

____

____
Trustee

____

ALL CREDITORS AND PARTIES IN INTEREST

A COPY OF THE APPLICATION BY ______________________
WITH SUPPORTING DOCUMENTATION MAY BE OBTAINED FROM RICHARD J. MILLER & ASSOCIATES, P.C. UPON WRITTEN REQUEST.

UNITED STATES BANKRUPTCY COURT
NORTHERN DISTRICT OF NEW YORK

In re:	IN BANKRUPTCY NO. ____________
______________,	
Debtor.	APPLICATION TO VACATE STAY

TO: HON. JUSTIN J. MAHONEY, Bankruptcy Judge.

The application of __________________, by its attorney, Richard J. Miller & Associates, P.C., respectfully represents:

1. ________________ filed a petition under Chapter __________ of the Bankruptcy Code on ________________, 19____.

2. This is an application to obtain relief from the stay as provided by Rule 601 of the Bankruptcy Code.

3. On ____________________, 19____, the applicant herein acquired a security interest in the personal property described in the attached security agreement, as indicated on the attached notice of recorded lien, to a motor vehicle, to wit: __________.

4. The total market value of the vehicle is $______________, as demonstrated by the NADA rating attached hereto.

5. The original amount of the secured debt was $____________________, as evidenced by the attached retail installment contract, and the present balance due is $____________________, as of ____________________, 19____.

6. No payment has been made on said obligation since ____________________, 19____, and, as a result of such default, the

applicant is entitled to the possession of said vehicle or to be paid such unpaid balance.

7. ____________________ does not have, and has not been offered, adequate protection for its interest in the vehicle described in the attached security agreement.

8. The debtor(s) has/have no equity in the vehicle listed in the attached security agreement, and it appears that the value of said property is less than the balance due to the applicant.

9. The debtor(s) has/have no reasonable prospect for reorganization.

10. Said personal property is believed not to be included in the assets of this bankruptcy estate, and the applicant is entitled to the possession thereof or to be paid the unpaid balance.

11. If applicant is not permitted to obtain possession of said personal property or to be paid the unpaid balance, it will suffer irreparable injury, loss and damage due to the deterioration and rapid depreciation of the vehicle and the potential loss of collateral by fire and malicious mischief.

WHEREFORE applicant prays for the entry of an order modifying the stay granted pursuant to 11 U.S.C., Section 362 to permit it to obtain possession of the motor vehicle described herein pursuant to its duly perfected security interest therein, and that it have such other and further relief as to the Court may seem just and proper.

Dated: Albany, New York

____________________, 19____

By: ______________________

RICHARD J. MILLER &
ASSOCIATES, P.C.
Attorney for Applicant
One Commerce Plaza, P.O. Box 2
Albany, New York 12260
Phone: (518) 465-7591

UNITED STATES BANKRUPTCY COURT
NORTHERN DISTRICT OF NEW YORK

In re:	IN BANKRUPTCY NO. ____________
____________,	
Debtor(s).	ORDER VACATING STAY

At Albany, New York in said District on ____________________, 19____.

Upon the application by ________________________ to modify the stay herein granted pursuant to 11 U.S.C., Section 362 to permit it to obtain possession of the motor vehicle described therein pursuant to its duly perfected security interest, and the matter having come on regularly to be heard at Court Room 311, United States Post Office and Court House, Albany, New York before the undersigned on ____________________, 19____, at which time there appeared Richard J. Miller & Associates, P.C. (____________________, of counsel), in support of said application and on behalf of ____________________, and no one appearing in opposition thereto, and the debtor(s) having failed to interpose an answer to the application served, and the Court having considered the matter then before it, and due deliberation having been had;

NOW, on reading and filing the notice of motion and application, it is, on motion of Richard J. Miller & Associates, P.C., attorney for the applicant;

ORDERED that the stay provided in favor of the debtor(s) by 11 U.S.C., section 362 of the Bankruptcy Code be, and the same hereby is vacated and annulled as to the applicant, effective ten (10) days subsequent to the entry of this order.

____

BANKRUPTCY JUDGE

EXHIBIT 4

UNITED STATES BANKRUPTCY COURT
NORTHERN DISTRICT OF NEW YORK

In re:

______________, In Bankruptcy No. ______________

Debtors.

Adversary No. ______________

Plaintiff,

-against-

ANSWER TO COMPLAINT BY TRUSTEE TO OBTAIN PAYMENTS MADE

______________,

Defendant.

Defendant ______________________________, for its answer to the plaintiff's complaint:

1. Denies the allegations contained in paragraphs 3, 4, 5 and 8 of the complaint.

2. Lacks knowledge or information sufficient to form a belief as to the allegations contained in paragraphs 6 and 7 of the complaint.

FIRST DEFENSE:

3. The Court herein lacks jurisdiction over the subject matter, and over the person of the defendant.

SECOND DEFENSE:

4. On January 10, 1983, the debtors herein tendered a check to the defendant in the sum of $550.

5. As a result of said payment, the debtors' insurance with the defendant was reinstated. A copy of said notice of reinstatement of insurance policy, dated January 10, 1983 is attached hereto and marked Exhibit "A."

6. The debtors herein filed a voluntary petition in bankruptcy pursuant to Chapter 7 of the Bankruptcy Code on April 11, 1983.

7. The aforementioned payment to the defendant herein was made 91 days prior to said filing date, and is thus excluded from preference treatment pursuant to 11 U.S.C. section 547.

WHEREFORE defendant ______________________________ demands judgment and that the allegations and specifications contained in the said complaint herein be dismissed with the costs and disbursements of this action.

Date: Albany, New York
November 28, 1983

RICHARD J. MILLER &
ASSOCIATES, P.C.
Attorney for Defendant
One Commerce Plaza
P. O. Box 2
Albany, New York 12260
Phone: (518) 465-7591

EXHIBIT 5

UNITED STATES BANKRUPTCY COURT
NORTHERN DISTRICT OF NEW YORK

In re: IN BANKRUPTCY NO. ______________

______________,

Debtor.

NOTICE OF MOTION TO DISMISS THE CHAPTER 11 PROCEEDING

SIRS:

PLEASE TAKE NOTICE that upon the annexed application of Hudson Valley Paper Company, by its attorney, Richard J. Miller & Associates, P.C., the undersigned will move this Court at the United States Post Office and Court House, Room 311, Albany, New York on February 21, 1984, at 12:45 o'clock in the afternoon, or as soon thereafter as counsel can be heard, for an order dismissing the Chapter 11 proceeding herein on the grounds more particularly set forth in the demand for relief requested in the annexed application, and for such other and further relief as may seem just and proper.

PLEASE TAKE FURTHER NOTICE that unless an answer to the application is served and filed together with proof of service at least one (1) day before the return date hereof, the relief demanded in the application will be deemed consented to.

Dated: Albany, New York
January 18, 1985

Yours, etc.

RICHARD J. MILLER & ASSOCIATES, P.C.
Attorney for Hudson Valley Paper Company
One Commerce Plaza, P. O. Box 2
Albany, New York 12260

TO: DONALD G. HATT, ESQ.
Attorney for Debtor
11 North Pearl Street
Albany, New York 12207

UNITED STATES BANKRUPTCY COURT
NORTHERN DISTRICT OF NEW YORK

In re:	IN BANKRUPTCY NO. ____________
____________	
Debtor.	APPLICATION FOR ORDER DISMISSING THE CHAPTER 11 PROCEEDING

TO: HON. JUSTIN J. MAHONEY, Bankruptcy Judge.

The application of Hudson Valley Paper Company, by its attorney, Richard J. Miller & Associates, P.C., respectfully represents:

1. The applicant is a party in interest in the above-entitled case, to wit, an unsecured creditor of the debtor in the sum of $3,525.29.

2. On or about June 21, 1981, the debtor herein filed a petition for reorganization pursuant to Chapter 11 of the Bankruptcy Code.

3. Applicant hereby requests the dismissal of the Chapter 11 proceeding herein on the grounds that there has been unreasonable delay by the debtor that is prejudicial to creditors, and that the debtor has exhibited an inability to effectuate a plan of reorganization.

4. It is in the best interest of creditors that the case be dismissed.

WHEREFORE applicant prays for an order pursuant to Section 1112(b) of Title 11, U.S. Code, dismissing the case, and for such other and further relief as is just.

Dated: Albany, New York

January 18, 1984

HUDSON VALLEY PAPER COMPANY

By: ______________________

Eileen V. Turner
RICHARD J. MILLER & ASSOCIATES, P.C.
Attorney for Applicant
One Commerce Plaza, P.O. Box 2
Albany, New York 12260
Phone: (518) 465-7591

UNITED STATES BANKRUPTCY COURT
NORTHERN DISTRICT OF NEW YORK

In re: IN BANKRUPTCY
NO. ______________

______________,

Debtor.

CONDITIONAL ORDER DISMISSING CHAPTER 11 PROCEEDING

At Albany, New York, in said District on March 1, 1984.

The debtor named herein having filed a petition under Chapter 11 of the Bankruptcy Code on June 21, 1981, and Hudson Valley Paper Company having made an application to dismiss said Chapter 11 proceeding, and a preliminary hearing having been scheduled by the Court and the matter having come on regularly to be heard before this Court at United States Post Office and Court House, Albany, New York on February 21, 1984 at 12:45 o'clock in the afternoon, at which time there appeared Richard J. Miller & Associates, P.C. (Eileen V. Turner of counsel), in support of the application, and State Bank of Albany and Union National Bank having appeared by their respective attorneys, and Donald G. Hatt, Esq. having submitted an answer to the application and having appeared on behalf of the debtor, and there being no other appearances, and the Court having considered the matter then before it, and due deliberation having been had;

NOW, on reading and filing the notice of motion and application herein, on motion of Richard J. Miller & Associates, P.C., attorney for the applicant, it is:

ORDERED that the Chapter 11 proceeding herein be dismissed, unless the debtor files its disclosure statement and plan of reorganization with this Court on or before April 21, 1984.

Dated: Albany, New York
March 1, 1984

____
BANKRUPTCY JUDGE

EXHIBIT 6

UNITED STATES BANKRUPTCY COURT
NORTHERN DISTRICT OF NEW YORK

In re:	IN BANKRUPTCY NO. ____________
______________,	
Debtor.	NOTICE AND REAFFIRMATION AGREEMENT

NOTICE: THE OBLIGATION ASSIGNED TO DESCRIBED BELOW IS DISCHARGEABLE UNDER APPLICABLE BANKRUPTCY LAWS. YOU ARE NOT LEGALLY OBLIGATED TO REAFFIRM SUCH OBLIGATION. IF YOU REAFFIRM SUCH OBLIGATION, YOUR LIABILITY ON SUCH OBLIGATION WILL BE FULLY RESTORED AND ENFORCEABLE IN ACCORDANCE WITH ITS TERMS.

Each of the undersigned acknowledges that he has read the above and, understanding that he is not legally obligated to do so and understanding the nature and consequences of his actions, hereby REAFFIRMS the following obligation ("Obligation"):

1. Name of Purchaser(s):

2. Name of Seller:

3. Date of Obligation:

4. Original Amount of Obligation:

5. Earned Attorney's Fees:

6. Current Balance of Obligation (including attorney's fees):

7. Contract Number:

8. Payment Schedule:

This reaffirmation agreement does not affect the terms of payment of the original Installment Sale Contract, a copy of which is attached hereto.

Each of the undersigned acknowledges that the amount set forth above after the words "Current Balance of Obligation" remains unpaid on the Obligation, and that the payment of the Obligation in accordance with its terms does not impose an undue hardship on him or his dependents, is in his best interest and is entered into in good faith, and accordingly, each of the undersigned hereby REAFFIRMS AND AGREES that he is indebted and obligated unto __________, and any assignee of ______________, for the Current Balance of the Obligation set forth above and further agrees that he shall be bound by the terms and conditions of the Installment Sale Contract evidencing and securing said obligation, or any extension, renewals or modifications thereof.

This agreement shall become enforceable upon approval by the United States Bankruptcy Court pursuant to 11 U.S.C. sec. 524(c)(4), subject to the right of rescission pursuant to 11 U.S.C. sec. 524(c)(2).

Dated: ____________, New York

SIGNATURES	WITNESSES
____________________________	____________________________
____________________________	____________________________
____________________________	____________________________

_______________________ hereby agrees that the reaffirmation described above may be made in accordance with the foregoing terms.

____

By: _______________________

Its: _______________________

UNITED STATES BANKRUPTCY COURT
NORTHERN DISTRICT OF NEW YORK

In the Matter of:	IN BANKRUPTCY NO. ____________
____________,	
Debtor.	NOTICE OF MOTION FOR AUTHORITY TO ENTER INTO, AND APPROVAL OF, REAFFIRMATION AGREEMENT

SIR:

PLEASE TAKE NOTICE that upon the annexed application of ____________________, by its attorney, Richard J. Miller & Associates, P.C., the undersigned will move this Court at Court Room No. 311, United States Post Office and Court House, Albany, New York on ____________________, 1984, at __________ o'clock in the ____________ noon, or as soon thereafter as counsel can be heard, for an order approving and authorizing the debtor to enter into a reaffirmation agreement pursuant to 11 U.S.C. sec. 524 as more particularly set forth in the annexed application, and for such other and further relief as may seem just and proper.

PLEASE TAKE FURTHER NOTICE that unless an answer to the application is served and filed, together with proof of service at least one (1) day before the return date herein, the relief demanded in the application will be deemed consented to.

Dated: Albany, New York
_______________, 19____

Yours, etc.

RICHARD J. MILLER &
ASSOCIATES, P.C.
Attorney for _______________
One Commerce Plaza, P. O. Box 2
Albany, New York 12260
Phone: (518) 465-7591

TO: __________________________

Attorney for Debtor ______

____
____

Trustee

UNITED STATES BANKRUPTCY COURT
NORTHERN DISTRICT OF NEW YORK

In the Matter of:	IN BANKRUPTCY NO. ________________
________________,	
Debtor.	APPLICATION FOR AUTHORITY TO ENTER INTO, AND APPROVAL OF, REAFFIRMATION AGREEMENT PURSUANT TO U.S.C. SEC. 524

TO: HON. JUSTIN J. MAHONEY, Bankruptcy Judge.

The application of ________________________________, by its attorney, Richard J. Miller & Associates, P.C., respectfully represents:

1. The debtor filed a petition in bankruptcy in this Court on ______________________________, 19 ______.

2. At the time of said filing, the debtor was indebted to ______________________________ in the sum of $________________; said indebtedness has a current balance of $________________________ and is scheduled as a dischargeable indebtedness in these proceedings.

3. The transaction giving rise to the indebtedness was the purchase of a ______________ described as a ________________________, pursuant to a certain retail installment contract in the nature of a security agreement dated ____________________, a copy of which is attached hereto and marked Exhibit "A."

4. The debtor has entered into a reaffirmation agreement with the applicant herein, ______________________; a copy of said agreement is attached hereto and marked Exhibit "B."

5. The said reaffirmation agreement was made before the granting of a discharge pursuant to 11 U.S.C. sec. 727.

6. Applicant believes that payments made pursuant to the said reaffirmation agreement will not create undue hardship on the debtor or the debtor dependents.

7. Applicant believes that reaffirmation would be in the debtor's ________________ best interest since the property pledged as security cannot be purchased elsewhere except at much greater expense.

8. The debtor understands that he has a right to redeem the said property pursuant to 11 U.S.C. sec. 722, but said debtor lacks the funds necessary to exercise said right.

WHEREFORE applicant prays that the annexed order, for which no prior application has been made, be entered.
Dated: Albany, New York

____________________, 19____

By: ________________________

RICHARD J. MILLER &
ASSOCIATES, P.C.
Attorney for Applicant
One Commerce Plaza, P.O. Box 2
Albany, New York 12260
Phone: (518) 465-7591

UNITED STATES BANKRUPTCY COURT
NORTHERN DISTRICT OF NEW YORK

In the Matter of:	IN BANKRUPTCY NO. _______________
_______________,	
	ORDER
Debtor.	

At Albany in said District on _________________________, 1984.

Upon the application by ____________________________ for authority for the debtor to enter into, and approval of, a reaffirmation agreement pursuant to 11 U.S.C. sec. 524, and the matter having come on regularly to be heard at Court Room No. 311, United States Post Office and Court House, Albany, New York before the undersigned on ____________________________, 1984, at which time there appeared Richard J. Miller & Associates, P.C., in support of the said application and on behalf of ___________________________, and the debtor herein, by attorney, ___________________________;

And the Court having informed the debtor of the legal effect and consequences of the reaffirmation agreement and of any defaults thereunder and that the execution of said reaffirmation agreement is not required by the Bankruptcy Code or other law;

And it appearing that the reaffirmation agreement does not impose any undue hardship on the debtor or dependents of the debtor and is in the best interest of said debtor; and the Court having considered the matter then before it, and due deliberation having been had thereon, it is:

ORDERED that the debtor herein be, and he is hereby authorized to execute the reaffirmation agreement.

____

BANKRUPTCY JUDGE

EXHIBIT 7

UNITED STATES BANKRUPTCY COURT
NORTHERN DISTRICT OF NEW YORK

In re: IN BANKRUPTCY
NO. ____________

______________,

Debtor.

NOTICE OF MOTION FOR AUTHORITY TO REDEEM PROPERTY

SIRS:

PLEASE TAKE NOTICE that upon the annexed application of General Motors Acceptance Corporation, by its attorney, Lynn, Lynn & Miller, P.C., and upon the annexed application of __________________, by his attorney, Roger H. Mallery, the undersigned will move this Court at Court Room No. 311, U.S. Post Office and Court House, Albany, New York on ______________________, 1983, at _________ o'clock in the ______________noon, or as soon thereafter as counsel can be heard, for an order authorizing the debtor herein to redeem one (1) 1978 Chevrolet Pick-Up, bearing vehicle identification number CCD4481127100, subject to the security interest of General Motors Acceptance Corporation the sum of $2,200 pursuant to 11 U.S.C. sec. 722 as more particularly set forth in the annexed application, and for such other and further relief as may seem just and proper.

PLEASE TAKE FURTHER NOTICE that unless an answer to the application is served and filed, together with proof of service, at least one (1) day before the return date herein, the relief demanded in the application will be deemed consented to by all parties in interest.

Dated: Albany, New York
June ____, 1983

Yours, etc.

LYNN, LYNN & MILLER, P.C.
Attorney for General Motors
Acceptance Corporation
99 Washington Avenue
Albany, New York 12210
Phone: (518) 465-7591

TO: ROGER H. MALLERY, ESQ.
Attorney for Debtor
20 Main Street
Cobleskill, New York 12043

SAMUEL P. FRANKEL, ESQ.
Trustee
153 Barrett Street
Schenectady, New York 12305

UNITED STATES BANKRUPTCY COURT
NORTHERN DISTRICT OF NEW YORK

In re: IN BANKRUPTCY
NO. ____________

____________,

Debtor.

APPLICATION FOR AUTHORITY TO REDEEM PROPERTY

TO: HON. JUSTIN J. MAHONEY, Bankruptcy Judge.

The application of General Motors Acceptance Corporation, by its attorney, Lynn, Lynn & Miller, P.C., respectfully represents:

1. The debtor herein filed a petition for relief under Chapter 7 of the Bankruptcy Code on December 28, 1982.

2. At the time of said filing, the debtor was indebted to General Motors Acceptance Corporation in the sum of $3,050.82; said indebtedness has current balance of $2,542.35 and is scheduled as a dischargeable indebtedness in these proceedings.

3. The transaction giving rise to the indebtedness was the purchase of one (1) 1978 Chevrolet Pick-Up, bearing vehicle identification number CCD4481127100, pursuant to a retail installment contract in the nature of a security agreement dated May 27, 1982, a copy of which is attached hereto and marked Exhibit "A."

4. The debtor has indicated an intention to redeem said property by paying to General Motors Acceptance Corporation the sum of $2,200.

5. General Motors Acceptance Corporation is the holder of the claim described, which has been allowed in the sum of $3,050.82.

6. The said 1978 Chevrolet Pick-up has an approximate value of $2,600.

7. Applicant believes that the payment to be made pursuant to the redemption sought will not create undue hardship on the debtor or the debtor's dependents.

8. Applicant believes that the suggested redemption would be in the debtor's best interest, since the property pledged as security cannot be purchased elsewhere except at a much greater expense.

9. Applicant finally represents to this Court that no undue influence or coercion has been brought against the debtor for the purpose of compelling him to redeem the property under review.

WHEREFORE applicant prays for an order authorizing the debtor to redeem the said property upon payment to the applicant and for such other and further relief as is just, for which relief no previous application has been made.

Dated: Albany, New York
June 10, 1983

____

Eileen V. Turner
LYNN, LYNN & MILLER, P.C.
Attorney for General Motors
Acceptance Corporation
99 Washington Avenue
Albany, New York 12210
Phone: (518) 465-7591

UNITED STATES BANKRUPTCY COURT
NORTHERN DISTRICT OF NEW YORK

In re: IN BANKRUPTCY NO. ____________

______________,

Debtor. APPLICATION FOR AUTHORITY TO REDEEM PROPERTY

TO: HON. JUSTIN J. MAHONEY, Bankruptcy Judge.

The application of ________________________, by his attorney, Roger H. Mallery, respectfully represents:

1. Pursuant to an order, dated and filed on April 22, 1983, the stay provided in favor of the debtor by 11 U.S.C. sec. 362 of the Bankruptcy Code was vacated as to General Motors Acceptance Corporation on May 12, 1983, with respect to one (1) 1978 Chevrolet Pick-Up, bearing vehicle identification number CCD4481127100 which the debtor owned at the time of the filing of his petition in this case.

2. Such automobile is subject to a security interest of General Motors Acceptance Corporation to secure an indebtedness of $4,067.76. The secured claim of such financing company has been allowed in the amount of $3,050.82, the balance of the debtor's obligation at the time of his filing of a petition under Chapter 7 of the Bankruptcy Code.

3. Before the filing of the petition herein, the said automobile was used primarily for business, and if the debtor is permitted to redeem it, it will be so used hereafter.

4. Debtor wishes to redeem said automobile by paying to General Motors Acceptance Corporation the sum of $2,200.

WHEREFORE debtor prays for the entry of an order requiring General Motors Acceptance Corporation, upon payment to it of the sum of $2,200 to release its security interest in said automobile, and that the debtor have such other and further relief as is just.

Dated: Cobleskill, New York
June 15, 1983

____

Roger H. Mallery
Attorney for Debtor
20 Main Street
Cobleskill, New York 12043

UNITED STATES BANKRUPTCY COURT
NORTHERN DISTRICT OF NEW YORK

In re:

______________,
Debtor.

IN BANKRUPTCY NO. __________

ORDER AUTHORIZING DEBTOR TO REDEEM PROPERTY

____________________________, the debtor above named, by his attorney, Roger H. Mallery, having made application for an order authorizing him to redeem certain property pursuant to the provisions of section 722 of Title 11, United States Code, and the same having come on to be heard before me on October 20, 1983, at 10 o'clock in the forenoon,

NOW, on reading the said application, dated June 15, 1983, the notice of motion and application of General Motors Acceptance Corporation, by its attorney, Richard J. Miller & Associates, P.C., respectively, dated June 10, 1983, and due proof of service thereof on Roger H. Mallery, attorney for ____________________________, the debtor herein, and on Samuel P. Frankel, Trustee, and after hearing Richard J. Miller & Associates, P.C., attorney for General Motors Acceptance Corporation, in support of said applications, and no one appearing in opposition thereto, and due consideration having been had, and it appearing to the satisfaction of the undersigned that the property sought to be redeemed consists of tangible personal property intended primarily for personal, family or household use, and is subject to a lien by General Motors Acceptance Corporation securing a dischargeable consumer debt that is exempted under section 522 of said Title 11, and that the amount of the allowed secured claim held by General Motors Acceptance Corporation is $3,050.82, it is:

ORDERED that the applications of the debtor and General Motors Acceptance Corporation be, and the same hereby are granted; and it is further

ORDERED that said debtor be, and he hereby is authorized to redeem the property described in the aforementioned applications as a 1978 Chevrolet Pick-Up, bearing vehicle indentification number CCD4481127100, by paying to General Motors Acceptance Corporation, the holder of the said lien on said property, the sum of $2,200.

Dated: Albany, New York
October 20, 1983

____

BANKRUPTCY JUDGE

EXHIBIT 8

UNITED STATES BANKRUPTCY COURT
NORTHERN DISTRICT OF NEW YORK

In re: IN BANKRUPTCY
NO. ____________

_______________,

Debtor. ORDER

At Albany, in said District on the ________ day of _________________, 19____.

On the annexed application of _______________________________, by its attorney, Richard J. Miller & Associates, P.C., the consents of __________________, the attorneys for the debtors herein, and __________________________, the Trustee herein, for authority to abandon certain property of the debtor, and it appearing that __________________ has a valid security interest in, and is permitted to obtain possession of such property, it is:

ORDERED that the debtor, __________________________, and the Trustee be, and they hereby are permitted and authorized to disclaim title to and to abandon certain property of the debtor consisting of a __________, serial number ____________, located at ______________ to ____________; and it is further

ORDERED that the entry of this order shall be deemed to constitute an abandonment of said property by said debtor and Trustee.

____

BANKRUPTCY JUDGE

UNITED STATES BANKRUPTCY COURT
NORTHERN DISTRICT OF NEW YORK

In re: IN BANKRUPTCY NO. ____________

____________,

Debtor.

APPLICATION TO ABANDON PROPERTY

TO: THE HON. JUSTIN J. MAHONEY, Bankruptcy Judge.

The application of ________________ by its attorney, Richard J. Miller & Associates, P.C., respectfully shows to the Court as follows:

1. ________________ filed a petition under Chapter ________ of the Bankruptcy Code on ________________, 19____.

2. On ________________, 19____, the plaintiff acquired a security interest in the personal property described in the security agreement annexed hereto, as indicated on the attached notice of recorded lien, to a motor vehicle, to wit: ________________.

3. The total market value of the vehicle is $________________.

4. The original amount of the secured debt was $__________, as evidenced by the retail installment contract annexed, and the present balance due is $______ as of ________________, 19____.

5. No payment has been made on said obligation since __________, 19____, and as a result of such default, the plaintiff is entitled to the possession of said vehicle or to be paid such unpaid balance.

6. Said personal property is believed now to be included in the assets of this bankruptcy estate, and the plaintiff is entitled to the possession thereof or to be paid the unpaid balance.

WHEREFORE applicant prays that the debtor, ______________, and the Trustee be directed to abandon said vehicle which is the subject of this application and that it have such other and further relief as is just.

Dated: Albany, New York

__________________, 19____

By: ____________________

RICHARD J. MILLER &
ASSOCIATES, P.C.
Attorney for Applicant
One Commerce Plaza,
P. O. Box 2
Albany, New York 12260
Phone: (518) 465-7591

UNITED STATES BANKRUPTCY COURT
NORTHERN DISTRICT OF NEW YORK

In re:	IN BANKRUPTCY NO. ____________
______________, Debtor.	CONSENT TO ORDER AUTHORIZING ABANDONMENT OF PERSONAL PROPERTY

TO: HON. JUSTIN J. MAHONEY, Bankruptcy Judge.

______________________ , the attorney for the debtor herein, hereby consents to the abandonment of ________________ , serial number ______ to ______, and does hereby state that the debtor does not intend to redeem the said vehicle, claim said vehicle as an exemption in the bankruptcy proceedings herein, or reaffirm the obligation as represented by the retail installment contract dated ___________, 19____.

The attorney for the debtor therefore prays that the Court grant the request of ________________ as set forth in the proposed order annexed hereto and made a part hereof.

Dated: ________________, New York

________________, 19____

____

Attorney for Debtor

UNITED STATES BANKRUPTCY COURT
NORTHERN DISTRICT OF NEW YORK

In re: IN BANKRUPTCY NO. ______________

________________,

Debtor.

CONSENT TO ORDER AUTHORIZING ABANDONMENT OF PERSONAL PROPERTY

TO: HON. JUSTIN J. MAHONEY, Bankruptcy Judge.

I, ____________________________, being the duly qualified Trustee herein, hereby consent to the application of ____________________________, ____________________ and pray that the Court grant the request therein as set forth in the proposed order annexed hereto and made a part hereof.

Dated: ____________________, New York

____________________, 19____

____

TRUSTEE

EXHIBIT 9

UNITED STATES DISTRICT COURT
WESTERN DISTRICT OF NEW YORK

In Re:

______________________________ , IN BANKRUPTCY
NO. ____________

Bankrupt.
NEW YORK STATE HIGHER EDUCATION
SERVICES CORPORATION,
Plaintiff,
-against- COMPLAINT
Defendant.

---

1. Plaintiff is a New York corporation created by section 652 of the New York State Education Law.

2. This is an adversary proceeding to determine the dischargeability of a debt pursuant to Bankruptcy Rules 409 and 701 (7).

3. On or about September 5, 1978, the defendant above named was duly adjudicated a bankrupt in this Court.

4. The question of the defendant's general discharge has not, as of this date, been determined.

5. The defendant is indebted to the plaintiff in the sum of $1,567.57, with interest from August 19, 1977, for money lent in the State of New York pursuant to Article 14 of the New York State Education Law, and said debt is founded upon a claim from which a discharge in bankruptcy would not be a release under the provisions of 20 U.S.C. 1087-3.

6. On or about July 30, 1971, and September 2, 1972, defendant made two applications for student loans, pursuant to the provisions of Article 14 of the New York State Education Law. The applications were approved on, respectively, August 30, 1971, and October 2, 1972, the money was advanced to the defendant, and to evidence the debt, a promissory note was executed by the defendant to Manufacturers and Traders Trust Co., Buffalo, New York. Copies of the applications and the promissory note are attached hereto and marked Exhibits "A" and "B."

7. Defendant defaulted in paying the bank under the terms of the note, whereupon it became the duty of the plaintiff, under Article 14 of the Education Law, to assume the obligation. Plaintiff did assume said obligation and paid to Manufacturers and Traders Trust Co. $2,579.30, on or about December 13, 1974. A copy of the Default Loan Action Record evidencing such payment is annexed hereto and marked Exhibit "C."

8. By the terms of the aforesaid note, the money owing to the plaintiff was to become due and payable nine months after the defendant completed her course of education, or terminated her enrollment from the educational institution, whichever event first occured. By reason of the fact that the defendant herein completed her educational course and graduated in September of 1973, the note became due and payable nine months thereafter on June 30, 1974.

9. An action to recover this indebtedness was commenced in Supreme Court, Albany County, resulting in a judgment entered in the Albany County Clerk's office on January 27, 1976, for a total of $2,680.91. Since then, defendant has paid installments totaling $1,330.00, $216.66 of which has been apportioned to interest and $1,113.34 of which has been apportioned to the principal, thereby leaving a balance due and owing to the plaintiff of $1,567.57 with interest at 6 percent from August 19, 1977.

10. By reason of the provisions of 20 U.S.C. 1087-3, defendant is precluded from discharging this debt in bankruptcy since the commencement of the repayment period occured less than five years prior to the adjudication in bankruptcy.

WHEREFORE plaintiff prays for an order determining said debt to be non-dischargeable in accordance with the provisions of the Bankruptcy Act as made and provided, and for such other and further relief as to the Court may seem just and proper.

Dated: Albany, New York
October 30, 1978

NEW YORK STATE
HIGHER EDUCATION
SERVICES CORPORATION

By ____________________________
Richard J. Miller
LYNN & LYNN, P.C.
Attorney for Plaintiff
99 Washington Avenue
Albany, New York 12210
Phone: (518) 465-7591

EXHIBIT 10

UNITED STATES BANKRUPTCY COURT
NORTHERN DISTRICT OF NEW YORK

In Re:

_______________,

Debtor.

BANKRUPTCY
NO. ____________

OBJECTION
TO COMFIRMATION
OF PLAN

TO: HON. JUSTIN J. MAHONEY, Bankruptcy Judge:

Central National Bank, Canajoharie, a secured creditor of the debtor above-named, by Lynn, Lynn and Miller, its attorney, hereby objects to the confirmation of the plan dated September 21, 1981, filed by the said debtor, and specifies the following as grounds of objection:

The deferred cash payments to be received by Central National Bank, Canajoharie, over a seventy-two month period with interest at sixteen (16%) percent per annum pursuant to a promissory note in an amount equal to the proceeds of pre-petition sales, as provided in Article Four of the said plan, do not have a present value equal to the amount of the secured claim of Central National Bank, Canajoharie, as represented by the value of its collateral.

Dated: Albany, New York
October , 1981

____
Matthew J. Barbaro
LYNN, LYNN AND MILLER, P.C.
Attorney for Central National
Bank, Canajoharie
99 Washington Avenue
Albany, New York 12210
Phone: (518) 465-7591

EXHIBIT 11

UNITED STATES BANKRUPTCY COURT
NORTHERN DISTRICT OF NEW YORK

	BANKRUPTCY NO.
In re:	______________
______________,	ORDER DETERMINING VALUE AND FIXING CLAIM
Debtor.	

At Albany, in said District, on the day of , 19 .

The debtor named herein having filed a petition pursuant to Chapter 13 of the Bankruptcy Code, and General Motors Acceptance Corporation having brought on a motion for valuation hearing and to determine claim, and a preliminary hearing having been scheduled by the Court and the matter having come on regularly to be heard before this Court in Court Room No. 2, United States Post Office and Court House, Albany, New York, on December 16, 1980, at 2:00 o'clock in the afternoon, at which time there appeared Lynn, Lynn and Miller, P.C. (Matthew J. Barbaro, of counsel), in support of the application and on behalf of General Motors Acceptance Corporation, and Robert E. Littlefield, Trustee, and no other parties having appeared, and the parties hereto desiring to settle their differences, and the Court having considered the matter then before it, and due deliberation having been had;

NOW on reading and filing the notice of motion and application for valuation hearing and to determine claim, dated October 14, 1980, respectively, and the stipulation in support of this order signed by counsel to the respective parties in interest and the Trustee herein, it is, on motion of Lynn, Lynn and Miller, P.C., attorney for General Motors Acceptance Corporation;

ORDERED that the value of one 1974 Cadillac, vehicle identification number 6D47R4Q137080 be, and it hereby is fixed at $1,000; and it is further

ORDERED that the claim of General Motors Acceptance Corporation be, and the same hereby is accepted and filed as secured to the extent of the sum of $1,000; and it is further

ORDERED that the debtor herein be, and he hereby is directed to amend his plan so as to list the claim of General Motors Acceptance Corporation as secured to the extent of the sum of $1,000; and it is further

ORDERED that the debtor herein pay to General Motors Acceptance Corporation the sum of $1,000 in accordance with the terms and provisions of the said plan as amended herein; and it is further

ORDERED that General Motors Acceptance Corporation and their respective counsel, and the Trustee herein, be, and they hereby are authorized to do all things and execute any and all papers and documents which may be necessary to carry into effect the various agreements reached and approved by this Court.

____
BANKRUPTCY JUDGE

UNITED STATES BANKRUPTCY COURT
NORTHERN DISTRICT OF NEW YORK

In re:	BANKRUPTCY NO. ____________
____________,	STIPULATION IN SUPPORT OF ORDER DETERMINING VALUE AND FIXING CLAIM
Debtor.	

IT IS HEREBY STIPULATED AND AGREED that the annexed order may be presented to the Court herein, signed and entered without notice.

Dated: Albany, New York
, 19

____

Dated: , New York
, 19

____
MORRIS STRAUSS, ESQ.
Attorney for Debtor
227 Mohawk Avenue
Scotia, New York

Dated: Albany, New York

, 19

GENERAL MOTORS
ACCEPTANCE CORPORATION

By: ______________________

Dated: Albany, New York

, 19

____

Matthew J. Barbaro
LYNN, LYNN & MILLER, P.C.
Attorney for General Motors
Acceptance Corporation
99 Washington Avenue
Albany, New York 12210
Phone: (518) 465-7591

Dated: Albany, New York

, 19

____

ROBERT E. LITTLEFIELD,
TRUSTEE
150 State Street
Albany, New York 12207

EXHIBIT 12

UNITED STATES DISTRICT COURT
NORTHERN DISTRICT OF NEW YORK

	BANKRUPTCY NO.
In the Matter of	______________
______________	ORDER TO SHOW CAUSE
Bankrupt.	

At Albany, New York, in said District on September 1978.

On reading and filing the annexed application of Donald G. Hatt, Trustee herein, dated September , 1978, and on all prior proceedings heretofore had herein; it is

ORDERED that the creditors of the within bankrupt and all other parties in interest show cause before this Court at Court Room No. 2, United States Post Office and Court House, Albany, New York, on the day of September 1978 at o'clock in the noon, or as soon thereafter as counsel can be heard, why an order should not be made and entered herein authorizing and empowering the Trustee to accept the sum of $36,600 in full settlement of an action now pending in the civil counterpart of this Court initiated by the Trustee named herein, as plaintiff, against Manufacturers Hanover Trust Company/Capital Region, as defendant; and it is further

ORDERED that mailing a copy of this notice to all creditors and parties in interest at least ten (10) days prior to the return date of this motion shall be deemed good and sufficient service.

____
BANKRUPTCY JUDGE

UNITED STATES BANKRUPTCY COURT
NORTHERN DISTRICT OF NEW YORK

In the Matter
of

______________,

Bankrupt.

BANKRUPTCY NO.

____

APPLICATION FOR ORDER AUTHORIZING COMPROMISE OF CLAIM

TO: HON. JUSTIN J. MAHONEY, Bankruptcy Judge.

The application of Donald G. Hatt respectfully shows:

1. In am the duly appointed, qualified and acting Trustee in Bankruptcy herein, having been appointed by order of this Court and having qualified by filing my bond.

2. Subsequent to the filing of the petition in bankruptcy herein and on July 15, 1977, I filed suit against Manufacturers Hanover Trust Company/Capital Region to set aside as a preference a certain transfer made by the bankrupt of its property to said lending institution in the nature of a security interest, to order said defendant to account for and to reconvey, return and re-transfer to me as plaintiff the aforesaid property by reason of the preferential transfer made to it, and to have judgment for the value of the said property if it were found that the defendant named had converted said property by reason of its repossession and sale of same pursuant by the bankrupt in favor of the bank.

3. Thereafter, counsel to the said defendant filed an answer in response to the complaint served in connection with the action initiated by me in Federal Court. By way of an affirmative defense and a setoff and counterclaim, the defendant claimed a priority as a secured creditor with respect to the bankrupt's property and the proceeds thereof, and also pleaded facts to establish a deficiency balance resulting from the aforesaid sale of the bankrupt's property by the defendant, which balance allegedly remains due and owing to the said defendant.

4. Subsequent thereto, a reply was filed in response to the defendant's answer.

5. It is my understanding that the attorneys for the defendant have suggested the following compromise so as to avoid further, extended litigation and resolve the issues at hand without excessive costs to the respective parties in interest:

(a) The defendant named is willing to pay to me, as Trustee for the Estate of the above named bankrupt, the sum of $36,600 in full settlement of the action brought by me as Trustee against the said defendant on condition that I move to expunge the late claims filed on June 28, 1977, by Insurance Company of North America in the sum of $35,926.61 and North River Insurance Company on August 29, 1977 in the sum of $353.42.

(b) On condition that the claim of Marjal Realty Corp. be amended and reduced from the sum of $11,200 to $5,775.

(c) On condition that the settlement sum be placed in a cash collateral amount at the defendant bank, and that such sum shall not be paid to the Trustee until the aforementioned late claims of Insurance Company of North America and the North River Insurance Company have been expunged, the aforementioned claim of Marjal Realty Corp. has been amended, the Bankruptcy Court has granted an order approving the settlement and the papers for the accounting by the Trustee have been prepared and are ready for submission to the Bankruptcy Court and will be so submitted to said Court immediately upon payment of the settlement sum by the defendant bank.

(d) That my attorney and I not object to the defendant's assertion of its rights subordinating the claim of ______________ to the bank's claim under the promissory note of the bankrupt dated July 31, 1973 in the principal amount of $45,000.

6. It is suggested that there is an immediate advantage to accepting the compromise as presented by the defendant bank. The only matter which remains unresolved in the administration of this estate is the action now pending against Manufacturer's Hanover Trust Company/Capital Region. Depositions have not yet been taken by the respective parties in interest, and a trial note of issue has not yet been filed with the Clerk of the Court. It is anticipated that the pre-trial proceedings and the time that it will take the Federal Court to reach this matter for trial will involve approximately two years. Moreover, if litigation is pursued there will be significant costs and expenses in the nature of legal fees incurred by the estate and to the detriment of creditors.

7. If the compromise suggested is rejected, any funds which may become available to creditors necessarily will be reduced in amount and will not become available for at least two years. Further, there is the possibility that the bank may prevail in the priority position claimed by it, thereby eliminating any possible dividend to the creditors of the estate. If the bank's proposal is agreed to at this time, the sum of $36,600 will be placed in a cash, collateral account upon the filing of the final accounting of the Trustee, and these funds then will be distributed to creditors without further delay.

8. It is my opinion that the settlement proposal suggested is reasonable and should be approved. It is proper and in the best interest of the creditors of the bankrupt estate that the controversy herein be settled by the acceptance by your applicant of this compromise.

9. No prior application has been made for the relief sought herein to any judge or court.

WHEREFORE I respectfully pray for the annexed order requiring all creditors and parties in interest to show cause why the offer of Manufacturers Hanover Trust Company/Capital Region should not be accepted in full settlement of the action now pending in the United States District Court for the Northern District of New York.

Dated: Albany, New York
September , 1978

____

DONALD G. HATT, Trustee

UNITED STATES DISTRICT COURT
NORTHERN DISTRICT OF NEW YORK

In the Matter
of

______________,

Bankrupt.

BANKRUPTCY NO.

____

ORDER AUTHORIZING COMPROMISE OF CLAIM

At Albany, New York, in said District, on November 30, 1978.

On reading and filing the show cause order, dated September 1978, the application of Donald G. Hatt, Trustee herein, dated September 11, 1978, and on proof of due service of the said order to show cause, and the matter having come on regularly to be heard before this Court in Court Room No. 2, United States Post Office and Court House, Albany, New York, on November 30, 1978, at 11:30 o'clock in the forenoon, at which time there appeared Lynn & Lynn, P.C. (Richard J. Miller, of counsel), in support of the application and on behalf of the Trustee, Donald G. Hatt, the Trustee named, and Zubres, D'Agostino & Hoblock (Daniel J. Tyson, of counsel), also in support of the application and on behalf of Manufacturers Hanover Trust Company/Capital Region, as defendant in the action brought by the Trustee now pending in the civil counterpart of this Court, and no other parties having appeared, and there being no opposition thereto, and the Court having considered the matter then before it, and due deliberation having been had;

NOW, on motion of Lynn & Lynn, P.C., attorney for the Trustee herein, and on motion of Zubres, D'Agostino and Hoblock, attorney for Manufacturers Hanover Trust Company/Capital Region; it is

ORDERED that Lynn & Lynn, P.C., as counsel to the Trustee herein, be, and it hereby is authorized to settle the action now pending in the civil counterpart of this Court initiated by the Trustee named herein, as plaintiff, against Manufacturers Hanover Trust Company/Capital Region, as defendant, as follows:

1. The defendant, Manufacturers Hanover Trust Company/Capital Region, shall pay to the Trustee for the estate of the above named bankrupt the sum of $36,600 in full settlement of the action brought by the Trustee, Donald G. Hatt, against the said defendant on condition that the Trustee move to expunge the late claims filed on June 28, 1977, by Insurance Company of North America in the sum of $35,926.61 and North River Insurance Company on August 29, 1977, in the sum of $353.42; and further

2. The sum of $36,600 shall be paid by the said defendant to the Trustee herein only on condition that the claim of Marjal Realty Corp. be amended and reduced from the sum of $11,200 to $5,775; and further

3. The sum of $36,600 shall be paid by the said defendant to the Trustee herein only on condition that the settlement sum be placed in a cash collateral account at the defendant bank, and that such sum shall not be paid to the Trustee until the aforementioned late claims of Insurance Company of North America and the North River Insurance Company have been expunged, the aforementioned claim of Marjal Realty Corp. has been amended, the Bankruptcy Court has granted an order approving the settlement described and the papers for the accounting by the Trustee have been prepared and are ready for submission to the Bankruptcy Court, thereby causing payment of the settlement sum by the defendant bank to the Trustee immediately upon the filing of the final accounting with the Court; and further

4. The sum of $36,600 shall be paid by the said defendant to the Trustee herein only on condition that the Trustee and his attorney, Lynn & Lynn, P.C., not object to the defendant's assertion of its rights subordinating the claim of ______________________ as filed with this Court to the defendant's claim under a promissory note made by the bankrupt dated July 31, 1973, in the principal amount of $45,000; and it is further

ORDERED that the Trustee, Donald G. Hatt, and his attorney, Lynn & Lynn, P.C., be, and they hereby are authorized to do all things and execute any and all papers and documents which may be necessary to carry into effect the compromise approved herein; and it is further

ORDERED that notice of this order authorizing compromise of the action now pending is dispensed with as and in the best interests of this estate.

____

BANKRUPTCY JUDGE

EXHIBIT 13

UNITED STATES BANKRUPTCY COURT
NORTHERN DISTRICT OF NEW YORK

In re:	IN BANKRUPTCY NO. ____________
____________, Debtor	ORDER TO SHOW CAUSE

Upon the annexed application of Ford Motor Credit Company, a creditor of the debtor herein, dated September 21, 1981, by its attorney, Lynn, Lynn & Miller, P.C., and upon all prior proceedings hereinbefore had, it is:

ORDERED that the debtor herein and the duly appointed Trustee of the estate, Thomas M. Whalen III, show cause before this Court at Court Room No. 2, United States Post Office and Court House, Albany, New York, on September , 1981, at o'clock in the noon, or as soon thereafter as counsel can be heard, why the debtor and the Trustee named herein should not be required to provide Ford Motor Credit Company with adequate protection for the purpose of securing the outstanding obligations of the debtor owed to Ford Motor Credit Company, or, in the alternative, deliver to Ford Motor Credit Company, forthwith, the vehicles hereinafter described in order to allow for protective custody by Ford Motor Credit Company, as more fully set forth in the application annexed hereto, pending a final determination of the action brought by Ford Motor Credit Company to vacate the stay afforded the debtor herein, now pending before this Court; and it is further

ORDERED that delivering in hand a copy of this notice to Thomas M. Whalen III, the Trustee of the estate, at 35 State Street, Albany, New York, and to Harvey and Harvey, Mumford & Kingsley, the attorneys for the debtor herein, at 29 Elk Street, Albany, New York, on or before September , 1981 shall be good and sufficient service.

Dated: Albany, New York
September , 1981

BANKRUPTCY JUDGE

UNITED STATES BANKRUPTCY COURT
NORTHERN DISTRICT OF NEW YORK

In re:	IN BANKRUPTCY NO. ____________
______________,	APPLICATION FOR ADEQUATE PROTECTION OR IMMEDIATE POSSESSION
Debtor.	

TO: HON. JUSTIN J. MAHONEY, Bankruptcy Judge.

The application of Ford Motor Credit Company, by Richard J. Miller, of counsel to Lynn, Lynn & Miller, P.C., its attorney, respectfully represents:

1. I am an attorney and an officer of the professional corporation of Lynn, Lynn & Miller, P.C., and I am duly authorized to practice before this Court. This office represents Ford Motor Credit Company (hereinafter "FMCC"), a secured creditor of the debtor named.

2. On April 21, 1981, __________________ filed in this Court a petition for an arrangement pursuant to Chapter 11 of the Bankruptcy Code; on September 18, 1981, the proceeding was converted to one under Chapter 7 of the Code.

3. ______________ was engaged in the business of selling new and used automobiles and trucks at retail. On or about January 25, 1974, FMCC and ____________ entered into an Automotive Wholesale Plan Application For Wholesale Financing And Security Agreement in the

nature of an inventory financing floor plan transaction whereby the debtor was extended credit by FMCC for the acquisition of vehicles for resale in its business. A copy of the Wholesale Financing and Security Agreement is attached hereto and marked Exhibit "A."

4. Pursuant to the Wholesale Financing and Security Agreement and in order properly to protect its security interest in the subject property held by the debtor, FMCC caused duly executed financing statements (Standard Form UCC-ls) to be filed with the Saratoga County Clerk and the Secretary of State of the State of New York; further, FMCC retained and continues to retain the manufacturer's statements of origin pertinent to the vehicles as hereinafter described. Copies of the financing statements and the manufacturer's statements of origin are attached hereto and marked Exhibits "B" and "C."

5. By reason of the foregoing, FMCC acquired a purchase money security interest in the trucks more fully described in the Wholesale Inventory List (Dealer Run Schedule) attached hereto and marked Exhibit "D."

6. Following the delivery, receipt and resale of certain of the vehicles made available to the defendant pursuant to the parties' inventory financing agreement, ____________________ defaulted in its contract with FMCC and continues to remain in default at this time. The property which comprises the inventory of the debtor and serves as FMCC's collateral consists of eight separate and distinct units identified in the schedule attached hereto and marked Exhibit "D."

7. By reason of the filing of the petition herein under Chapter 7 of the Bankruptcy Code, FMCC is stayed from pursuing the recovery of its loss by taking possession of its collateral and, generally, from enforcing its rights under the Wholesale Financing And Security Agreement of January 25, 1974.

8. The total market value of the eight vehicles is $275,000. There is presently due from the debtor of FMCC on the security instrument the sum of $299,692.72. *See* Exhibit "D."

9. FMCC has made a thorough inventory of the remaining eight vehicles covered by said security instrument, and it appears that the value of said property is markedly less than the balance due to FMCC. As indicated above and allowing for the resale at auction of the remaining eight vehicles, the potential loss anticipated by FMCC amounts to $24,693.72, plus interest. *See* Exhibit "D."

10. The debtor's business is defunct. The vehicles presently are subject to deterioration, and, due to the current instability of the economy as reflected in the automobile industry, the remaining eight units on hand are suffering rapid depreciation. FMCC's collateral is subject to loss by fire, malicious mischief and theft by reason of the fact that the business has ceased all operations and the dealership has been vacated.

11. Taking into consideration the balance due on the obligation owed by ______________ to the plaintiff, there is no equity in the subject vehicles, and, therefore, they are of no value to the estate and only would cause an undue and unnecessary administration expense to the Trustee.

12. The Trustee is unable to, and lacks the means with which to, provide adequate protection for FMCC's interest in the property. FMCC does not have and has not been offered adequate protection for its interest in the vehicles described in the attached wholesale inventory list.

13. Since there is no equity in the subject vehicles, FMCC is requesting that the Trustee herein provide adequate protection for the purpose of securing the outstanding obligation of the debtor or, in the alternative, surrender the vehicles to FMCC immediately to allow for complete and adequate protective custody, pending a final determination of the adversary proceeding initiated by FMCC to vacate the stay herein, now before this Court.

14. FMCC is threatened with irrevocable injury. The situation is inequitable and unjust considering FMCC's interest, and it constitutes a taking and deprivation of property without due process of law.

WHEREFORE, on behalf of the applicant, I pray for the annexed order to show cause, together with such other and further relief as may be just, for all of which no previous application has been made to this Court or any other Court other than in the context of the adversary proceeding brought on to vacate the stay herein, which presently is pending before this Court but has not yet been heard.

Dated: Albany, New York
September 21, 1981

____

Richard J. Miller
LYNN, LYNN & MILLER, P.C.
Attorney for Ford Motor
Credit Company
99 Washington Avenue
Albany, New York 12210
Phone: (518) 465-7591

UNITED STATES BANKRUPTCY COURT
NORTHERN DISTRICT OF NEW YORK

In re:	IN BANKRUPTCY NO. ______________
______________,	ORDER
Debtor.	

At Albany, New York, in said District on September 23, 1981.

The debtor named herein having filed a petition for an arrangement pursuant to Chapter 11 of the Bankruptcy Code on April 21, 1981, and the proceeding having been converted to one under Chapter 7 of the Code on September 18, 1981, and Ford Motor Credit Company having brought an application for adequate protection or, in the alternative, immediate possession of its collateral consisting of certain vehicles comprising a portion of the assets of the estate, and a hearing having been scheduled by the Court and the matter having come on regularly to be heard before this Court in Court Room No. 2, United States Post Office and Court House, Albany, New York, on September 23, 1981, at 10:15 o'clock in the forenoon, at which time there appeared Lynn, Lynn & Miller, P.C. (Richard J. Miller, of counsel), in support of the application and on behalf of Ford Motor Credit Company, Thomas M. Whalen III, the Interim Trustee of the estate, and McNamee, Lochner, Titus and Williams, P.C. (Robert E. Biggerstaff, of counsel), as attorney for First National Bank of Glens Falls, a creditor of the estate, and no other parties having appeared, and the parties hereto desiring to settle their differences, and the Court having considered the matter then before it, and due deliberation having been had;

NOW, on reading and filing the order to show cause and application submitted thereof, dated September 21, 1981, respectively, and the stipulation in support of this order signed by counsel to Ford Motor Credit Company and the Interim Trustee herein, it is, on motion of Lynn, Lynn & Miller, P.C., attorney for Ford Motor Credit Company, and on motion of Thomas M. Whalen III, as Interim Trustee;

ORDERED that the stay provided in favor of the debtor by Rule 601 of the Bankruptcy Code be, and the same hereby is vacated and annulled in part as to Ford Motor Credit Company to the extent hereinafter set forth and upon the following conditions:

1. For the purposes of affording Ford Motor Credit Company adequate protection, the applicant named is authorized to take protective custody of the vehicles hereinafter described upon the entry of this order:

One (1) 1980 Ford L8000 Diesel, bearing serial no. K80SVHJ6724

One (1) 1981 Ford F700 Diesel, bearing serial no. 1FDNK74N3BVJ23322

One (1) 1981 Ford LN700 Diesel, bearing serial no. 1FDNR7OU4BVJ20132

One (1) 1981 Ford LN700 Diesel, bearing serial no. 1FDXR7OU2BVJ20784

One (1) 1981 Ford LT900 Diesel, bearing serial no. 1FDYU9OX5BVJ27236

One (1) 1981 Ford LY900 Diesel, bearing serial no. 1FDYU9OX7BVJ12527

One (1) 1981 Ford LNT90 Diesel, bearing serial no. 1FDYW9OW7BVJ28261

One (1) 1981 Ford CLT 90000 D, bearing serial no. 1FDYX98X6BVJ20758

2. The expense of transporting and storing the subject vehicles herein shall be borne by Ford Motor Credit Company, and, further, Ford Motor Credit Company shall be responsible for insuring whatever interest may be attributable to the respective parties hereto.

3. Once in the protective custody of Ford Motor Credit Company, the vehicles shall not be removed from this State, from their location, transferred, sold, pledged, assigned or otherwise disposed of by Ford Motor Credit Company or permitted to become subject to a security interest or lien other than the one now claimed by Ford Motor Credit Company or permitted to become subject to a security interest or lien other than the one now claimed by Ford Motor Credit Company until further ordered by this Court, and, to this end, Ford Motor Credit Company, its agents, employees and all other persons acting on its behalf are restrained and enjoined hereby pending a further determination by this Court; and it is further

ORDERED that Ford Motor Credit Company, its counsel and Thomas M. Whalen III, as the Interim Trustee of the estate, be, and they hereby are authorized to do all things and execute any and all papers and documents which may be necessary to carry into effect the provisions allowing for the protective custody permitted Ford Motor Credit Company; and it is further

ORDERED that the stay provided in Rule 601 of the Bankruptcy Code be, and the same hereby shall continue and remain extant in all other respects.

____

BANKRUPTCY JUDGE

UNITED STATES BANKRUPTCY COURT
NORTHERN DISTRICT OF NEW YORK

In re:	IN BANKRUPTCY NO. ________
____________,	STIPULATION IN SUPPORT OF ORDER OF SEPTEMBER 23, 1981
Debtor.	

IT IS HEREBY STIPULATED AND AGREED that the annexed order may be presented to the Court herein, signed and entered without notice.

Dated: Albany, New York
September 23, 1981

____

Richard J. Miller
LYNN, LYNN & MILLER, P.C.
Attorney for Ford Motor
Credit Company
99 Washington Avenue
Albany, New York 12210
Phone: (518) 465-7591

Dated: Albany, New York
September 23, 1981

____

Thomas M. Whalen III
TRUSTEE
35 State Street
Albany, New York 12207
Phone: (518) 434-8131

EXHIBIT 14

UNITED STATES BANKRUPTCY COURT
NORTHERN DISTRICT OF NEW YORK

In re:	BANKRUPTCY NO. __ (Chapter 11)
________________, Debtor.	ORDER APPROVING EMPLOYMENT OF ATTORNEY

Upon consideration of application of the Creditors' Committee for approval of its employment of Lynn, Lynn & Miller, P.C., as attorney to represent it in this case, and it appearing that the members of the law firm of Lynn, Lynn & Miller, P.C., are duly admitted to practice in this Court, and the Court being satisfied that the firm represents no interest adverse to said Committee or to the Estate in the matters upon which it is to be employed, it is

ORDERED that employment by the Creditors' Committee of Lynn, Lynn & Miller, P.C., for the sole purpose of the Chapter 11 proceeding herein to represent it in the case is approved; and it is further

ORDERED that the compensation of Lynn, Lynn & Miller, P.C., for its services in behalf of the Committee shall be hereafter fixed by the Court.

Dated: Albany, New York
June 21, 1982

____
UNITED STATES BANKRUPTCY JUDGE

UNITED STATES BANKRUPTCY COURT
NORTHERN DISTRICT OF NEW YORK

In re:	BANKRUPTCY NO. __ (Chapter 11)
______________,	APPLICATION TO APPOINT ATTORNEY
Debtor.	

The application of the Creditors' Committee respectfully represents:

1. The debtor filed a voluntary petition under Chapter 11 of the Bankruptcy Code on March 1, 1982, and on April 16, 1982, this Creditors' Committee was appointed.

2. At a scheduled meeting of the Committee at which a majority of the members were present, it was decided that the Committee would seek approval of the Court of its employment of Lynn, Lynn & Miller, P.C., a law firm with members duly admitted to practice in this Court, as its attorney.

3. The Committee has selected Lynn, Lynn & Miller, P.C., for the reason that it has had much experience in matters of this character and your Committee believes that it is well-qualified to represent it in this proceeding.

4. The professional services the said Lynn, Lynn & Miller, P.C., is to render are:

(a) To give the Committee legal advice with respect to its duties and powers in this case;

(b) To assist it in its investigation of the acts, conduct, assets, liabilities and financial condition of the debtor, the operation of the debtor's business and the desireability of the continuance of such business, and any other matter relevant to the case or to the formulation of a plan;

(c) To participate with it in the formulation of a plan;

(d) To assist it in requesting the appointment of a Trustee or Examiner, should such action become necessary; and

(e) To perform such other legal services as may be required and in the interest of the creditors.

5. To the best of the Committee's knowledge, Lynn, Lynn & Miller, P.C., represents no other entity in connection with this case, is a disinterested party, and represents or holds no interest adverse to the interest of the Estate with respect to the matters in which it is to be employed.

WHEREFORE the Committee prays that its employment of Lynn, Lynn & Miller, P.C., for the sole purpose of the Chapter 11 proceeding herein to represent it in this case under Chapter 11 of the Bankruptcy Code be approved, and that it have such other and further relief as is just.

Dated: Albany, New York
June 14, 1982

____
Nelson Kenney
Chairman of the Creditor's Committee
c/o International Built-On Systems, Inc.
2 Oakwood Street
Albany, New York 12205

CHAPTER FOURTEEN

MISCELLANEOUS PROVISIONS

Bruce B. Roswig, Esq.

I. JUDGMENT BY CONFESSION

One problem with the traditional methods of suing on collection claims is that they take increasing amounts of time. Not only are there statutory waiting periods for appearance or answer, CPLR Rule 320(a), sec. 3012(a), and for entry of a default judgment, CPLR sec. 308, but time can also be lost in drafting papers and achieving service of process. Meanwhile, assets may be lost and debtors may disappear. One way to circumvent these obstacles is through judgment by confession.

A confession of judgment is simply an agreement to let judgment be entered without legal action. It may be taken for money due or to become due, or to secure the plaintiff against a contingent liability, or both. CPLR sec. 3218 (a). The defendant must execute an affidavit authorizing the entry of judgment and stating the county where he/she resides; if the debtor is a nonresident, the affidavit must designate the county where entry is authorized. CPLR sec. 3218 (a) (1). If the judgment is for money due or to become due, the affidavit must recite the factual basis for the debt. CPLR sec. 3218 (a) (2). If it is taken for security, the underlying facts must be set forth, and they must show that the sum confessed does not exceed the amount of liability. CPLR sec. 3218 (a) (2). The judgment itself follows the usual form, except that costs are limited to $15. CPLR sec. 3218 (b). It must be entered within three years after the affidavit is executed, but not after the death of the defendant. CPLR sec. 3218 (b). If the judgment is filed before the total debt accrues, execution is limited to the amount owing, and successive executions may be issued as the balance becomes due. CPLR sec. 3218 (c).

A judgment by confession against one joint debtor is not a bar to a plenary action against the others. CPLR sec. 3218 (d).

PRACTICE GUIDES

A sample form appears as Appendix "A" to this chapter. The top portion is a promissory note, and serves as the evidence of liability. The lower section is the statutory affidavit. If the confession of judg-

ment expires, the note will still survive as a basis for suit, a point which may be useful if the statute of limitations becomes a problem.

There is no bar to successive confessions of judgment. Thus, if the instrument secures installments of more than three years, the file should be diaried accordingly, and a new confession should be obtained before the old one expires.

A confession of judgment is prohibited in some transactions such as retail installment contracts for consumer goods. Personal Property Law, secs. 302 (13) (b), 403 (2) (c). Hence, the law should always be consulted before the instrument is accepted, so that the client will not be subjected to penalties.

II. CONTEMPT PROCEEDINGS

Collection devices are of little value if they may be ignored with impunity. To protect the creditor against persistent scofflaws, the statute provides that a person may be held in contempt of court for the refusal or willful neglect to obey a subpoena, restraining notice, or a court order, for false swearing in answers to oral or written questions, and for removing a posted notice of sale before the return day. CPLR sec. 5251.

The proceeding is handled as a motion, which may be served by mail, except that the application must contain a warning of possible arrest and imprisonment. Judiciary Law, sec. 756. On the return day, the Court must inform the offender that he/she has a right to counsel, and may assign an attorney if the offender lacks the means to retain one. Judiciary Law, sec. 770. If the wrong is established, the Court must issue an order. Judiciary Law, sec. 770. Where the offender has not appeared, the order must include a provision giving the party ten days to eliminate the contempt. If he/she fails to do so, then thecourt must, upon proper proof, issue a warrant of arrest. Judiciary Law, sec. 772. The Court may also impose a fine, which may not exceed the complainant's costs and expenses plus $250.00. Judiciary Law, sec. 773.

If the offender appears and satisfies the judge that he/she has no means or property subject to levy, the application must be denied, without prejudice to renewal on notice, upon proof that the offender's circumstances have changed. Judiciary Law, sec. 770.

PRACTICE GUIDES

The most frequent use of contempt is for failure of a judgment debtor to answer a subpoena. It is a good idea to give the sheriff a copy of a questionnaire along with instructions for serving the debtor. A sample letter to the sheriff is included as Appendix "B."

Because a contempt proceeding is so cumbersome, it should be requested only when it is reasonably likely to elicit information or other specific results. The fine alone may not be worth the effort, and may be uncollectible in any event.

III. RECEIVERSHIPS

If the judgment creditor cannot levy on property of the debtor, or does not wish to do so, the statute offers an alternative remedy, the appointment of a receiver. Generally, this approach is used when an asset has more income value than sale value, or when it consists of an intangible such as a cause of action that needs to be sued. In other words, a receiver is appointed when the creditor needs someone to stand in place of the debtor and collect revenue for application to the judgment. *See* Siegel, Practice Commentaries to CPLR sec. 5228, ¶ C5228: 2.

The CPLR allows for three kinds of receivers. The first is the temporary receivership, a provisional remedy which applies only when the moving party has an apparent interest in property which is the subject of the action, CPLR sec. 6401 (a), and which usually ceases at final judgment. CPLR sec. 6401 (c). The second is a receivership aimed at enforcing a judgment directed at specific property. CPLR sec. 5106. The third empowers the receiver, after judgment, to administer, collect, improve, lease, repair, or sell any real or personal property of the debtor. CPLR sec. 5228.

An order appointing a receiver has priority, from the date of filing, over a subsequent levy against the same personal property. CPLR sec. 5234 (c).

PRACTICE GUIDE

A receivership can be time-consuming and expensive, and it is not often used in the average collection practice. The attorney should avoid the temptation to become carried away with sophisticated procedural devices, and should look for the most direct means to produce cash for the client. The recievership should be reserved for situations in which the more traditional devices are unavailable, impractical, or nonproductive.

IV. PRIORITIES AMONG JUDGMENT CREDITORS AND OTHERS

In the race to recover assets, the debtor may not be the creditor's only adversary. Others may claim prior rights to the same property.

New York gives judgments different treatment against real and personal property. A judgment is a lien on real estate from the date of docketing, CPLR sec. 5203, and competing rights are determined by the order of docketing. CPLR sec. 5236 (g) (1). A judgment becomes a lien on personalty when an execution is delivered to the sheriff, CPLR sec. 5202, and the order of delivery determines priority among judgment creditors. CPLR sec. 5234 (b). Income executions also share in the order of delivery. CPLR sec. 5231 (h).

A restraining notice does not create a lien, and has no bearing on priorities. Siegel, Practice Commentaries to CPLR sec. 5222, ¶ C5222: 8.

The same distinctions do not necessarily govern other classes of creditors. For example, a state tax warrant is the equivalent of a judgment, and may even be listed in the judgment book of the County Clerk. But unlike private judgments, it becomes a lien on both real and personal property from the date of filing. Tax Law, sec. 692 (d), (e); *Marine Midland Bank-Central v. Gleason*, 47 N.Y.2d 758, 417 N.Y.S.2d 458, 391 N.E.2d 294, (1979). Similarly, a federal tax lien is perfected upon filing, 26 U.S.C.A. sec. 6323(a), and against personalty, takes precedence over an earlier, unexecuted private judgment. *Dean Constr. Co. v. Simonetta Concrete Constr. Corp.*, 37 F.R.D. 242, 246 (S.D.N.Y. 1965).

The same pattern applies to competition with secured creditors under the Uniform Commercial Code. A perfected security interest has priority over a subsequent execution on a judgment. *GMAC v. Stotsky*, 60 Misc. 2d 451, 303 N.Y.S.2d 463 (1969). *See* Uniform Commercial Code sec. 9-301 (2)-(4).

PRACTICE GUIDE

Often a debtor may submit a payment proposal in return for a stipulation not to enter judgment. A creditor should not agree without a detailed financial statement and a search of the public record. If there is a danger of competing interests, withholding judgment may endanger the creditor's priority against real property, and may hinder his/her ability to execute quickly if payments cease.

V. SATISFACTIONS

When a judgment is wholly or partly paid, the creditor must execute a full or partial satisfaction, respectively, must file it with the clerk, and must mail a copy to the debtor within ten days after filing. CPLR sec. 5020 (a). An attorney of record may execute the satisfaction within ten years after the entry of judgment. CPLR sec. 5020 (b). If transcripts have been filed with other county clerks, their records must be cleared with certificates issued by the county of original entry. CPLR sec. 5020 (d).

PRACTICE GUIDE

It is common for a smaller case to be sued in a city court, and for a transcript to be filed with the County Clerk after judgment. Although it would seem logical to satisfy the judgment in both places, the practice, at least upstate, is to file the satisfaction only with the county clerk. In fact, city court clerks have been known to refuse satisfactions where transcripts have been issued.

Although the statute appears to require that a satisfaction be filed for each partial payment, this practice is generally not followed when a judgment is paid in regular installments over a period of time. Otherwise, a literal reading of the section might lead to the filing of hundreds of partial satisfactions every month or every week by each county clerk, a result which the Legislature could not have intended. It is noteworthy that while there is a $100 penalty for disobedience, this fine applies only to full satisfactions. CPLR, sec. 5020(c). A more sensible interpretation would be that an installment arrangement is really a single transaction divided into segments, so that a satisfaction would not be needed until the last amount is received. The partial satisfaction does have some utility, however; it is common for enforcement officers to return executions partially satisfied, and for dockets to be marked accordingly. **See *CPLR sec. 5021(b). Again, though, the officer does not satisfy each remittance individually, but instead, waits until all possibilities of further moneys have been exhausted.***

VI. DEBT COLLECTION PRACTICES

Every collection lawyer should become familiar with sections 600 through 603 of the General Business Law, which govern debt collection procedures. Unlike the federal statute, 15 U.S.C.A. sec. 1692a(6), which applies only to bill collectors, the New York enactment prohibits conduct by both a "principal creditor" and "his agent"; this language, on its face, is broad enough to include attorneys, and since each violation is a misdemeanor, General Business Law sec. 602(1), it would be risky to assume otherwise.

The law applies only to "consumer" claims, defined as those arising out of credit extended for personal, family, or household purposes. General Business Law sec. 600(1).

The statute, declares that neither principal nor agent may, General Business Law sec. 601:

a. Simulate an enforcement officer;

b. Knowingly charge any collection fee, attorney's fee, or court cost or expense unless such amounts are legally due and owing;

c. Disclose or threaten to disclose any knowingly false information about the debtor's reputation for credit worthiness;

d. Communicate or threaten to communicate the nature of a consumer claim to the debtor's employer prior to judgment, except to enforce a wage assignment;

e. Disclose or threaten to disclose a contested debt without including the fact that it is disputed;

f. Communicate with the debtor or his family at unreasonable hours;

g. Threaten any action which the creditor does not actually take in the usual course of business;

h. Pursue a right with knowledge that it does not exist;

i. Use a communication which falsely simulates government process.

PRACTICE GUIDE

The most frequent question from clients is whether they may call debtors at work before judgment is entered. The answer seems to be that they may do so if they do not disclose the debt to the employer,

but the procedure can be very delicate in practice, requiring extreme caution. Subject to the same restriction, there appears to be no prohibition against serving the debtor with a summons and complaint at his/her place of employment.

VII. REMITTING TO THE CLIENT

The last and most important step in the collection process is distributing the proceeds. When the money is first received, it must be deposited in one or more identifiable bank accounts containing no funds of the attorney except as may be required to cover bank charges; costs and expenses may first be deducted. At an appropriate time, the legal fee may be withdrawn and the balance may be sent to the client. *See* Code of Professional Responsibility, Canon 9, Disciplinary Rule DR 9-102 (A). *See also* 22 NYCRR secs. 603.15, 691.12, 806.18, 1022.5 (Uniform Rule for Preservation of Client Funds).

PRACTICE GUIDES

Most accounts are collected in installments over months or even years. The most common procedure is to prepare a monthly itemized statement showing the receipts and disbursements for all claims of a particular client. The fee is computed on the total collections, and the client receives a check for the net amount after deducting fees and disbursements.

An office with a substantial collection practice will spend a great amount of its time recording receipts and disbursements. Often a check from an obligor will not identify the creditor. A common system is to have cards arranged alphabetically by debtors, so that the payments can be readily identified. If a firm serves several creditors, it may also need a ledger system which groups the debtors according to clients. While this dual system requires duplicate recording, it serves distinct purposes. The cards are used in the day-to-day collection process, while the ledgers are employed in drawing monthly remittances. Another consideration is newly promulgated 22 NYCRR, **supra** ***which***

among other things requires a "ledger book or similar record for all escrow accounts, with specified details on incoming and outgoing money. While the usual collection cards and ledgers may suffice, this author recommends that some additional sheets be created with categories corresponding to those set forth in the Rule. Experience shows that a little extra time during the month can save more time at the end, and can simplify the process of accounting to clients.

APPENDIX A

$______________ Syracuse, N. Y., ______________ 19______

As stated below, after date, I (we jointly and severally) promise to pay to the order of ____

________________________ $ ________________________
Value Received.

Due at the office of Payable ______________________

____

Syracuse, N. Y. In the event of a default the full amount shall become due.

____

____

COURT
COUNTY OF ONONDAGA-STATE OF NEW YORK

____

	)	
	)	STATEMENT
Plaintiff	)	and
	)	CONFESSION
vs.	)	of
	)	JUDGMENT
Defendant	)	

____

The defendant above named of ________________________ County of ____________ , N.Y., does hereby confess judgment in this action in favor of ____________________________ , Plaintiff, for the sum of $ ________ , and authorize judgment to be entered therefor against the defendant.

This confession of judgment is for debt justly due to the plaintiff arising upon the following facts: Security for promissory note executed herewith by the defendant.

Dated: ________ 19 ______________________________________

STATE OF NEW YORK)
COUNTY OF ONONDAGA) SS:
CITY OF SYRACUSE)

____defendant above named, being duly sworn, says that the above statement and confession of judgment and the matters of fact therein set forth are true.

Sworn to before me ______ 19 . __________________________

____

Comm'r of Deeds, Syracuse, N. Y.
Notary Public Comm. expires

APPENDIX B

(Date)

(Name and Address of Sheriff)

Re:

Dear Sheriff:

We herewith enclose the original and one copy of the contempt order and an examination sheet in each of the above-captioned matters.

Please serve the copies on the defendants as follows: (Names and addresses of defendants)

We would also appreciate your handing the examination sheets to the defendants and advising them that they are required by law to complete the questionnaires and return them to this office along with their respective fines within ten (10) days after the service of the papers. Please try to impress upon them that if they fail to do either, a warrant for their arrest may be issued within the very near future.

We await your affidavits and bills for service.

Thank you.

Very truly yours,

(SEPARATE LETTER FOR EACH DEBTOR)

TABLE OF AUTHORITIES

CASES

STATUTES

Federal Statutes

Bankruptcy Rules

United State Code

New York State Statutes

Administrative Code (NYCRR)

INDEX

ABOUT THE AUTHORS

GABRIEL J. FERBER, ESQ.

Mr. Ferber is a partner in the firm of Davis, Nesper & McElvein. His primary areas of practice are Commerical Litigation, Administrative and Municipal Law. He is a 1976 graduate of SUNY at Buffalo Law School. Mr Ferber. is a member of the New York State, Erie County, Florida, and American Bar Associations and the Commerical Law Committees of America, and is the author of "Collection of Taxes under the Real Property Tax Law: Recommendation For Change," 2 Certiorari 24 (1976).

RONALD FORSTER, ESQ.

Mr. Forster is Senior Partner in the firm of Forster & Garbus. He received his law degree from Brooklyn Law School in 1968. Mr. Forster is a member of the New York State and Queens County Bar Associations, the Association of the Bar of the City of New York, the Brandeis Association and the Commerical Lawyers Conference. He has lectured in the past at New York State Bar Association programs on Enforcement and Monetary Judgments.

RAYMOND L. FINK, ESQ.

Mr. Fink is a partner in the firm of Gross, Shaman, Silver, Laub & Giljillan, P.C. His primary areas of practice are Secured Transactions, Bankruptcy, Banking Law and Commerical Litigation. Mr. Fink received his law degree from the University of Toledo in 1977. He is a member of the New York State and Erie County Bar Associations, the Bankruptcy Subsection of the Banking, Corporate and Business Law Committee, the National Association of Credit Managers, Educational Committee, and served as vice chairman of the Commercial Law & Bankruptcy Committee during 1984 and 1985. Mr. Fink frequently lectures for Erie County and New York State Bar Associations regarding Bankruptcy and Commercial matters.

MICHAEL J. KAPLAN, ESQ.

Mr. Kaplan is presently a clerk in the U.S. Bankruptcy Court of the Western District of New York. He received his law degree from Boston University in 1977. Mr. Kaplan is a member of the Erie County Bar Association and the National Conference of Bankruptcy Clerks. He has spoken at New York State Bar Association programs on Mortgage Foreclosures & Mechanic's Liens. From 1972 to 1981 Mr. Kaplan was Senior Editor of Lawyers' Cooperative Publishing Co. and has written numerous articles for them.

MARVIN KRUMHOLZ, ESQ.

Mr. Krumholz is a partner in the firm of Sennett & Krumholz. He graduated from Brooklyn Law School in 1952. Mr. Krumholz is a member of the Bank Lawyers Conference and the Commercial Law League. He has lectured for both the New York State Bar Association and the New York County Lawyers' Association, and has served as a panelist for the Group Interchange seminar on Collection Practice. Mr. Krumholz is a expert in collections of claims and judgments.

ROBERT B. FRANK, ESQ.

Mr. Frank practices consumer and commercial credit law at Citibank, N.A., Northeast Division Legal Department, where he is a Vice President. He has been with Citibank since 1967. He attended law school at Fordham. Mr. Frank is a member of the Business Law Committee of the Banking, Corporation and Business Law Section of the New York State Bar Association. He is also a member of the Legal Advisory Board of the Consumer Credit Division of the State Bankers Association. In the past, Mr. Frank has lectured at programs on "Collections and Enforcement of Money Judgments" for the New York State Bar Association; and Truth-In-Lending, and Legal Form and Procedures for Commercial Loans for the Banking Law Institute.

JACK L. GETMAN, ESQ.

Mr. Getman is a partner in the Buffalo firm of Goldman, Costa, Getman and Biryla. He is a member of the Banking, Corporations and Business Law Secion, the Real Property Law Section and the Insurance Law Section of the New York State Bar Association. He is also a member of the Erie County Bar Association, the Commercial Law League and the American Arbitration Association. Mr. Getman has served as a panelist for several programs including "Collection and Enforcement of Judgments" and was Chairman of the Erie County Bar Association's Continuing Legal Education Program on Commercial Law. He is co-author of the pamphlet "Guidelines for Enforcement of Civil Judgments and Issuance of Civil Process."

RICHARD J. MILLER, ESQ.

Mr. Miller is president of Richard J. Miller & Associates, P.C., of Albany. His primary areas of practice are Collection and Commercial Litigation. He attended Providence College and received his J.D. from Albany Law School. He is a member of the American Bar Association and the Albany County

Bar Association. He is also a member of the Business Law Committee of the Banking, Corporation and Business Law Section of the New York State Bar Association. He has been a lecturer on several topics, including Consumer Debt Collection and the Enforcement of Money Judgments in both 1982 and 1985. In addition, Mr. Miller is very active in various organizations in his community.

BRADLEY E. ROCK, ESQ.

Mr. Rock is a partner in the Smithtown, New York firm of Schechter Schecter & Kenney. A 1978 graduate of Cornell Law School, Mr. Rock's primary areas of practice include Commercial Litigation, Trials and Appeals as well as Corporate Counseling of Banks and Schools. He served as Vice President of the Suffolk Academy of Law during 1984-85 and was Editor-In-Chief of the Journal of the Suffolk Academy of Law from 1982-84. Mr. Rock is the author of several articles, including "Simultaneous Service of Interrogatories and Notice of Deposition," 190 NYLJ 61, 1983, and "Computer Failures and Article 4 of UCC," 189 NYLJ 45, 1983.

BRUCE B. ROSWIG, ESQ.

Mr. Roswig is a single practitioner working in the fields of Commercial Law, Zoning Litigation, and Motion and Appellate Practice. Upon graduating from Syracuse Law School in 1965, he served as Confidential Law Assistant to the Supreme Court, Appellate Division, Third Department. From 1967-83 he practiced with a Syracuse law firm. He is the author of "Creditors Are Still Victims of the Old Myths," *Credit & Financial Management*, February 1977. Mr. Roswig is a member of the American, New York State, and Onondaga County Bar Associations and is a former Chairman of the Public Education Committee of the Onondaga County Bar Association.

FRANCIS P. WEIMER, ESQ.

Mr. Weimer is a partner in the Buffalo firm of Aaron, Dautch, Sternberg & Lawson. His primary areas of practice are Commercial Law and Bankruptcy. Mr. Weimer is a member of the New York State and Erie County Bar Associations, and is on the Board of Directors at the National Association of Credit Management for Upstate New York. In addition, he is a member of the Erie County Bar Association Commerical Law Committee and the Commercial Law League of America. Mr. Weimer graduated from the University of Buffalo Law School in 1978.

BARRY ZARETSKY, ESQ.

Mr. Zaretsky is a Professor of Law at Brooklyn Law School. He is member of the American Bar Association Committee on Bankruptcy, Consumer Financial Services, and Commercial Financial Services, as well as the New York State Bar Association Committee on Alternative Dispute Resolution. He is a 1974 graduate of Michigan Law School. Professor Zaretsky has participated in the New York State Bar Association's Program on Collections and the Enforcement of Money Judgments in 1982 and 1984, and in programs for the Practising Law Institute on Bankruptcy and Commercial Law. He is co-author of *Debtors' and Creditors' Rights*, and has written numerous law review articles on Commercial Law and Bankruptcy.

RICHARD A. NICOLL, ESQ.

Richard A. Nicoll is partner of the national law firm of Hayt, Hayt & Landau. The firm is headquartered in Great Neck, New York and maintains offices in 12 states, Washington, D.C. and London, England. Mr. Nicoll, formerly with the Litigation Division of Bankers Trust Company, is the firm's partner-in-charge of business development. He has been a guest lecturer before many groups such as The Commercial Law League of America, The National Council of Higher Education Loan Programs, the New York State Organization of Bursars and Business Administrators, and the American Recovery Association. He is a member of the Nassau County and New York State Bar Associations and received his preparatory education at Drexel University and legal education at Brooklyn Law School. He is married and lives on Long Island with his wife and three children.

